WHOSE RIGHT IS IT?

THE SECOND AMENDMENT AND THE FIGHT OVER GUNS

WHOSE RIGHT IS IT?

THE SECOND AMENDMENT AND THE FIGHT OVER GUNS

HANA BAJRAMOVIC

Henry Holt and Company
New York

Henry Holt and Company, *Publishers since 1866*
Henry Holt® is a registered trademark of Macmillan Publishing Group, LLC
120 Broadway, New York, New York 10271 • mackids.com

Library of Congress Cataloging-in-Publication Data
Names: Bajramovic, Hana, author.
Title: Whose right is it? : the Second Amendment and
the fight over guns / Hana Bajramovic.
Description: First. | New York : Henry Holt Books for Young Readers, 2020. |
Audience: Ages 10–14 | Audience: Grades 10–12 | Summary: "Timely middle-grade
nonfiction documenting and discussing the Second Amendment and
the rise of the NRA"—Provided by publisher.
Identifiers: LCCN 2019037069 | ISBN 9781250224255 (hardcover)
Subjects: LCSH: Firearms—Law and legislation—United States—Juvenile literature. |
United States. Constitution. 2nd Amendment—Juvenile literature. |
Gun control—United States—Juvenile literature.
Classification: LCC KF3941 .B35 2020 | DDC 344.7305/33—dc23
LC record available at https://lccn.loc.gov/2019037069

Our books may be purchased in bulk for promotional, educational, or business use. Please contact
your local bookseller or the Macmillan Corporate and Premium Sales Department at (800) 221-7945
ext. 5442 or by email at MacmillanSpecialMarkets@macmillan.com.

First edition, 2020 / Designed by Kay Petronio
Printed in the United States of America by LSC Communications, Harrisonburg, Virginia

1 3 5 7 9 10 8 6 4 2

FOR ALISA

CONTENTS

Congrefs OF THE

begun and held at the

Wednesday the Fourth of March, one

THE Conventions of a number of the

oration of its powers, that further declaratory and restrictive clauses should be added: And as

RESOLVED by the Senate

concurring that the following Articles be proposed to the Legislatures of the several States, as

said Legislatures, to be valid to all intents and purposes, as part of the said Constitution

ARTICLES in addition to, a

of the several States, pursuant to the fifth Article of the original Constitution.

Article the first... After the first enumeration required by the first Article of the Constitution

which, the proportion shall be so regulated by Congress, that there

until the number of Representatives shall amount to two hundred,

nor more than one Representative for every fifty thousand persons.

Article the second... No law, varying the compensation for the services of the Senators an

Article the third... Congress shall make no law respecting an establishment of religion,

afsemble, and to petition the government for a redrefs of grievance

A well regulated Militia, being necefsary to the security of a

red in any house, wi

A NOTE ON LANGUAGE

Throughout this book, I have chosen not to name any of the killers in mass shootings, many of whom perpetrated the murders in the hope of becoming famous. The focus should be on the victims and survivors, not on those who killed them.

INTRODUCTION

I t was Valentine's Day 2018. High school junior Tori Gonzales was finally feeling well enough to go back to school after being sick for a while. She saw her boyfriend, Joaquin Oliver, who gave her a bouquet of flowers. Actually, he wasn't her boyfriend. He told her, "I hope you know you're not my girlfriend. You're my soul mate."

It would be the last day she ever saw him. That afternoon, a nineteen-year-old boy walked into Marjory Stoneman Douglas High School in Parkland, Florida, with an AR-15 rifle and opened fire into four classrooms. The shooter had purchased the gun legally, passing a background check that included a mental health question. By the time it was all over, he would kill seventeen students and staff—including Joaquin.

"I know I'm just a kid and kids don't know any better," Tori said, referring to her relationship with Joaquin, "but [it] was the purest form of love that there is. I'm so thankful that I had that, even if it was for such a short time." She still has the flowers Joaquin gave her on the day he died. She still wears his sweatshirt.

Anthony Borges, who was fifteen at the time of the shooting, was shot five times as he stood in the doorway to his classroom, shielding his fellow students with his own body. He's homeschooled now, not yet ready to return to the hallways of Marjory Stoneman Douglas High. He doesn't feel safe there.

And though Anthony's wounds have healed, he only recently learned to walk again. "It will never be like before," he said. "I used to get out of school and go play soccer. All I wanted was to play soccer professionally. I played forward. Now I don't do anything."

The average length of a mass shooting is about fifteen minutes, but Parkland was different. The first shot was fired at 2:21 p.m. The killer escaped the campus and was arrested around 3:40 p.m., but for a while the police weren't sure they had the right person. In total, the students at Parkland were on lockdown for three and a half hours. Three and a half hours that felt like three and a half years.

The night of the shooting, around 10:00 p.m., high school senior David Hogg appeared on Laura Ingraham's show on Fox News. She asked him about what had happened that day.

"So, the first thing that I heard was one single gunshot," he explained. "We initially thought it was a drill, but it turned out to be anything but." Ingraham asked him questions about the shooter, whether he had mental health issues, whether there was any armed security in the building. He explained what he knew.

"So, David, incredibly poised delivery of information tonight," she said, wrapping up the conversation.

"Can I say one more thing?" he asked.

"Yes," she replied.

"I don't want this to be another mass shooting. I don't want this just to be something that people forget," he said. "This is something that people need to look at and realize that there is a serious issue in this country that we all need to face. It's an issue that affects each and every one of us. And if you think it doesn't, believe me, it will, especially if we don't take action to step up."

CHAPTER 1

GUN VIOLENCE IN AMERICA

The era of mass school shootings began in 1999 at Columbine High School in Littleton, Colorado, when two boys killed twelve of their fellow students and a teacher before taking their own lives. Columbine wasn't the first high school mass shooting, but at that point, it was the worst in American history. And it started a trend.

Many other mass school shootings followed Columbine: at Virginia Tech in Blacksburg, Virginia, on April 16, 2007, where a shooter killed thirty-two people; at Sandy Hook Elementary School in Newtown, Connecticut, on December 14, 2012, where a shooter killed twenty-six people; at Parkland on February 14, 2018, where a shooter killed seventeen people; at Santa Fe High School in Santa Fe, Texas, on May 18, 2018, where a shooter killed ten people . . . The list goes on.

Columbine became a blueprint for later school shootings in large part because of the way it was reported. Major media outlets latched on to the story of the killers, repeating their names, exploring their psychology, and sharing their manifestos and home movies. As a result, many of the killers in later school shootings used Columbine as a model. Some even went so far as to wear trench coats, the clothing item for which the Columbine killers had become known.

People use the phrase all the time, but believe it or not, there's actually no agreed-upon definition of "mass shooting." For years the FBI has defined the term to mean four or more people killed by guns in "close geographical proximity" to one another. Congress defined "mass killing" as three or more killings in one incident (using any sort of weapon) after the 2012 tragedy at Sandy Hook Elementary. Other researchers exclude murders that occur during a robbery, gang violence, or domestic abuse when making their calculations. Because of these different definitions, the estimates of how many mass shootings occur vary greatly, from about four per year to a mass shooting every day.

One thing to keep in mind about school shootings is that while the ones you hear about in the news, like Columbine and Parkland, tend to occur at schools that are predominantly white, gun violence more frequently affects students of color. In understanding the racial disparities in school shootings, it's important to think about the difference between a *mass* school shooting and a school shooting that involves fewer victims.

There are, on average, three casualties when a shooting happens at a predominantly white school. While "that's twice the average of the number of shooting victims at predominantly Black and Hispanic schools," CNN reports, students of color face more *frequent* gun violence. For example, even though only about 15 percent of students in the United

MASS SHOOTING

More than 3 or 4 people killed (depending on your definition)

MASS SCHOOL SHOOTING

More than 3 or 4 people killed at a school

SCHOOL SHOOTING

Any sort of shooting at a school

States are Black, Black students "account for about a third of the students who have experienced a school shooting since 2009." A recent Pew Research Center survey found that Black and Hispanic students were markedly more worried about the possibility of a shooting happening at their schools.

"Those mass shootings, the headline-grabbing ones, are really, really a small fraction of them," says Chris Cole, a former FBI agent who is now the director of threat intervention services at the University of Wisconsin–Madison. "It's more of the everyday violence, that unfortunately I think we've become a bit immune to, that produce[s] the large numbers."

"In some ways," *New York Times* reporter Dana Goldstein writes, "the panic and dark legacy of Columbine brought to suburban and rural schools some of the fears and pressure that urban students of color had already been living under." The fear of school shootings means that students practice lockdown drills, pass through metal detectors, and wear clear backpacks. In a recent school shooter drill in Indiana, teachers suffered "bloody welts" after trainers used nonlethal pellet guns to shoot at them.

"There's a trauma that comes simply from being part of one of those drills," Chris Murphy, a Democratic senator from Connecticut, explains. Indeed, in a recent online survey, the American Psychological Association (APA) found that when a school implements safety measures such as lockdown drills, the proportion of parents who feel more stressed (36 percent) exceeds the proportion who feel less stressed (34 percent).

And these mass shootings, of course, don't just happen in schools— they also happen at concerts, in churches, in movie theaters, and at restaurants. In 2016, for example, a shooter killed forty-nine people at Pulse nightclub in Orlando, Florida, and in 2017 a shooter killed fifty-eight people at a country music festival in Las Vegas.

The threat of mass shootings outside school affects students in much the same way that school shootings do. The APA found that "for a majority of Gen Z youth [aged 15 to 21], gun violence—mass shootings and school shootings—are significant sources of stress." Indeed, "75 percent of those in this age group report mass shootings as a significant source of stress, and nearly as many (72 percent) say the same about school shootings or the possibility of them occurring."

DEADLIEST MASS SHOOTINGS IN AMERICA, 1999–2018

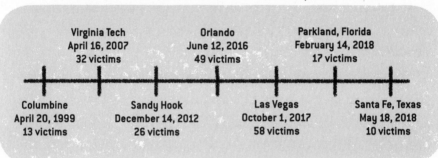

Virginia Tech
April 16, 2007
32 victims

Orlando
June 12, 2016
49 victims

Parkland, Florida
February 14, 2018
17 victims

Columbine
April 20, 1999
13 victims

Sandy Hook
December 14, 2012
26 victims

Las Vegas
October 1, 2017
58 victims

Santa Fe, Texas
May 18, 2018
10 victims

There are also plenty of gun deaths that have nothing to do with school shootings or mass shootings. Let's take a look at the statistics.

HOW MANY GUNS ARE PEOPLE BUYING? WHO'S BUYING THEM?

Gun ownership is falling: The percentage of households with guns has declined from 1977 to 2017, according to two different surveys.

PERCENTAGE OF AMERICAN HOUSEHOLDS THAT OWN GUNS

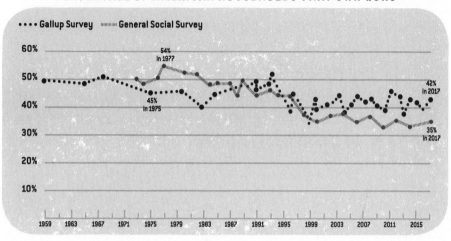

The number of guns sold per year increased until 2016, then fell in 2017 and 2018, likely because of President Donald Trump's election. As we'll learn in chapter 8, gun sales tend to spike when gun owners think their gun rights are under threat, not when they think their gun rights are safe.

GUN SALES IN AMERICA, 2000–2018

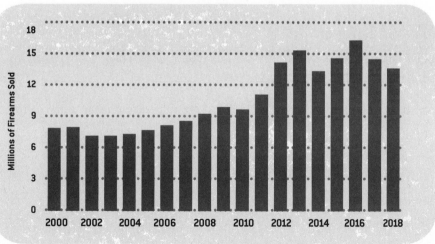

Gun owners often own more than one gun per person, which explains why the number of sales can increase in the same year that the number of households owning guns decreases. A recent Pew Research Center survey found that 66 percent of gun owners report owning more than one gun, and 29 percent report owning five or more guns.

Men (39 percent) are more likely to own a gun than women (22 percent); white people (36 percent) are more likely to own a gun than Black (24 percent) or Hispanic (15 percent) people; and gun ownership is more common in rural areas (46 percent) than in suburban (28 percent) or urban (19 percent) areas. The states with the highest gun ownership rates tend to be largely rural and in the South, Midwest, or West, while those with the lowest gun ownership rates tend to be less rural and on the East or West Coast.

HOW MANY PEOPLE ARE DYING BECAUSE OF GUNS?

The Centers for Disease Control and Prevention reports that in 2017, the most recent year for which it has data, there were 39,773 firearms deaths—the highest number in fifty years. (And there are about five to seven gun injuries for every gun death.) Of these deaths, 1,814 were children aged 1 to 17. In fact, in 2017 more children died from gunshots than on-duty police officers and active duty military combined.

While policymakers often focus on homicides when they talk about gun control, suicides actually account for the majority of gun deaths. In 2017, for example, about 60 percent of gun deaths were suicides, while about 37 percent were homicides. Guns were involved in 51 percent of all suicides that year.

Some people think that gun availability is unrelated to suicide; they argue that people who want to die by suicide will find any way to do it. But studies show that when guns are less prevalent, there are fewer gun suicides, at least among young adults.

This is for two main reasons: First, guns are the deadliest means of suicide—about 80 to 90 percent of gun suicide attempts end in death—

while other means of suicide are less deadly. And second, particularly among young people, the suicidal impulse may pass. The availability of a gun, however, makes it much easier to follow through on that impulse.

There are also firearms accidents, which accounted for 486 gun deaths in 2017. These deaths are most common among children and young adults—about half of those who die because of a gun accident are under thirty years old. Accidental deaths often occur when guns aren't stored safely in the home.

As you can see, there's also a pretty good amount of overlap between gun ownership and gun death rates: The states with the most guns also tend to be the states with the most gun deaths. (Note that "gun deaths" include homicides, suicides, and accidents.) We'll look at these statistics again on pages 179–89, when we analyze whether these gun deaths are preventable.

PERCENTAGE OF GUN OWNERS PER STATE IN AMERICA

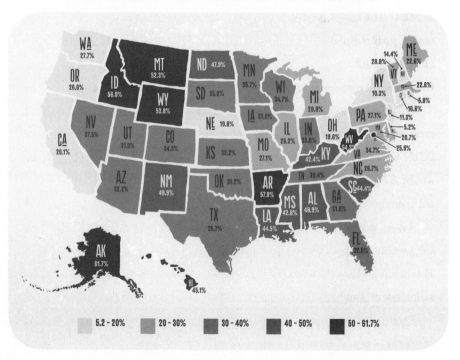

| | 5.2 - 20% | | 20 - 30% | | 30 - 40% | | 40 - 50% | | 50 - 61.7% |

GUN DEATH RATES BY STATE PER 100,000 PEOPLE IN 2017

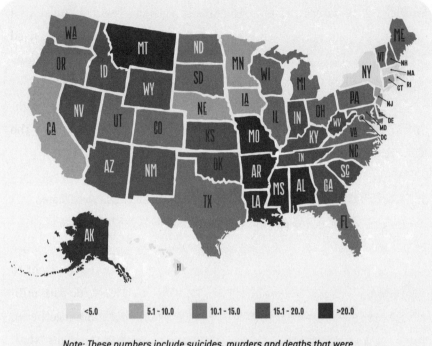

| <5.0 | 5.1 - 10.0 | 10.1 - 15.0 | 15.1 - 20.0 | >20.0 |

Note: These numbers include suicides, murders and deaths that were unintentional, involved law enforcement, or had undetermined circumstances.

Given all these guns, and all this gun violence, what's getting in the way of passing gun control laws? Three letters: NRA. The National Rifle Association, the most powerful gun rights organization in the country.

The NRA blocks laws that interfere with gun rights, and it spends millions of dollars to help elect candidates who support gun rights. In 2016, for example, the NRA spent over $11 million to support Republican Donald Trump and almost $20 million to oppose Democrat Hillary Clinton. (There are also a few other, smaller pro-gun lobbying groups, like Gun Owners of America and the National Association for Gun Rights, which say that they're even *more* pro-gun than the NRA.)

Shortly after the Parkland shooting, Wayne LaPierre, the NRA's chief executive, said the solution to the problem of school shootings isn't stricter gun laws—it's more armed security in schools. In his view, and in the view of many gun rights supporters, a good guy with a gun stops a bad guy with a gun. For that reason, LaPierre argues that schools need armed guards or even armed teachers. His solution is to add *more* guns in schools.

LaPierre and the NRA believe that gun control violates the "right to keep and bear arms" guaranteed by the Second Amendment to the Constitution. That amendment reads as follows:

> A well regulated Militia, being necessary to the security of a free State, the right of the people to keep and bear Arms, shall not be infringed.

Sort of a winding sentence. It seems to say people have the right to own "arms," or guns. But it's not clear what that right has to do with militias, which are military forces made up of citizens that come together to fight when they're needed. And what does it mean that the right "shall not be infringed"—can there be any laws restricting it?

The NRA says no. The NRA believes that the right to keep and bear arms belongs to every individual, not to state militias, and that there can't be any gun control laws that infringe on that right. In its view, even a minor gun control law is just a slippery slope to total gun confiscation. As Wayne LaPierre put it: "The anti-gunner's formula for surrendering our Second Amendment freedoms is clear: First, enact a nationwide firearms waiting period"—in other words, a period of time a person has to wait before buying a gun—"second, after the waiting period fails to reduce crime, enact a nationwide licensing and registration law; and the final step, confiscate all registered firearms."

LaPierre and the NRA believe that things like licensing requirements can lead to a gun registry—a list of all gun owners—which would make it easier for the government to seize all privately held weapons.

(This is the potato chip theory of gun control—once you start you can't stop.) For this reason, the NRA fights anything that gets in the way of gun rights, no matter how small. Even small-scale, reasonable gun control can seem impossible given the strength of the pro-gun lobby.

So how did America get into this mess? Did the nation's founders support every individual's right to have guns? And how have we gotten to the point where twelve hundred teens and young adults died from gun violence in the twelve months after the Parkland shooting alone?

Answering those questions means examining the history of gun laws in America. When we do that, we realize that gun control laws in this country have coexisted with gun rights for hundreds of years.

The aim of this book is to trace our nation's history with guns, to examine how our relationship with the Second Amendment has changed over time, and to analyze the forces that have shaped that relationship. Of course, there are limitations to my telling of this story—hundreds of books could be written about guns in America. Indeed, something new happens in the world of guns and gun policy every day. This book means to capture the most relevant information to explain how we've gotten to where we are today: schools filled with metal detectors, clear backpacks, and active shooter drills.

These may seem like modern phenomena, but to start this story, we have to go back in time—all the way to 1688 and the Glorious Revolution.

THE EARLY HISTORY OF THE GUN

The AR-15 rifle used in the Parkland shooting caused wounds that were unrecognizable to a trained trauma surgeon; the bullets fired from that rifle are three times as powerful as those fired from a 9mm handgun. The AR-15 looks nothing like the guns European settlers brought across the Atlantic when they colonized the Americas.

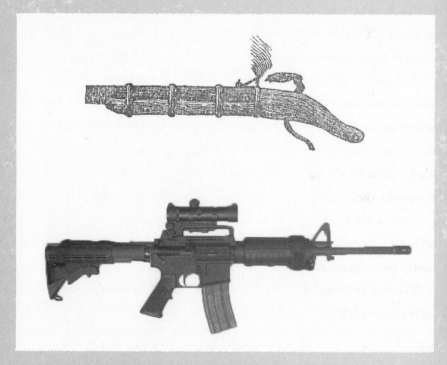

The matchlock, above; a Colt AR-15, below. [Wikimedia Commons]

The first guns in the world were probably cannons, which used explosive gunpowder (likely discovered around the 900s in China) to hurl projectiles in combat. The next major development occurred in fourteenth-century Europe when craftsmen, in an effort to create small, portable cannons, developed the first hand-carried arms. These weapons were only somewhat mobile, very unwieldy, and a definite risk to the shooter. They were called hand cannons, fire sticks, or hand gonnes.

The matchlock, developed in the fifteenth century by European gunsmiths, was the first *mechanical* firing device. The term "matchlock" encompasses guns known as arquebuses, harquebuses, calivers, and muskets. When a lever on the matchlock was pulled, a burning match was lowered into the flashpan, which ignited the powder that sent the bullet flying. Before the matchlock, the shooter had to hold a flame to a hole in the barrel, which then ignited the powder. But the matchlock allowed both hands to remain on the gun, which helped with aim. The matchlock was a success thanks to a combination of relative ease of use and low cost.

Then, in the early sixteenth century, the wheel lock appeared. The wheel lock was self-igniting; when the shooter pulled the trigger, a rough-edged steel wheel struck a piece of pyrite, which ignited a spark. This made the wheel lock easier to use and more reliable than the matchlock. Of course, the complicated craftsmanship that went into the wheel also made it more expensive. For this reason, even after the wheel lock was invented, the matchlock was still more popular as a military firearm.

In the early seventeenth century, the flintlock was developed in France. Like the wheel lock, it was self-igniting—it ignited a spark by striking flint on steel. Unlike the wheel lock, it didn't use an expensive wheel. By the mid-1600s, the flintlock had been adopted throughout Europe.

Guns first came to the Americas as harquebuses hauled over by Spanish explorers and conquistadores in the fifteenth century, and subsequently as matchlocks, wheel locks, and flintlocks with English settlers. In the eight hundred years of their existence, guns have become deadlier and deadlier, enabling the devastating forms of destruction we see today.

CHAPTER 2

TWO REVOLUTIONS

Picture this: It's 1685 in England, and you're Catholic. You've been discriminated against all your life. Protestants don't trust Catholics—there's a rumor going around that the pope is planning to overthrow the king and take control of the British Empire. As a Catholic, you can't run for public office, and you can't lead troops in the military. You keep hoping things will change.

The king is Protestant, as are most members of Parliament, the group of people who make laws for the country. A pamphlet that's been going around explains the horrors that Protestants think will ensue if a Catholic ruler comes to power:

> First, Imagine you see the whole Town in a flame, occasioned this second time by the same Popish malice which set it on fire before. . . . Your Trading's bad, and in a manner lost already, but then the only Commodity will be Fire and Sword; the only object, Women running with their hair about their ears, Men cover'd with blood, Children sprawling under Horses feet, and only the walls of Houses left standing.

After King Charles II dies, James II becomes king of England, Scotland, and Ireland. But here's the thing—James is Catholic.

Even King James II doesn't know what to do with his hands in pictures.
[Wikimedia Commons / Bolton Museum and Art Gallery, Lancashire, UK]

Suddenly, things are looking up for you! James supports freedom of worship for Catholics—you're hopeful that James might make a difference in your life and help you feel more accepted.

But it soon becomes clear that James is power hungry and has no regard for anyone but himself, Catholic or not. A few months after

James takes power, in the summer of 1685, James Scott, Duke of Monmouth—the illegitimate son of Charles II—attempts to dethrone the Catholic king. Even though Monmouth's attempt fails, the whole thing makes James realize that he needs to expand the size of the army and appoint Catholics to positions of power within it. When the archbishop of Canterbury—the leader of the Church of England—complains to James about these decisions and asks him to rethink them, James throws him in prison.

Then, in a bold move, James decides to take guns away from the people who don't support him. He doesn't even need to pass any new laws: the Militia Act of 1662 says that the king's officers can take weapons away from anyone they think is "dangerous to the Peace of the Kingdom." James uses this as an excuse to disarm Protestants, who he worries are plotting to overthrow him.

In 1687, James issues his first of two Declarations of Indulgence, which establish freedom of religion and eliminate the penalties against Catholics. Later that year, he formally dissolves Parliament, the government body that could have checked his powers. He starts putting together a new Parliament full of people who support only him.

The Protestants are getting more and more nervous, but they're sure this whole Catholic thing will end soon enough. James doesn't have any sons, and his two daughters, Mary and Anne, are both Protestant. Then, on June 10, 1688, James's wife gives birth to a baby boy. James announces that the boy will be raised Catholic.

If James has a Catholic son, that means Catholic reign in England could continue for a long time—maybe forever. That could be good for you! (Remember, you're a Catholic.)

The birth of James's son really makes Protestants panic. And so the Glorious Revolution begins.

The Tower of London, where the archbishop of Canterbury was imprisoned.
[Wikimedia Commons / British Museum]

THE GLORIOUS REVOLUTION, 1688

In 1688, seven English noblemen decided to send a letter to James's daughter Mary and her Dutch husband, William of Orange, asking for help overthrowing James. James had an army of twenty thousand men, so if he was going to be overthrown, it had to be by someone with the manpower to match that. The noblemen's letter, dated June 30, 1688, went like this:

> We have great reason to believe we shall be every day in a worse
> condition than we are, and less able to defend ourselves, and therefore
> we do earnestly wish we might be so happy as to find a remedy before
> it be too late for us to contribute to our own deliverance.

After explaining how bad things were with James as king, the

noblemen promised that if William and Mary came to overthrow James, they would help out:

> These considerations make us of the opinion that this is a season in which we may more probably contribute to our own safeties than hereafter (although we must own to your Highness there are some judgments differing from ours in this particular), insomuch that if the circumstances stand so with your Highness that you believe you can get here time enough, in a condition to give assistances this year sufficient for a relief under these circumstances which have been now represented, we who subscribe this will not fail to attend your Highness upon your landing and to do all that lies in our power to prepare others to be in as much readiness as such an action is capable of, where there is so much danger in communicating an affair of such a nature till it be near the time of its being made public.

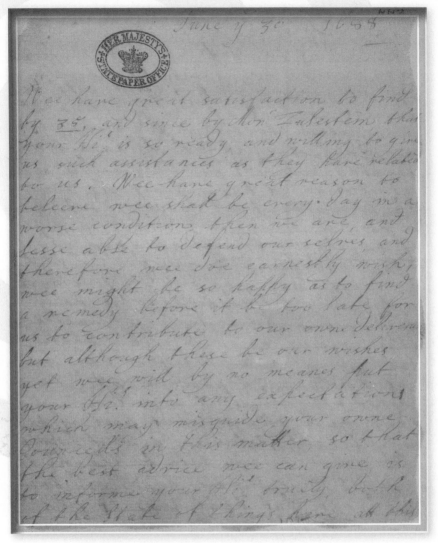

A copy of the letter from the English noblemen. (Contains public sector information licensed under the Open Government Licence v3.0.)

And so William and Mary, with the help of a Dutch army, came to England, where they were met by a group of English volunteers. James thought he could fight them off, but several of his own men—including John Churchill, his good friend and the lieutenant general of the army—changed their minds and took William's side. Even Princess Anne, James's other daughter, joined William and Mary's group of volunteers.

So James gave up. On December 23, 1688, fearing for his safety, he ran away to France. The overthrow of King James II would soon become known as the Bloodless Revolution or the Glorious Revolution.

In early 1689, after the Glorious Revolution, Parliament appointed William and Mary, who were Protestant, to be king and queen—but first they had to promise to follow Parliament's laws and respect the rights of their citizens. These promises were incorporated into the Declaration of Rights of February 1689, which became the official English Bill of Rights in December 1689.

An engraving of William and Mary from 1703.
[Wikimedia Commons / Private Collection of S. Whitehead]

Adam Winkler, historian, law professor, and author of the book *Gunfight: The Battle Over the Right to Bear Arms in America*, explains that a lot of the rights in this document were clearly reactions to things James had done: The new right "to petition the King" would've allowed the archbishop to complain about James's policies without being punished. The new right to due process of law would've prevented James from arresting people for no good reason. And, importantly, the Bill of Rights created a new right where "subjects which are Protestants may have arms for their defence suitable to their conditions and as allowed by law," which would've stopped James from disarming people.

Well, sort of. Two things are important in that last provision. First, only Protestants could own weapons. Indeed, soon after the English Bill of Rights was adopted, Parliament passed a law that said Catholics could not stockpile weapons. And second, even for Protestants, the right was only as "suitable to their conditions"—in other words, it was limited to the upper class.

James had been removed from power in part because he tried to take guns away from Protestants. But once the Protestants came to power again, they did the exact same thing to Catholics.

Almost a hundred years later and a whole ocean away, the English Bill of Rights would serve as a model for America's Declaration of Independence and for the American Constitution's own Bill of Rights.

PRE-REVOLUTIONARY AMERICA

America's history with guns started even before the Constitution was written. Even though early Americans expected to be able to own a gun, they didn't think the right was unlimited; gun rights and gun control coexisted peacefully during the birth of America.

Part of the reason most men expected to be able to own a gun was because of the militia. Militias were "military forces drawn from the citizenry," lawyer and historian Michael Waldman explains—people would come together and fight when they were needed. The colonists formed militias as soon as they arrived in America; all free, able-bodied white men (usually between eighteen and forty-five) were required to serve.

Most colonies required that every man in the militia own a firearm that he could use in military service. Government officials enforced this requirement several times a year at "musters," where they inspected every militia-eligible man's gun. (This is where today's phrase "pass muster" comes from. It means "gain approval or acceptance.") "Muster days were important festive occasions," historian Saul Cornell explains, which "drew citizens together for celebration and revelry." In some colonies, government officials even went door-to-door making a list of the guns people owned, a practice that would enrage today's gun rights supporters.

The colonists far preferred the militia to a standing army. Back in Britain, the king had an army of paid soldiers. But the king could use that army to oppress people, as James did. Early Americans thought a militia, made up of citizens, would better protect the rights of everyday people.

But not *all* people. When British colonists arrived in America, they arrived in a land that was already occupied by millions of Indigenous people. Taking control of the colonies meant waging war on the native population, and waging war meant the colonists needed a group of people who were armed and willing to fight. That's where the militia came in.

While the militia would protect the rights of the British colonists, these armed citizen groups would be used to oppress the rights of others. As historian Roxanne Dunbar-Ortiz, author of *An Indigenous People's History of the United States*, writes in her book on the Second Amendment: "The militias referred to in the Second Amendment were intended as a means for white people to eliminate Indigenous communities in order to take their land, and for slave patrols to control Black people."

These militias were initially created to repel invasions and suppress insurrections, which Dunbar-Ortiz explains meant "the destruction and control of Native peoples, communities, and nations." And soon these militias formed the basis for what were known as "slave patrols." A 1727 Virginia law, for example, required that militias draw on their ranks to create these patrols. The law suggested that "great danger may happen to the inhabitants of this dominion, from the unlawful concourse of negros" and that the patrols should break up any unusual gathering of Black people. Patrols often stopped and questioned enslaved Black people and asked them to show their "passes"—letters that said they had permission to go where they were going. (Not unlike the modern stop-and-frisk laws in many states, where police can stop, search, and detain anyone who looks suspicious.)

Hand in hand with arming the militias went disarming the groups they wanted to control: Most colonies forcibly disarmed law-abiding Indigenous and Black people, arguing that these groups were "dangerous."

Pennsylvania, for example, prohibited "any Negro" from carrying "any Guns, Sword, Pistol, Fowling-piece, Clubs, or other Arms or weapons whatsoever" without "his Masters special licence."

Virginia demanded that "no negro, mulatto, or indian whatsoever" should "presume to keep, or carry any gun, powder, shot, or any club, or other weapon whatsoever, offensive or defensive."

And South Carolina law stated that "every master, mistress or overseer" must "cause all his negro houses to be searched diligently and effectually, once every fourteen days" for "guns, swords, clubs, and any other mischievous weapons, and finding any, to take them away."

Basically, the white people in power—the ones who were making the laws—used "dangerous" to describe any group they oppressed, and disarmed them accordingly.

Sometimes white people were considered "dangerous," too. Before the American Revolution, some colonies required people to swear their loyalty to the British before they could buy a weapon. Once the Revolution began, the script flipped: People had to pledge their allegiance to the Revolution to buy a gun.

But not all gun laws during this time were about oppressive disarmament—a whole bunch were passed for safety reasons. In 1686, for example, New Jersey prohibited people from carrying weapons because legislators thought this would lead to "great Fear and Quarrels." In 1771, New Jersey banned what it considered dangerous weapons: guns rigged with a string so that the shooter didn't have to pull the trigger. New Hampshire prohibited guns from being fired at night "unless in case of alarm, approach of an enemy, or other necessary defense." And several colonies had laws that allowed gunpowder, which was very flammable, to be stored only on the top floor of buildings.

That's just the tip of the iceberg. Historian Robert Spitzer and lawyer and researcher Mark Frassetto have extensively documented and cataloged the number of states that had these sorts of laws between 1607 and 1790. (A few notes at the outset: First, as Spitzer notes, even though the table on the next page indicates that these are "state" gun laws, some were enacted when the states were colonies, and some are local or municipal laws. And second, keep in mind that in 1790 there were only thirteen states.)

Number of States with Various Gun Laws, by Category (1607–1790)

TYPE OF LAW	DESCRIPTION OF TYPE OF LAW	NUMBER OF STATES
Brandishing Laws	Criminalized the threatening use of weapons, which typically included pistols and certain sorts of knives.	2
Carry Laws	Restricted people from carrying weapons in certain circumstances. In the eighteenth century, these laws focused on the general carrying around of firearms, usually in crowded places.	4
Dangerous Weapons Laws	Prohibited particularly dangerous or unusual weapons, like guns rigged with a string so that the shooter didn't have to pull the trigger.	1
Firing Weapons	Prohibited firing weapons in certain locations, such as within city limits, or at certain times, like at night.	9
Manufacturing, Inspection	Allowed state inspectors to make sure weapons were working correctly.	2
Registration, Taxation Laws	Required that gun sales or dealers be registered and taxed some gun sales.	2
Storage Laws	Said that guns and gunpowder had to be stored safely.	1

There were lots and lots of gun laws during this era—some meant to oppress Black and Indigenous people, and others that were safety based. But while the colonists were fine creating their own gun laws, they were *not* about to let the British do the same. When the British tried to disarm the colonists, a revolution began.

One thing to keep in mind as you read about the laws that were motivated by racial bias: Just because gun control laws were frequently racist, that doesn't mean there should be no gun control laws now. As Adam Winkler put it: "Property law was once profoundly racist, allowing racially restrictive covenants; voting law was once profoundly racist, allowing literacy tests; marriage law was once profoundly racist, allowing no interracial marriage. Does that mean we should never have laws regulating property, voting, or marriage?" No—it just means these laws must be applied equally to all people.

THE AMERICAN REVOLUTION

In 1773, Britain was deeply in debt because of foreign wars, and it began taxing the colonists in America on things like sugar, newspapers, and tea to make money. The colonists were frustrated by these taxes, in part because there was no one in Parliament fighting for what Americans wanted. This practice was known as taxation without representation, and the colonists were sick of it.

In protest, a group of American colonists sneaked onto East India Company ships and threw almost £10,000 worth of British tea into Boston Harbor. (That's more than $1.8 million in today's dollars.)

In response to the Boston Tea Party, Parliament passed a series of laws that were meant to make the American people obedient. These later became known as the Coercive Acts. The acts required the town to pay for all the destroyed tea and said the port of Boston would be closed until it did. The acts also appointed General Thomas Gage as the military governor of Boston, which meant the town would be occupied by thousands of British soldiers. Per King George III's orders, guns and ammunition were no longer allowed to be exported to the colonies.

Gage was afraid there would be an armed uprising and asked the British for twenty thousand troops to help him keep control of New

Americans throwing the Cargoes of the Tea Ships into the River, at Boſton

An engraving from 1789 of the Boston Tea Party. (Notice how back in the day, the letter s used to look like the letter f—weird, huh?). [Wikimedia Commons / W. D. Cooper]

England. But that was too expensive; they told Gage he should instead arrest and disarm rebellious colonists. So in April 1775, Gage sent seven hundred soldiers to confiscate the colonists' guns and ammunition from an arsenal in Concord, a town sixteen miles northwest of Boston. Someone, however, had tipped the Americans off.

On April 18, 1775, the night before the British were planning to head to Concord, a group of men including Paul Revere went from house to house warning people: *The British are coming. The British are coming . . . to get your guns.* General Gage was planning to disarm the colonists, and the midnight riders were trying to stop him.

The next morning, the British troops marched toward Concord, where they thought they would surprise the colonists and confiscate their guns. Instead, they were met by American militiamen at Lexington and then again at Concord, and it was on that day, April 19, 1775, that the Revolutionary War began.

You could argue that America's fight for independence from the British started with guns. That's why the issue of arms was at the tip-top of all the founders' minds when they wrote America's founding documents.

THE CONSTITUTION AND THE BILL OF RIGHTS

In 1781, late in the Revolutionary War, America ratified its first constitution: the Articles of Confederation and Perpetual Union. The national government was a single legislature with little power and no executive, known as the Congress of the Confederation. Even though it seems weird today to think of a government without a president, there was a time when our country didn't have one. The states functioned like independent countries—historian Gordon S. Wood compares the United States at this time to the modern-day European Union.

In 1783, after America won its independence from Britain, the economy took a turn for the worse. State taxes skyrocketed, and a lot of people went bankrupt. The Congress of the Confederation, however, was too weak to fix anything, which made people realize that America needed a stronger central government if it wanted to stay stable.

In the spring of 1787, states sent delegates to the Constitutional Convention in Philadelphia to discuss the issue. James Madison, a politician from Virginia, had been very eager to get to the Constitutional Convention—so eager that he got there ten days early. Before other folks arrived, he studied up on world governments—including ancient Greece, the Roman Empire, Switzerland, and the Netherlands—to come up with the outline of his ideal political system. In his view, there needed to be a strong central government to correct the errors of the Articles of Confederation, which had given the states too much freedom. But to prevent that government from becoming tyrannical, power needed to be spread across three branches—judicial, legislative, and executive.

James Madison was born on March 16, 1751, the oldest son of a wealthy Virginia family. He grew up on his family's plantation, where Black people were enslaved, and graduated from the College of New Jersey (now Princeton University), where he studied moral philosophy. Madison has been described by various historians as "scholarly, sickly, astute, and shy," a "painful public speaker, tending to mumble," and "weak of voice." Nevertheless, he decided to become a politician. He served in the Virginia government and the Continental Congress. After the Constitution was ratified, he was elected to the House of Representatives, where he

[Wikimedia Commons / The White House Historical Association]

drafted the Bill of Rights. Before being elected the fourth president of the United States (1809–1817), he also served as secretary of state. Madison died in 1836 at the age of eighty-five.

The fifty-five delegates were merchants, farmers, planters, and lawyers. Most were Protestants, and most were wealthy. George Washington, who had become famous during the Revolutionary War and was then the "most revered man in the nation," according to Pulitzer Prize–winning historian Alan Taylor, was elected to preside over the convention.

To avoid pressure from the public and encourage honest debate, the convention was held in secret—reporters and visitors couldn't attend the proceedings. The delegates even closed all the windows in the building to make sure no one was eavesdropping. Since it was summer, they deliberated in the heat.

After four months of intense (and sweaty) deliberation, they had a plan. They decided that the Constitution would be based on Madison's idea

A painting of the 1787 Constitutional Convention at the Pennsylvania State House, now known as Independence Hall (by Junius Brutus Stearns, 1856).
[Wikimedia Commons / Virginia Museum of Fine Arts]

for a government with three branches: executive, legislative, and judicial. But that wasn't the end of the matter. Before the Constitution could become law, it had to be ratified, or approved, by nine of the thirteen states. And this was way back before internet or TV, so in order to distribute the document, the delegates printed it in newspapers throughout the country.

A lot of people, particularly older people, were worried about Madison's vision for a strong central government. They were afraid that the new Constitution would lead to the return of a monarchy and that America would become just like Britain. In particular, the new Constitution allowed Congress to "provide for organizing, arming, and disciplining, the Militia" of the individual states. This clause was supposed to give Congress the power to call up state militias in case a foreign country invaded, but people were afraid it could be used by the federal government to take over state militias and take away their weapons.

And as we discussed before, the colonists much preferred the militia to a standing army, which they worried could lead to tyranny. Early Americans thought a militia, made up of citizens, would better protect their rights.

Starting in December 1787, five states—Delaware, Pennsylvania, New Jersey, Georgia, and Connecticut—ratified the Constitution, one after another. But once those five signed on, others were slow to follow.

Many states recommended adding a Bill of Rights like the one in England and those in some state constitutions, which would list basic political rights that the government couldn't take away, like freedom of speech and religion, the right to a speedy trial, and protection from unreasonable searches and seizures. In particular, five states recommended adding the right to bear arms because of their fear that militias would be disarmed; New Hampshire specifically recommended including a provision that "Congress shall never disarm any Citizen unless such as are or have been in Actual Rebellion."

To win over these states, the supporters of the Constitution promised that if the document was ratified, they would immediately propose those amendments. Massachusetts, Maryland, and South Carolina all signed on, which added up to eight states. The delegates needed just one more.

Finally, in June 1788, New Hampshire ratified the Constitution. The remaining states—Virginia, New York, North Carolina, and Rhode Island—would all sign on eventually. The Constitution was now the law of the land.

A year after ratification, just as he had promised, James Madison proposed a Bill of Rights, which was ultimately approved by three-quarters of the states in December 1791. These rights included the freedom of speech and religion, the right to due process, and many more—including the right to bear arms.

FEDERALISM

Have you ever heard your parents mention that they have to pay both state and federal taxes? Or have you noticed that some laws are state laws, passed by state governments, while other laws are federal laws, passed by Congress? State and federal governments share power and work in parallel; they each have their own laws, constitutions, and court systems. The complicated interplay between state and federal governments is known as "federalism."

The Constitution spells out certain express, or enumerated, powers belonging to the federal government. These include the right to regulate goods and services that travel between states (interstate commerce), the right to declare war, and the right to impose taxes. Whatever governmental powers that the Constitution does not specifically grant to the federal government, such as the power to make laws for public safety and to create school systems, are reserved for the states. And if state and federal laws conflict, Article VI of the Constitution—the Supremacy Clause—says that you have to follow the federal law.

State constitutions work separately from the federal Constitution. They might look a lot like the U.S. Constitution, but they don't have to.

There are also separate state and federal courts. Federal courts can only hear certain sorts of cases: cases about federal laws and cases between citizens of different states. This separation developed because federal courts were seen as better able to interpret federal law and because people worried a state court might treat its own citizens better than citizens of other states. State courts, on the other hand, have general jurisdiction, which means they can hear all sorts of cases.

★ THE BILL OF RIGHTS ★		
	AMENDMENT	**TRANSLATION**
I	*Congress shall make no law respecting an establishment of religion, or prohibiting the free exercise thereof, or abridging the freedom of speech, or of the press, or the right of the people peaceably to assemble, and to petition the Government for a redress of grievances.*	This amendment is chock-full of rights. First, it says that the government can't establish a state religion. This clause, called the Establishment Clause, often comes into play when local governments put up a Christmas display around the holidays—the U.S. Supreme Court has said that such displays are okay only if they also include items from other religions, like Jewish menorahs. The First Amendment also says that the government can't stop you from practicing your religion—for example, it usually can't pass a law saying that your religious traditions are illegal (though there are some exceptions). Next, the amendment says that the government can't punish you for speaking your mind (freedom of speech) or stop journalists from speaking theirs (freedom of press). Of course, there are limits to this: You can't falsely yell "Fire!" in a crowded theater because it would be a threat to public safety, for example, and journalists can't publish things they know are lies. The First Amendment also promises freedom of assembly, which means the government can't prevent you from joining organizations, clubs, or political parties, no matter how unpopular those groups may be. And finally, the amendment says you can ask the government to make right a wrong it has committed against you—that's what it means to petition for a redress of your grievances.
II	*A well regulated Militia, being necessary to the security of a free State, the right of the people to keep and bear Arms, shall not be infringed.*	Much more to come on this one.
III	*No Soldier shall, in time of peace be quartered in any house, without the consent of the Owner, nor in time of war, but in a manner to be prescribed by law.*	The Third Amendment says that during peacetime, soldiers aren't allowed to walk up to your house and demand that you let them stay with you. (This was more of a problem before the Revolutionary War, when British soldiers would demand that the colonists house and feed them.)

IV	The right of the people to be secure in their persons, houses, papers, and effects, against unreasonable searches and seizures, shall not be violated, and no Warrants shall issue, but upon probable cause, supported by Oath or affirmation, and particularly describing the place to be searched, and the persons or things to be seized.	The Fourth Amendment tells government officials (often police officers) that they can't stop and search you, your house, or your possessions unless they have a good reason to believe you've done something wrong. And they can't get a warrant to do so unless they explain to a judge very specifically who or what needs to be searched.
V	No person shall be held to answer for a capital, or otherwise infamous crime, unless on a presentment or indictment of a Grand Jury, except in cases arising in the land or naval forces, or in the Militia, when in actual service in time of War or public danger; nor shall any person be subject for the same offense to be twice put in jeopardy of life or limb; nor shall be compelled in any criminal case to be a witness against himself, nor be deprived of life, liberty, or property, without due process of law; nor shall private property be taken for public use, without just compensation.	The Fifth Amendment protects your right to a grand jury in cases when you're accused of a felony—in other words, more serious cases. A grand jury is a group of people who look at the evidence against you and decide whether you should be brought to trial—the idea is that people should be protected from false accusations of very serious crimes; you shouldn't have to go to trial at all if there isn't enough evidence. The Fifth Amendment also says you can't be tried twice for the same crime and that you can't be forced to testify against yourself, which means you have the "right to remain silent." The amendment next says you've got a right to "due process" before the government takes away your life, liberty, or property, which just means the government has to follow fair legal procedures when it punishes you or takes things from you. Finally, the amendment talks about eminent domain, which can come up, for example, when the government wants to build a highway but your house is in the way. The Fifth Amendment's Takings Clause says the government can only force you to move elsewhere if it pays you a fair amount for your property.

VI	In all criminal prosecutions, the accused shall enjoy the right to a speedy and public trial, by an impartial jury of the State and district wherein the crime shall have been committed, which district shall have been previously ascertained by law, and to be informed of the nature and cause of the accusation; to be confronted with the witnesses against him; to have compulsory process for obtaining witnesses in his favor, and to have the Assistance of Counsel for his defense.	The Sixth Amendment says you have a right to trial by jury in criminal cases, and that trial has to be speedy—you can't sit waiting for it forever. Your trial has to be in the same place where the crime was committed, you have to know what you were charged with, and you're entitled to question (or "confront") the people who accuse you at your trial. You also have the right to a lawyer to help you defend yourself.
VII	In Suits at common law, where the value in controversy shall exceed twenty dollars, the right of trial by jury shall be preserved, and no fact tried by a jury, shall be otherwise re-examined in any Court of the United States, than according to the rules of the common law.	The Seventh Amendment says you also have a right to a jury trial in civil (in addition to criminal) cases, as long as the property involved is worth more than twenty dollars. Of course, twenty dollars was a lot more money back then—about five hundred dollars in today's money.
VIII	Excessive bail shall not be required, nor excessive fines imposed, nor cruel and unusual punishments inflicted.	The Eighth Amendment says that if you're arrested, the judge can't set unreasonably high bail. Bail is the money you have to pay to be released while you're waiting for your trial to finish, which is returned to you as long as you show up to all your court appearances. Fines also can't be too high, and you can't be punished in ways that are "cruel and unusual," like torture. Many people think the death penalty is cruel and unusual punishment and so should be prohibited by the Eighth Amendment, but the U.S. Supreme Court disagrees.

IX	The enumeration in the Constitution, of certain rights, shall not be construed to deny or disparage others retained by the people.	The Ninth Amendment reminds people that they have more rights than just those listed in the Bill of Rights.
X	The powers not delegated to the United States by the Constitution, nor prohibited by it to the States, are reserved to the States respectively, or to the people.	Finally, the Tenth Amendment explains that if the Constitution doesn't explicitly give the federal government certain powers, and doesn't explicitly prohibit states from wielding certain powers, then they belong to the states or to the people. These are called reserved powers.

As we learned in chapter 1, the right to bear arms is guaranteed by the Second Amendment in the Bill of Rights. That's the part of the Constitution that talks about the use and ownership of guns in this country:

A well regulated Militia, being necessary to the security of a free State, the right of the people to keep and bear Arms, shall not be infringed.

But whose right is it? The militia's or the people's?

Let's break this famous passage down.

"A well regulated Militia"—got it. A militia is a military force composed of regular people, which could be called up at a moment's notice. And it's "well regulated" because the government can, for example, inspect all militiamen's guns at public musters.

And then we have . . .

". . . being necessary to the security of a free State." There's actually some disagreement on what "State" means here. Some scholars argue that when the Amendment uses the word "state," it's referring to individual states, like Arkansas or New Jersey. Others suggest that the phrase "free State" was common in the eighteenth century and meant a "free country." Either way, a militia was thought to be "necessary" for "security" because it could suppress insurrections and repel invasions.

Let's put those two clauses together: "A well regulated Militia, being necessary to the security of a free State." So before the Second Amendment talks about guns at all, it seems to just be noting that the militia would be useful for security reasons.

But then it says, "the right of the people." And then, near the end of the sentence, the Second Amendment finally tells us what right it actually seeks to protect: the right "to keep and bear Arms." Arms are weapons, and to "keep and bear" them just means you're allowed to have them.

And this is where it gets . . . confusing. Does "the people" here include *everyone*, or just men in the "well regulated militia"? Again, the Second Amendment protects the right to keep and carry weapons, including guns. But whose right is it? The militia's or the people's? This wonky sentence structure has resulted in endless debate and turmoil in the last few decades of American history.

The Constitution uses the phrase "right of the people" two other times: the First Amendment protects the "right of the people peaceably to assemble," and the Fourth Amendment protects the "right of the people . . . against unreasonable searches and seizures." When the First and Fourth Amendments use the phrase "right of the people," they clearly refer to a right that belongs to *everyone*—not one that might require membership in a militia or other organization. Which makes sense. When your teacher says, "all the *people* in this class get an A," wouldn't you be surprised if she meant only white men, ages eighteen to forty-five, who are part of a militia?

But then why does the Second Amendment include the militia clause in the first place? It must mean *something*.

Finally, the amendment says that right "shall not be infringed." In other words, hands off my guns!

A well regulated Militia, being necessary to the security of a free State, the right of the people to keep and bear Arms, shall not be infringed.

So there's definitely a right to bear arms. But whose right is it?

Until the twentieth century, almost everyone thought the answer to that question was the militia. America in the colonial era was full of gun laws. Some of these were safety based, while others were intended to disarm the people colonists considered dangerous—usually Black and Indigenous people.

But when the British tried to disarm the Americans, a revolution ensued. That revolution was a lot like the Glorious Revolution in England a century prior; in both cases, people rebelled against a British king who was trying to disarm them.

When the founders were drafting the documents that would create their new country, they had all of this history in mind. They created an amendment—the Second Amendment—that was supposed to prevent government tyranny by making sure state militias would never be disarmed.

In 2008, the U.S. Supreme Court would declare that the Second Amendment wasn't actually supposed to be about militias. It was always, the court would declare, about an *individual* right. But as we'll see, state governments passed a whole bunch of gun regulations in the years after the Bill of Rights was ratified. Even with the ink still fresh on the Bill of Rights, the founders definitely felt that the right to own guns could—and should—be limited.

THE ORIGINS OF THE GUN INDUSTRY

In the colonial era, guns were made one by one by independent gunsmiths. These guns were heavy, unbalanced, "cranky and imperfect," and there weren't nearly enough of them. In fact, America was so "undergunned" during the Revolutionary War that it had to buy guns from France. "The gun industry emerged out of the need for more domestically produced guns," writes historian Pamela Haag, "especially more guns for the national defense."

Remington, founded in 1816 in upstate New York, is America's oldest firearms company. Legend has it that the company was started by Eliphalet Remington II after he "forged his first gun barrel and with his own hands produced the finished gun," possibly because his father wouldn't buy him one—though some people doubt whether that story is accurate.

For years, barrel-making was Remington's main focus, but in 1845 the company struck a deal with the U.S. Army for five thousand rifles, which was quickly followed by an order for another thousand. After these initial government deals, the Remington Armory was built so that the company could handle its increased orders. In 1856, Eliphalet's three sons came to work with their father, and the company's name changed to E. Remington and Sons.

Although Eliphalet died shortly after the Civil War began, the company was taken over by his sons and became a major manufacturer of weapons for the North. In all, the company sold over two hundred thousand weapons to the army and navy during the conflict. "Anticipating a decline in the demand for military arms" after the war ended, the company changed "from the manufacture of implements of war to those of peace," such as sewing machines, bicycles, typewriters, and farm equipment.

The Remington Factory around 1874. [Wikimedia Commons / Case, Leon, et al. [1874] The Great Industries of the United States. J.B. Burr and Hyde, p. 818]

In 1836, a man named Samuel Colt was issued a patent that improved the functionality of the revolver and built a factory in Paterson, New Jersey. His gun allowed for repeated fire without the need to reload, which made it more reliable than its predecessors. Despite his patent, Colt's initial sales were slow, and by 1842, the company had gone bankrupt.

It wasn't until the outbreak of the Mexican-American War in 1846 that Colt returned to the arms business. By chance, Colt had presented his gun to Captain Samuel H. Walker, who used the revolver during his time with the Texas Rangers. The two men worked together to produce a gun called the Walker Colt. Colt sold a thousand of them to the U.S. government, which enabled him to restart his business. In the 1850s, Colt's business was booming, owing in large part to his sales to international markets. By 1855, Colt was able to build an enormous factory in Hartford, Connecticut.

Samuel Colt died in 1862, but his business continued to boom as a provider of weapons to both the North and the South throughout the Civil War.

Colt believed business was business, and even though the *New York Times* accused him of treason for selling guns to the southern states, Colt's company "was busy shipping arms to the South up to the last possible moment" in boxes labeled HARDWARE.

Smith & Wesson was founded in 1852 in Connecticut by Horace Smith and Daniel Baird Wesson. The company was sold to clothing manufacturer Oliver Winchester, who renamed it the New Haven Arms Company, headquartered in New Haven, Connecticut. (Smith and Wesson, meanwhile, refounded their company in 1856 in Springfield, Massachusetts.) The Civil War saved the New Haven Arms Company, which sold guns only to the Union, from bankruptcy. Later, the company would be renamed yet again: the Winchester Repeating Arms Company.

After the Civil War, gun demand plummeted throughout the country. Smith & Wesson made about fifteen guns per month in 1867, and the gun industry as a whole was "fighting to stay afloat." So gun manufacturers looked elsewhere for business—including the Ottoman Empire, Mexico, Egypt, Cuba, Sardinia, and Russia. "The development of an 'American' gun culture," writes Haag, "was bound up inextricably—and quite necessarily—with non-US, international markets." In other words, American gun culture wouldn't exist today if it weren't for these non-American gun sales.

CHAPTER 3

SLAVERY AND THE CIVIL WAR

In January 1811, Charles Deslondes decided to rebel. Unable to live through another day of slavery, he led a group of several hundred enslaved Black people toward New Orleans, Louisiana, chanting "freedom or death" and pillaging and burning plantations along the way. Inspired by the recent revolution of enslaved people in Haiti, their plan was to found an independent Black republic.

They almost succeeded. But just before they reached New Orleans, they were confronted by a well-armed white militia. Though there were between two hundred and five hundred rebels, only about half carried guns. A few minutes into the confrontation with the white militia, the rebels had run out of ammunition, but the militia kept shooting. Almost one hundred enslaved people lost their lives. When the rebels who survived the battle fled, the militia hunted them down and killed them, cutting their heads off and placing them on poles along the river.

Guns, in Charles Deslondes's rebellion, were power. Indeed, in the years leading up to the Civil War, guns defined what it meant to be a citizen. White people—who enjoyed all the privileges of citizenship— were allowed to own them. Black people were not. The Civil War was a

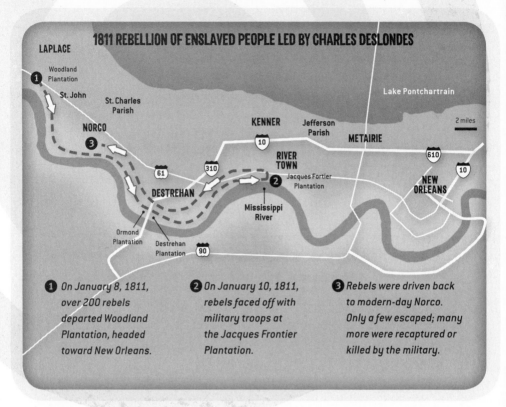

1811 REBELLION OF ENSLAVED PEOPLE LED BY CHARLES DESLONDES

LAPLACE

Woodland Plantation ❶

St. John

St. Charles Parish

NORCO

❸

KENNER

Jefferson Parish

METAIRIE

Lake Pontchartrain

2 miles

10

RIVER TOWN

61

310

❷

Jacques Fortier Plantation

DESTREHAN

Mississippi River

610

10

NEW ORLEANS

Ormond Plantation

Destrehan Plantation

90

❶ On January 8, 1811, over 200 rebels departed Woodland Plantation, headed toward New Orleans.

❷ On January 10, 1811, rebels faced off with military troops at the Jacques Frontier Plantation.

❸ Rebels were driven back to modern-day Norco. Only a few escaped; many more were recaptured or killed by the military.

fight over freedom for enslaved Black people, but it was also a fight over their right to own guns.

And just as in the colonial period, gun laws in the years before the Civil War went beyond those meant to unfairly disarm and oppress people. Throughout this era, there were also generally applicable gun laws, meant to cut down on gun violence and keep people safe.

BLEEDING KANSAS AND BEECHER'S BIBLES

Starting in the 1600s, Black people were kidnapped from Africa and taken to America in chains, on boats. Millions died during the journey. Once they arrived in America, they were forced into slavery, and frequently whipped, beaten, and murdered. They were abused and treated as if they were less than human. Nikole Hannah-Jones, a staff writer at the *New York Times Magazine*, explains that America had a "brutal system of slavery unlike anything that had existed in the world before." Slavery in America "was not conditional but racial. It was heritable and permanent, not temporary, meaning generations of black people were born into it and passed their enslaved status onto their children." And while many white people knew that slavery directly contradicted the principles of freedom they had fought for in the Revolutionary War, they got around the contradiction by falsely claiming that Black people were inferior to white people. By arguing that Black people "were a caste apart from all other humans," Hannah-Jones explains, white people were able to keep believing that "the 'we' in the 'We the People' was not a lie."

After the Constitution was ratified, the United States grew westward; by 1860, there were thirty-three states in the Union. White settlers were taking land from Indigenous people, slaughtering and displacing people who had lived there for centuries. In all this, they had the government's support—it wasn't just the actions of individual people taking land on their own.

As these settlers moved westward, a debate erupted over the new western states: Should slavery be allowed within their borders? Mostly in the North, people began to demand that slavery be abolished in the western territories. Many southerners, by contrast, worried that the existence of slavery in America—the backbone of their economy—was in danger.

In 1854, the U.S. Congress passed the Kansas-Nebraska Act, which was based on a principle of "popular sovereignty": It allowed settlers in the territories of Kansas and Nebraska to make their own decisions about whether to allow slavery. The Kansas-Nebraska Act effectively repealed the Missouri Compromise of 1820, which had outlawed slavery in any new states north of Missouri's southern border. The Kansas-Nebraska Act upset many people in the North, since it opened up more of the western territories to slavery. A June 1854 edition of the *Burlington Free Press* in Vermont reprinted the viewpoint of an opponent to the act:

> But the deed is done. The wrong to the North is consummated. A solemn compact is violated. The South having pledged itself that Slavery should never cross a certain line of latitude [after] Missouri was admited into the Union as a Slave State, has broken its pledge. Territory, by a solemn engagement set aside for freedom, is given up to Slavery.

After the Kansas-Nebraska Act passed, politicians who opposed it came together to form a new political party: the Republicans. The Republican Party's founding principle was its opposition to the Kansas-Nebraska Act and slavery; it was at that point the "liberal" party.

Soon pro- and antislavery settlers in Kansas began to fight over whether slavery would be allowed in Kansas. By 1856, the fight grew so violent that it became known as Bleeding Kansas.

People throughout the country were invested in what was happening in Kansas. If they supported slavery, they wanted it to exist in Kansas; if they were opposed to slavery, they wanted it to be a free state. Henry Ward Beecher—the "most famous preacher in America"—wanted it to be a free state. (His sister, by the way, was Harriet Beecher Stowe, who wrote *Uncle Tom's Cabin*.)

Henry Ward Beecher believed that the antislavery settlers in Kansas needed guns, specifically Sharps rifles, to fight against the proslavery settlers, arguing that there was "more moral power in one of those instruments, so far as the slaveholders of Kansas were concerned, than in a hundred Bibles." (Remember, he's a preacher! That's saying a lot.) Beecher's supporters sent hundreds of rifles to Kansas, but they labeled the boxes BIBLES so that they wouldn't be seized by proslavery forces on the way there. Soon enough, people started calling Sharps rifles "Beecher's Bibles."

POLITICAL PARTIES

Today, the United States has two primary political parties: Democrats, who are more liberal (the political left), and Republicans, who are more conservative (the political right). Democrats tend to be more interested in change, while Republicans tend to be more interested in maintaining things as they are. Generally, Democrats tend to support a strong federal government, while Republicans support states' rights. When candidates say they belong to a particular party, that helps voters understand what they stand for.

The Constitution doesn't require political parties; nevertheless, the United States has had a two-party system almost since the beginning. The first political parties were the Federalist Party, which supported a strong federal government, and the Democratic-Republican (or Jeffersonian Republican) Party, which supported states' rights and wanted to limit federal power.

A political cartoon from 1848 depicting the growing divides within the Whig Party.
[Wikimedia Commons / Library of Congress Prints and Photographs Division]

The Federalist Party started to lose appeal with voters in the early 1800s, and so for a while the only party was the Democratic-Republicans.

It wasn't until the 1830s that a second party, the Whig Party, emerged; around this same time, the Democratic-Republicans splintered and were replaced by the Democratic Party. The Whigs came together around their shared hatred of President Andrew Jackson, a Democrat notorious for his horrible treatment of Indigenous people. The Whigs also supported industry and modernization, which the Democrats thought would hurt rural farmers.

By the 1850s, the Whig Party was divided over many issues, including slavery. Antislavery Whigs joined with antislavery Democrats and other anti-slavery politicians to form the Republican Party.

Throughout the Civil War and for several decades after it, the Republican Party was the more liberal party, advocating for the abolition of slavery and the rights of free Black people. Over time, the parties' ideologies shifted: The Democratic Party began moving left, and the Republican Party began moving right. That's how we got to the two parties we have today.

There have always been smaller "third parties," such as the Libertarian Party, whose mission is to reduce the size of the government, and the Green Party, whose mission is largely focused on preserving the environment.

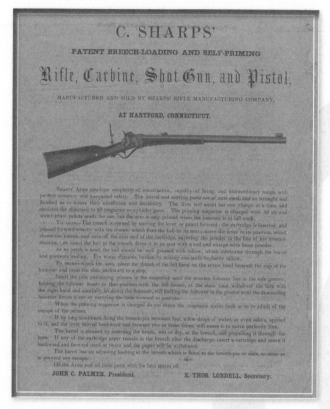

An advertisement for Sharps rifles, circa 1855. [Kansas State Historical Society]

On the other side of the argument was Andrew Pickens Butler, a senator from South Carolina. Butler, who strongly supported slavery and cowrote the Kansas-Nebraska Act, proposed a plan for the federal government to disarm the antislavery settlers in Kansas by sending a posse comitatus (a group of armed citizens who are summoned to help local law enforcement, similar to a militia) to seize their guns:

> The President of the United States is under the highest and most
> solemn obligations to interpose; and, if I were to indicate the man-
> ner in which he should interpose in Kansas, I would point out the old
> common law process. I would serve a warrant on Sharpe's rifles, and if
> Sharpe's rifles did not answer the summons, and come into court on a

day certain, or if they resisted the sheriff, I would summon the posse comitatus, and would have Colonel Sumner's regiment to be a part of that posse comitatus.

Several weeks later, Senator Charles Sumner of Massachusetts angrily called Butler a disgrace and said his plan violated the Second Amendment:

Really, sir, has it come to this? The rifle has ever been the compan-
ion of the pioneer, and, under God, his tutelary protector against the
red man and the beast of the forest. Never was this efficient weapon
more needed in just self-defence, than now in Kansas, and at least
one article in our National Constitution must be blotted out, before the
complete right to it can in any way be impeached. And yet, such is the
madness of the hour, that, in defiance of the solemn guaranty, embod-
ied in the Amendments to the Constitution, that "the right of the people
to keep and bear arms shall not be infringed," the people of Kansas
have been arraigned for keeping and bearing them, and the Senator
from South Carolina has had the face to say openly, on this floor, that
they should be disarmed—of course, that the fanatics of Slavery, his
allies and constituents, may meet no impediment. Sir, the Senator is
venerable with years . . . but neither his years, nor his position, past or
present, can give respectability to the demand he has made, or save
him from indignant condemnation, when, to compass the wretched
purposes of a wretched cause, he thus proposes to trample on one of
the plainest provisions of constitutional liberty.

Sumner said the right to bear arms was one of the "plainest provisions of constitutional liberty," in part because rifles were necessary for
antislavery settlers to protect themselves from "the fanatics of Slavery."

(But note that Sumner—who might seem like a good guy for condemning slavery—claims that settlers were also protecting themselves against the Indigenous people, when really the settlers were stealing Indigenous land.) As we'll see later, it was pretty rare at this time for the Second Amendment to be viewed as an individual liberty, rather than something tied to militia service.

Sumner had ruffled some feathers by condemning both slavery and Butler in his speech. In response, Preston Brooks, another congressman from South Carolina, attacked Sumner with a cane in the Senate while a third South Carolina congressman pulled out a gun to prevent bystanders from intervening. The men from South Carolina knew how powerful guns could be. And they weren't interested in disarming people equally; they were allowed to have guns, but opponents to slavery weren't.

DRED SCOTT AND JOHN BROWN

The miniature civil war in Bleeding Kansas was ripping the country apart along its center seam. That seam ripped even further in 1857,

A lithograph of Preston Brooks's 1856 attack on Charles Sumner. [Wikimedia Commons]

when the Supreme Court decided the case of *Dred Scott v. Sandford*.

Dred Scott, an enslaved Black man, was suing for his freedom. He argued that because he had previously lived in a free territory, he was entitled to his freedom in Missouri, a state where people were enslaved. At this time, lawsuits of this sort were relatively common; when Scott brought his case, about a hundred other enslaved people in Missouri had won their freedom by arguing that they became free by working or living in a free state.

Unfortunately, by the time Dred Scott's case made it to the Missouri Supreme Court, the court's composition had changed to majority Democratic and proslavery. (Remember, the Democrats were the more conservative party at this time.) The court's opinion made clear that the decision was a political one, given the worsening national tensions over slavery: "Times now are not as they were when the former decisions on this subject were made," the court wrote. "Since then, not only individuals but States have been possessed with a dark and fell spirit in relation to slavery. . . . Under such circumstances, it does not behoove the State of Missouri to show the least countenance to any measure which might gratify this spirit."

Scott then decided to bring his case in federal court, where he sued for battery and wrongful imprisonment. After losing his case in the trial court, Scott appealed to the U.S. Supreme Court, which was then majority Democratic and proslavery. The case was getting more attention because by that point it had shifted its focus to the constitutionality of the Missouri Compromise. "What had begun in 1846 as an attempt by Scott to gain freedom for himself and his family," writes law professor and historian Paul Finkelman, "had become a case with potentially monumental legal and political significance."

In a 7–2 ruling, the Supreme Court denied Scott's request for his freedom, holding that Scott had no right to sue in the first place. This was a horrible, hateful case; historian and lawyer Michael Waldman

An 1882 painting of Dred Scott based on an 1857 photograph.
[Wikimedia Commons / Missouri History Museum]

describes it as "the worst in American history." Writing for the majority, Chief Justice Taney said that Black people were "a subordinate and inferior class of beings" who "had no rights which the white man was bound to respect." He wrote that Black people weren't citizens of the United States and couldn't sue in federal court:

> We think ... that they are not included, and were not intended to be included, under the word "citizens" in the Constitution, and can therefore

claim none of the rights and privileges which that instrument provides for and secures to citizens of the United States. On the contrary, they were at that time considered as a subordinate and inferior class of beings, who had been subjugated by the dominant race, and, whether emancipated or not, yet remained subject to their authority, and had no rights or privileges but such as those who held the power and the Government might choose to grant them.

The majority opinion declared that Black people were not entitled to the rights of citizenship, including the right to bear arms. Akhil Reed Amar, a leading scholar of constitutional law, explains that Chief Justice Taney thought that "*if* free blacks were citizens, it would necessarily follow that they had a right of *private* arms bearing," and "for Taney all this wrongly meant that black citizenship could never be." At that time, the idea of Black people with guns was terrifying to white people, in part because they feared that those whom they oppressed would rebel.

Their fears came from rebellions like Charles Deslondes's, which weren't uncommon in the 1800s. In 1831 in Virginia, for example, an enslaved preacher named Nat Turner led a rebellion that killed fifty-five white people and instilled fear throughout the South. In response to revolts like these, groups of armed white people continued to patrol enslaved Black people during this era, enforcing curfews, demanding their passes, and breaking up gatherings. In particular, these patrollers sought to seize weapons from any Black people they saw.

An 1825 Florida law said that patrollers were allowed to "enter into all negro houses," free or not, and "lawfully seize and take away" any "arms, weapons, and ammunition." (Compare this to the Fourth Amendment, which was supposed to protect "the right of the people to be secure in their persons, houses, papers, and effects against unreasonable searches and seizures.") To keep Black people powerless, white patrollers took away their guns.

This practice wasn't limited to Black people who were enslaved; even free Black people were disarmed. Who were the free Black people at this time? Some were freed by "manumission"—a formal act of emancipation by an enslaver—while others had run away from slavery or immigrated from places such as the West Indies. In 1860, a tenth of the entire Black population was free—about 500,000 Black people.

In *Dred Scott*, Chief Justice Taney went further than the specific issue before him. He also said that the federal government couldn't prevent slavery from being imposed in the new western territories, holding several portions of the Missouri Compromise unconstitutional. This opinion affected more states than just the two mentioned in the Kansas-Nebraska Act, and it was more long-lasting: Before *Dred Scott*, Congress could always change its mind and pass a new law saying there wasn't going to be any more slavery in the West. But by ruling that the federal government could *never* prevent slavery from being imposed in the new western territories, the Supreme Court prevented this from happening.

Before the decision was even announced, Democratic President James Buchanan praised its outcome—an extreme breach of judicial ethics and a sign that the decision was a political one. Taney's goal was to "settle the issue of slavery in the territories once and for all," Finkelman explains, and he hoped that his decision would destroy the Republican Party. To the contrary, his decision would factor into Abraham Lincoln's election in 1860 and, eventually, the outbreak of the Civil War.

The opinion sparked a lot of anger from Republicans, who called the decision "wicked," "atrocious," and "abominable." In response to the *Dred Scott* decision and the Kansas-Nebraska Act, a white abolitionist named John Brown raided the town arsenal in Harpers Ferry, West Virginia, in 1859, hoping to ignite a rebellion of enslaved Black people. Many of his men were killed in the revolt, but he survived and was captured, tried, and hanged for treason.

One of the witnesses to Brown's death was "a young actor with seductive eyes and curly hair, already a fanatical believer in Southern nationalism," who went by the name of John Wilkes Booth. Keep that name in mind—you'll see it again.

A mural representing John Brown between pro- and antislavery forces.
[Wikimedia Commons / U.S. National Archives and Records Administration]

John Brown's raid at Harpers Ferry had struck a nerve. Southerners were already afraid of armed uprisings—one reason why they prohibited Black people from owning weapons. And Democrats fanned the flame of Harpers Ferry by suggesting that the Republicans supported John Brown's raid; the 1860 election was coming up, and Democrats wanted to win. Democrats began using the term "Black Republicanism" to tie their political opponents to John Brown and his support of Black people.

Harpers Ferry convinced more and more southerners that the North was going to destroy slavery. And when Abraham Lincoln was elected president in November 1860, that was the final straw.

PRESIDENT LINCOLN AND THE CIVIL WAR

Abraham Lincoln was a Republican and an opponent of slavery, but he wasn't an abolitionist. He opposed its expansion, but he didn't think slavery should be outlawed where it was already legal. And even though he thought slavery was wrong, he also thought there was "a physical difference between the white and black races which I believe will for ever forbid the two races from living together on terms of social and political equality." While his views on race changed during the Civil War, explains historian Eric Foner, "he never became a principled egalitarian in the manner of abolitionists such as Frederick Douglass and Wendell Phillips or Radical Republicans like Charles Sumner."

Still, southerners got nervous when he was elected president. In a February 1860 speech at Cooper Union that helped spark his presidential campaign, Lincoln had criticized the ruling in *Dred Scott*. He also addressed the incident at Harpers Ferry. Lincoln denounced the South's attempt to blame Republicans for John Brown's raid:

> You charge that we stir up insurrections among your slaves. We deny it; and what is your proof? Harper's Ferry! John Brown!! John Brown was no Republican; and you have failed to implicate a single Republican in his Harper's Ferry enterprise. . . .
>
> Some of you admit that no Republican designedly aided or encouraged the Harper's Ferry affair; but still insist that our doctrines and declarations necessarily lead to such results. We do not believe it. . . .
>
> Slave insurrections are no more common now than they were before the Republican party was organized. What induced the Southampton insurrection, twenty-eight years ago, in which, at least, three times as many lives were lost as at Harper's Ferry?

Abraham Lincoln, uncharacteristically beardless, an hour before he delivered his speech at New York City's Cooper Union.
[Wikimedia Commons / U.S. National Archives and Records Administration]

But Lincoln's denials didn't do much. Southern states were convinced that Lincoln would ban slavery, and so before he was even sworn in, South Carolina, Mississippi, Florida, Alabama, Georgia, Louisiana, and Texas all seceded from the Union. A few months later, Virginia,

Arkansas, North Carolina, and Tennessee would join them. These eleven states became known as the Confederacy, and the North became known as the Union.

In April 1861, Confederates fired the first shots of the Civil War at Fort Sumter, in Charleston, South Carolina. Lincoln thought the war would end in ninety days, but it dragged on for years. Millions of men would fight and become experienced with guns, almost two hundred thousand of them were Black.

On April 9, 1865, the South finally surrendered, although slavery wouldn't be officially abolished until December 1865 with the Thirteenth Amendment. The Union army let soldiers buy their muskets for a fair price, and many Black soldiers took them up on their offer. Worried about whether their rights would be respected, especially in the southern states, they took their guns home to protect themselves. They weren't able to keep them for long.

GENERAL RESTRICTIONS ON GUN OWNERSHIP

In the years before and during the Civil War, gun laws were often based on oppression and disarmament—but there were also plenty of generally applicable, safety-based gun laws. Bans on concealed weapons (weapons carried outside of plain view) emerged in 1813, when Kentucky and Louisiana first adopted them. They were soon followed by similar laws across the country:

★ An 1820 Indiana law said that "every person, not being a traveler, who shall wear or carry a dirk, pistol, sword in a cane, or other dangerous weapon concealed, shall upon conviction thereof, be fined in any sum not exceeding one hundred dollars."

★ An 1837 Arkansas law said that "every person who shall wear any pistol, dirk, butcher or large knife, or a sword in a cane, concealed as a weapon, unless upon a journey, shall be adjudged guilty of a misdemeanor." (A dirk is a sort of knife, often used in fighting.)

★ Virginia said in 1838 that it is against the law "to habitually or generally keep or carry about his person any pistol, dirk, bowie knife, or any other weapon of the like kind . . . hidden or concealed from common observation."

★ Alabama's 1839 concealed-carry law explained that its purpose was "to suppress the evil practice of carrying weapons secretly."

★ In Colorado, an 1862 law said that if "any person or persons shall, within any city, town, or village in this Territory, whether the same is incorporated or not, carry concealed upon his or her person any pistol, bowie knife, dagger, or other deadly weapon," that person "shall, on conviction thereof before any justice of the peace of the proper county, be fined in a sum not less than five, nor more than thirty-five dollars."

There were other sorts of gun laws during this period, too. In 1845, Connecticut said that anyone who fired a gun "within the limits of the city of New Haven, except for military purposes, without permission first obtained from the mayor of said city, shall be punished by fine not exceeding seven dollars, or by imprisonment in the county jail not exceeding thirty days." Alabama in 1856 and Kentucky in 1859 made it illegal to sell, give, or loan a weapon to a minor. And North Carolina (like other states) taxed in 1858 "every dirk, bowie-knife, pistol, sword-cane, dirk-cane and rife cane, used or worn about the person of any one at any time during the year, one dollar and twenty-five cents."

Historian Robert Spitzer and lawyer and researcher Mark Frassetto have cataloged the many sorts of gun laws in this era.

(Again, note that Spitzer and Frassetto list more categories than those mentioned here, and keep in mind that in 1867 there were thirty-seven states total.)

	Number of States with Various Gun Laws, by Category (1791–1867)	
TYPE OF LAW	**DESCRIPTION OF TYPE OF LAW**	**NUMBER OF STATES**
Brandishing	Criminalized the threatening use of weapons, which typically included pistols and certain sorts of knives.	3
Carry	Restricted people from carrying weapons around in certain circumstances. In the nineteenth century, these were mostly focused on the secret (or "concealed") carrying of weapons.	19
Dangerous Weapons	Prohibited particularly dangerous or unusual weapons, like guns rigged with a string so that the shooter didn't have to pull the trigger.	4
Firing Weapons	Prohibited firing weapons in certain locations, such as within city limits, or at certain times, like at night.	14
Manufacturing, Inspection	Allowed state inspectors to make sure weapons were working correctly.	10
Registration, Taxation	Said that gun sales or dealers had to be registered, and taxed some gun sales.	6
Storage	Said that guns and gunpowder had to be stored safely.	6

As you can see, there were plenty of generally applicable gun laws in the years before and during the Civil War, just as in the colonial era. "These laws weren't racist in origin," Adam Winkler explains, since at this time Black people in many states "were already prohibited from even owning a gun. The target of concealed carry laws was white people, namely violence-prone men who were a bit too eager to defend their honor by whipping out their guns. These laws, which might be thought of as the first modern gun control laws, had their origin in reducing criminal violence among whites."

The Civil War was a fight over the right for Black people to be free, but that fight was deeply interwoven with guns. When a miniature civil war erupted in Kansas over whether it should enter the Union as a free state, abolitionists sent "Beecher's Bibles" to antislavery settlers. When Dred Scott sued for his freedom, the U.S. Supreme Court said he wasn't a citizen because if he was, he would have the right to own guns. And when John Brown tried to lead an armed revolt against slavery, he helped spark the Civil War.

Throughout this era, Black people were prevented from owning firearms, but there were also generally applicable gun laws, some of which were targeted at white criminality. Laws like these make clear that the right to bear arms was always limited, sometimes *very* limited— even in the early days of our country. Legislation this restrictive would be totally unacceptable to the National Rifle Association today, which argues against any gun regulation, no matter how small. But the early NRA was very different.

THE ORIGINS OF THE NRA

The National Rifle Association's story begins in late summer of 1871, when Colonel William C. Church and General George W. Wingate founded the organization in the office of the *Army and Navy Journal* in lower Manhattan.

William C. Church, a foreign war correspondent for the *New York Times*, was born in Boston in 1836. During the Civil War, Church fought for the North. In 1863, he and his brother Francis founded a newspaper called the *United States Army and Navy Journal and Gazette of the Regular and Volunteer Forces—the Army and Navy Journal* for short.

The very first issue of the Army and Navy Journal.
[Wikimedia Commons / Army and Navy Journal]

In its first issue, the journal explained that its "one paramount aim" was to support the armed forces: "We believe in the Army. We believe it is a necessity to the Nation. . . . We have no other creed than the Army has—the creed of loyalty, the creed of nationality. Of party politics we know nothing and care nothing." As the *New York Times* put it in 1865, the Church brothers "sought to supply what hitherto we had been without—an organ devoted to the military and naval history and organizations of the United States." Church published editorial after editorial comparing the shooting skills of the American militia to the European troops he had seen as a foreign war correspondent, arguing that the Americans needed to improve.

George Wingate, who was born in New York City in 1840, was "deeply impressed by Church's editorials." Since childhood, Wingate had been interested in hunting and target shooting, and during the Civil War, he was horrified by the poor shooting skills of urban-dwelling Union soldiers. (Like Church, Wingate fought for the North.) Confederate soldiers, who tended to come from rural states where gun ownership and use were more common, were far more experienced with firearms. If the North had been better trained, Wingate thought, it might have won the war more quickly.

Wingate started looking for books that could help teach soldiers how to shoot, but he found nothing. So he reached out to Church, the man behind the *Army and Navy Journal*, to see whether he had any leads. Church agreed that there weren't any good sources available and suggested that Wingate put together a rifle training manual, which Church would then publish in the *Army and Navy Journal* in six parts between 1870 and 1871. Based on the interest in Wingate's *Manual for Rifle Practice*, the duo decided that an association should be organized in New York City "to promote and encourage rifle shooting on a scientific basis," modeled off a similar group in Great Britain that held rifle-shooting competitions. The National Guard, they thought, wasn't doing enough to encourage this reform, so "private enterprise must take up the matter and push it into life."

Not long after, Church invited Wingate and interested officers of the New York National Guard to the offices of the *Army and Navy Journal*, where they sketched out a plan for the NRA. They drew up a "certificate of incorporation"—a legal document necessary to start a company or corporation. On November 17, 1871, New York approved the certificate, issuing a charter for the NRA "to promote rifle practice, and for this purpose to provide a suitable range or ranges in the vicinity of New York, and a suitable place for the meetings of the Association in the city itself, and to promote the introduction of a system of aiming drill and target firing among the National Guard of New York and the militia of other States."

The NRA's first president was another Civil War veteran: General Ambrose Burnside. He, too, thought Americans needed to improve their shooting skills. "Out of ten soldiers who are perfect in drill and the manual of arms," he said, referring to his troops in the Civil War, "only one knows the purpose of the sights on his gun or can hit the broad side of a barn." Church became vice president, and Wingate became secretary, but Burnside was rarely around, so Church and Wingate effectively functioned as the group's leaders.

General Ambrose Burnside, first president of the NRA (1871–1872). The word "sideburns" comes from his name, believe it or not. [Library of Congress]

At its start, the NRA wanted to build a shooting range for target-shooting competitions, but the group didn't have much money. So Church and Wingate asked their friend New York State Assemblyman David W. Judd for help. Judd persuaded the New York legislature to pass a law giving the NRA money to buy a shooting range on Long Island, where the organization began sponsoring international target-shooting competitions. The land cost about $25,000 back then, which would be around $500,000 today.

Shooting competitions were held at Creedmoor, the NRA's range on Long Island.
[Library of Congress]

New York continued to support the NRA's target-shooting competitions until 1880, when Governor Alonzo Cornell told Wingate that rifle practice wasn't necessary anymore: "There will be no war in my time or in the time of my children," Cornell said. "Rifle practice for these men is a waste of money, and I shall not countenance in my presence anything as foolish as a discussion of the rifle shooting at Creedmoor." Without money from the government, the

NRA went dormant; in 1892, the NRA's board of directors voted to put all the NRA's records in storage.

But the NRA would come back to life a decade later. As journalist and historian Osha Gray Davidson explains in *Under Fire: The NRA and the Battle for Gun Control*, the NRA was reborn in 1901 "in response to the growing clamor for 'military preparedness.'" Davidson suggests the clamor was a response to the South African Boer War—which the British had nearly lost, in large part because the South Africans were excellent at rifle shooting—while historian Robert J. Spitzer believes it was in response to the 1898 Spanish-American War. Whatever the reason, there was a newfound interest in the group.

James A. Drain, the NRA's president in the early 1900s, worked to help the group spread across the country. The NRA was then centered on the East Coast, but he wanted to convert "the association to an umbrella organization for hunters, farmers, ranchers, sport shooters, and gun collectors everywhere," and so he helped found rifle club branches throughout the United States. For the next several decades, the NRA sponsored nationwide target-shooting contests and organized the first U.S. Olympic rifle team, which eventually won a gold medal. As we'll see in the next several chapters, however, the aim of the NRA would soon change.

CHAPTER 4

RECONSTRUCTION

fter the Union won the Civil War in 1865, many Black soldiers were able to take their guns home—but Black people were not yet officially considered citizens. During the period known as Reconstruction, the country began making progress toward equality. The Thirteenth, Fourteenth, and Fifteenth Amendments were passed, which ended slavery, guaranteed equal protection under the law, and granted Black men the right to vote. And for the first time in American history, Black people were able to serve in the government: In 1870, forty-two-year-old Hiram Revels of Mississippi became the first Black U.S. senator.

But the progress was short-lived. Soon southern states would pass the Black Codes, laws meant to keep Black people powerless, many of which also prohibited Black people from owning guns. Groups like the Ku Klux Klan emerged to terrorize Black people who sought equality and to disarm those who were able to own guns in the brief window after the Civil War. White people in the South were worried that the people they oppressed would rebel, so they continued to disarm Black people throughout the Reconstruction era and beyond.

PRESIDENTIAL RECONSTRUCTION AND THE BLACK CODES

In the last few years of the Civil War, President Lincoln thought a lot about how he would bring the South back into the Union. In a speech delivered at the White House on April 11, 1865—two days after the South surrendered—Lincoln described the difficulty of coming up with a plan to "reconstruct" the country.

He also proposed that *some* Black Americans deserved the right to vote: "It is also unsatisfactory to some that the elective franchise is not given to the colored man. I would myself prefer that it were now conferred on the very intelligent, and on those who serve our cause as soldiers." (Note that Lincoln didn't say he thought all Black people should vote—just those who had fought in the Civil War or who were educated enough. And remember that women couldn't vote at this time either.)

Lincoln's speech infuriated Confederate sympathizer John Wilkes Booth, who was in the audience—yes, *that* John Wilkes Booth, the one who had witnessed John Brown's hanging. After Lincoln's speech, Booth allegedly vowed that it was the last one Lincoln would ever make.

Three days later, on April 14, Booth assassinated President Lincoln at Ford's Theatre in Washington, D.C. using a pistol he had hidden in his pocket. Lincoln's successor would have to be the one to reconstruct the country.

Unfortunately, that successor was Andrew Johnson, who was vice president when Lincoln was assassinated. President Johnson was horribly racist, described at the time as holding "almost unconquerable prejudices against the African race." He fervently opposed Black suffrage, and in 1866, a critic described him as a "man of narrow mind, bitter prejudices, and inordinate self-estimation" who was "egotistic to the point of mental disease."

Johnson's plan for Reconstruction wasn't really a plan. He asked only that southern states do three things before they could return to the Union: abolish slavery, pay back their war debts, and pledge their allegiance to the Union. They certainly didn't have to allow Black people to vote. Under Johnson's plan, Foner writes, "the white South [had] a virtual free hand in regulating the region's internal affairs."

Johnson's permissiveness opened the door to the Black Codes, a series of laws enacted by southern states in 1865 and 1866 that were supposed to define the rights of Black people. The Black Codes clarified that Black people could sue, marry, and own property, but they also trapped Black people in an abusive labor system. Under the codes, Black people were required to sign exploitative labor contracts and could be arrested or fined if they left their jobs. The laws, which were designed to force Black people to work for the people who had previously enslaved them, essentially replaced the slavery that had existed before the war. Louisiana Republican Benjamin F. Flanders aptly surmised in 1865 that "the South's whole thought and time will be given to plans for getting things back as near to slavery as possible."

The Black Codes also prevented Black people from voting or being part of a jury. Several states also said that Black people had no right to bear arms. In Alabama, it was not "lawful for any freedman, mulatto, or free person of color in this State, to own fire-arms, or carry about his person a pistol or other deadly weapon." Florida's Black Code said Black people could not possess "any bowie-knife, dirk, sword, firearms or ammunition of any kind" without a license, or else they would be publicly whipped and the government would seize the weapon. And the Black Codes of Mississippi required that:

no freedman, free negro or mulatto . . . shall keep or carry fire-arms of any kind, or any ammunition, dirk or bowie knife, and on conviction thereof, in the county court, shall be punished by fine, not exceeding ten dollars, and pay the costs of such proceedings . . . and it shall be the duty of every civil and military officer to arrest any freedman, free negro or mulatto found with any such arms or ammunition, and cause him or her to be committed for trial in default of bail.

Some southern governments forcibly confiscated the weapons that Black soldiers had taken home from the war. George McKee, a Republican Representative from Mississippi, explained that he had "seen those muskets taken from them and confiscated under this Democratic law. The United States did not even protect the soldier in retaining the musket which it had given him, and which he had borne in its defense."

Lawmakers argued that disarmament was necessary to prevent an insurrection—the same argument they'd made before the war—but Black families needed the guns to protect themselves from widespread racial violence. In *Southern Horrors: Lynch Law in All Its Phases*, Black journalist and activist Ida B. Wells explained that guns were often the only way Black people could protect themselves: "The only case where the proposed lynching did *not* occur, was where the men armed themselves in Jacksonville, Fla., and Paducah, Ky., and prevented it. The only times an Afro-American who was assaulted got away has been when he had a gun and used it in self-defense."

In response to the Black Codes, Congress passed the 1866 Civil Rights Act, which sought to establish racial equality. It defined "all persons born in the United States excluding Indians," but including Black people, as citizens entitled to "full and equal benefit of all laws and proceedings for the security of person and property as is enjoyed by white citizens." In this way, the Civil Rights Act rejected the logic of *Dred Scott*. Andrew Johnson vetoed the act, but Congress overrode his veto, and the law passed on April 9, 1866—exactly a year to the day after the Civil War ended.

HOW DOES A BILL BECOME A LAW?

A bill can start in either chamber of Congress—the Senate or the House of Representatives. If more than half of the chamber in which it was introduced votes in favor of the bill, it moves on to the other chamber. If the bill then receives more than half of the vote in the second chamber, it moves on to the president's desk. The president can either sign the bill or veto it. ("Veto" means to reject something.) If the president signs the bill, it becomes law. And even if the president vetoes a bill, it might still become law: Congress can override the president's veto if two-thirds of each chamber vote in favor of the bill.

After the Civil Rights Act was passed, most Southern states modified their Black Codes so that they didn't explicitly mention race. But in practice, the laws that remained—like vagrancy laws, which required that people get jobs or be punished—were still enforced against only Black people.

RADICAL RECONSTRUCTION

Opposition to Johnson was brewing, particularly among Radical Republicans—the most liberal wing of the Republican Party. Radical Republicans thought that the Civil Rights Act was well and good but that there needed to be new constitutional amendments to more firmly guarantee equality.

So Representative John Bingham of Ohio proposed what would become the Fourteenth Amendment, ratified in July 1868. Like the

Civil Rights Act of 1866, the Fourteenth Amendment guaranteed that "all persons born or naturalized in the United States, and subject to the jurisdiction thereof, are citizens of the United States and of the State wherein they reside."

Some scholars argue that the whole point of the Fourteenth Amendment was to make sure that southern state governments couldn't disarm newly free Black people in the South, so that they could protect themselves against racial violence. Indeed, Akhil Reed Amar argues that Radical Republicans saw the Second Amendment as an individual right of self-defense, not a right belonging to the militia. "Between 1775 and 1866," he writes, "the poster boy of arms morphed from the Concord minuteman to the Carolina freedman."

Other scholars, including Michael Waldman, disagree, arguing that the drafters of the Fourteenth Amendment weren't suggesting that the Second Amendment bestowed an individual right and weren't opposed to gun laws that applied equally to people of all races. (Keep this disagreement in mind for chapter 9, when we discuss the case of *District of Columbia v. Heller*—it has to do with the whether the Second Amendment is a right belonging to the militia or to the people.)

In February 1869, Congress approved the Fifteenth Amendment (ratified in 1870), which guaranteed that a citizen's right to vote would not be denied "on account of race, color, or previous condition of servitude." Together, the Fourteenth and Fifteenth Amendments were meant to guarantee equal rights to the people who had recently been freed from slavery—or at least the men. Women of any race wouldn't be able to vote until 1920, when the Nineteenth Amendment was ratified.

By 1870, the country seemed to be making progress. Radical Reconstruction led to the first public school systems in the South, laws against racial discrimination, fairer tax laws, and the election of Black Americans to public office throughout the South. All in all, sixteen Black people served in the U.S. Congress during Reconstruction, nine of whom had previously been enslaved. Many others served as major state officials: governor, lieutenant governor, treasurer, superintendent of education, and secretary of state, for example. But the progress wouldn't last.

The first Black senator and representatives, elected during Radical Reconstruction.
[Library of Congress]

THE RISE OF THE KU KLUX KLAN AND WHITE SUPREMACY

Frightened by the gains Black people were making during Reconstruction, groups of white men, including the Ku Klux Klan, began to torment Black communities. The Ku Klux Klan was formed in Tennessee in 1868 by six white men who had fought for the Confederacy. Soon the group spread across the country as former Confederate soldiers started to use the name KKK. Eric Foner explains that the KKK sought to reestablish white supremacy in the South by aiming "to reverse the interlocking changes sweeping over the South during Reconstruction: to destroy the Republican party's infrastructure, undermine the Reconstruction state, reestablish control of the black labor force, and restore racial subordination in every aspect of Southern life."

The KKK "operated like a huge slave patrol," Roxanne Dunbar-Ortiz explains—though unlike before, it was now acting illegally. KKK members wore white robes and hoods and pretended to be ghosts of Confederate soldiers, terrorizing Black people with unchecked violence. They beat or murdered Black people for just about any reason: holding public office, managing to acquire an education, seeking to change employers, speaking disrespectfully to a white person, or even just being successful. As Foner explains, violence was often directed at Black people "who no longer adhered to patterns of behavior demanded under slavery." In particular, Black people in public office were threatened with daily violence.

In some states, like Texas, violence was particularly widespread. A report presented by the Committee on Lawlessness and Violence at the 1868–1869 Texas Constitutional Convention explained the atrocities committed against Black people and white supporters of the Union:

And when we come to examine the persecutions suffered by the freed people, the mass of testimony is so overwhelming that no man of candor can for a moment question the statement that they are, in very many parts of the State, wantonly maltreated and slain, simply because they are free, and claim to exercise the rights of freemen. Some months ago, in Panola county, a party of whites rode up to a cabin wherein some freed people were dancing, and deliberately fired upon them, killing four, one a woman, and seriously wounding several others. . . . In Fort Bend county [1867], the freed people were holding a fair to procure funds to finish their church, and while they were singing a hymn two white men rode by and fired their pistols into the church. . . . In [Falls] county, a few weeks ago, two armed white men, in open day, went to the house of a colored man and without any provocation murdered him. . . . And so the bloody story runs.

We mention some minor outrages. . . . Last week a colored woman was whipped in Parker county by a white man; and some time ago, in another county, a white man cut off the ears of a freed-woman. It is openly proclaimed by many of the perpetrators of these wrongs that their object is to compel the negroes to give up loyal leagues, and to get satisfaction out of them for supporting Yankees.

We could extend this account. We have selected these cases at random to exhibit the feeling of hatred cherished by a certain class of ex-rebels against Union men and freedmen; and we deem them sufficient to sustain our allegation, that there is a settled determination on the part of many to suppress the growth of loyalty, and, if possible, to expel or exterminate the white and colored Unionists in the State.

These attacks were rarely investigated by the police, and the perpetrators were almost never convicted. The Texas convention report went on, "It is our solemn conviction that the courts, especially juries, as a rule, will not convict ex-rebels for offenses committed against Union men and freedmen." Local officials in the South were often members of the KKK, and even when they weren't, witnesses were rarely willing to testify and Klan members would often lie in court. As one Florida sheriff put it at the time, "If a white man kills a colored man in any of the counties of this State you cannot convict him."

In addition to the widespread violence, the KKK sought to confiscate all guns from Black people. The KKK thought that if Black people had guns, then Black people could overcome those who were terrorizing them. As the Texas convention report noted, "bands of armed whites are traversing the county, forcibly robbing the freedmen of their arms, and committing other outrages upon them." At the same time, groups like

KKK members in their costumes, and carrying guns, from an 1868 edition of Harper's Weekly. [Wikimedia Commons / Missouri History Museum]

the KKK had "seized every gun and pistol found in the hands of the (so-called) freedmen" in parts of Mississippi, according to an 1866 issue of *Harper's Weekly.*

What about the Second Amendment? you might be thinking. *Doesn't it protect the right to bear arms?* Not always, it turns out. The Second Amendment only protects you when your guns are being taken away by the federal government—not by individual people or groups like the KKK.

The Supreme Court made this clear in an 1876 case called *United States v. Cruikshank.* Three years prior, in Colfax, Louisiana, a white mob attacked a group of Black people protesting voter intimidation, ordering the protestors to turn over their guns and eventually killing 150 Black people. As was typical at the time, local officials failed to prosecute Cruikshank and his white co-conspirators for murder of Black people, so the federal government charged them with conspiring to violate the Black protestors' civil rights, including their right to bear arms.

The federal jury convicted Cruikshank and two other men, but the ruling was overturned by the Supreme Court. The Supreme Court held that the Second Amendment applied only to Congress—not to state governments, and not to individuals:

> The second amendment declares that it shall not be infringed, but this, as has been seen, means no more than that it shall not be infringed by Congress. This is one of the amendments that has no other effect than to restrict the powers of the national government, leaving the people to look for their protection against any violation by their fellow-citizens of the rights it recognizes, to what is called . . . the "powers which relate to merely municipal legislation, or what was, perhaps, more properly called internal police," "not surrendered or restrained" by the Constitution of the United States.

In other words, the Supreme Court said that if your guns were being taken away by the KKK, the Second Amendment couldn't protect you. Instead, you'd have to ask local officials for help. And in southern states in this era, local officials were of little help to Black people; those officials were often members of the KKK themselves. As professor and historian Alexander DeConde explains:

> For gun owners, this ruling would have great significance. It upheld as principle the right of states to legislate firearms controls affecting individuals without fear of federal sanction. This decision also had a racist slant. It made federal prosecution of those who committed crimes against blacks, especially in areas where local authorities would not enforce the law, virtually impossible. Thus, in denying blacks a Second Amendment privilege, the court condoned white vigilantism.

Black people in the South couldn't turn to local law enforcement, so sometimes Black militias were formed to fight back against the KKK. They got their guns from the North or from liberal politicians in the South. In Bennettsville, South Carolina, armed Black people patrolled the streets to prevent Klan attacks. In Blount County, Alabama, white Union army veterans formed "the anti-Ku Klux" and threatened to attack the KKK.

Black militias, however, were rare, and they were often unable to fight back against the violence. Civil rights scholar and journalist Charles E. Cobb Jr. explains that "the overwhelming violence against blacks" in the South after the Civil War helps explain why "there were few black paramilitary units and they rarely attacked or fought back with arms against white-supremacist authority, even . . . where blacks were an overwhelming majority of the population." The scale of violence by groups like the KKK was just too large. "Overt displays of force, organization, and resistance by the black community," he writes, "might once again trigger an instantaneous and overwhelming reaction from white-supremacist power and its foot soldiers—who were everywhere in the South—with little prospect of federal intervention."

GENERAL RESTRICTIONS ON GUN OWNERSHIP

As before, however, there were also generally applicable, safety-based gun laws in this post–Civil War era. In 1871, Kentucky made it illegal for people to "carry concealed any deadly weapon upon their persons other than an ordinary pocket-knife." That same year Texas passed an Act to Regulate the Keeping and Bearing of Deadly Weapons, which prohibited the carrying of any "pistol, dirk, dagger, slung-shot, sword-cane, spear, brass-knuckles, bowie-knife, or any other kind of knife" without "reasonable grounds for fearing an unlawful attack on his person." And Wyoming in 1875 explicitly forbid anyone "to bear upon his person, concealed or openly, any fire arm or other deadly weapon, within the limit of any city, town or village."

As before, Mark Frassetto and Robert Spitzer have catalogued the number of states with such laws. (Note that in 1899 there were forty-five states total.)

TYPE OF LAW	DESCRIPTION OF TYPE OF LAW	NUMBER OF STATES
Ban	For the first time in this era, some states passed laws totally banning particular types of guns—typically pistols.	5
Brandishing	Criminalized the threatening use of weapons, which typically included pistols and certain sorts of knives.	13
Carry	Restricted people from carrying weapons around in certain circumstances. In the nineteenth century, these were mostly focused on the secret (or "concealed") carrying of weapons.	28
Dangerous Weapons	Prohibited particularly dangerous or unusual weapons, like guns rigged with a string so that the shooter didn't have to pull the trigger.	8
Firing Weapons	Prohibited firing weapons in certain locations, such as within city limits, or at certain times, like at night.	17
Manufacturing, Inspection	Allowed state inspectors to make sure weapons were working correctly.	9
Registration, Taxation	Said that gun sales or dealers had to be registered, and taxed some gun sales.	11
Storage	Said that guns and gunpowder had to be stored safely.	2

Number of States with Various Gun Laws, by Category (1868–1899)

Dodge City, 1878. The top sign reads: THE CARRYING OF FIRE ARMS
STRICTLY PROHIBITED. [Wikimedia Commons / Flickr]

Some scholars have argued that gun regulations during this era weren't intended to be applied to white people, suggesting that certain "statutes in Southern states restricting either the carrying of concealed pistols or prohibiting the sale of certain types of firearms [were] enacted with racial motives in mind." Other scholars disagree; in a 2016 article, Frassetto contends that this wasn't always the case. He suggests that the 1871 Texas law to regulate deadly weapons wasn't enacted for racist purposes—that instead it was meant to *protect* Black people from the horrifying violence that was being committed against them:

> In the face of aberrational homicide rates, the government of Texas under Governor Edmund Davis took action. This action was taken with the full support of the black community who it was intended to protect.

The law was also enforced in a racially neutral manner during the Davis administration. The Texas state police was a fully integrated police force closely aligned with the Republican governor and fully committed to protecting freedmen from violence perpetrated by whites.

Frassetto suggests that the key to the Texas law—the reason it protected, rather than harmed, the Black community—was that it was enforced by people who were trying to protect Black people from groups like the KKK (at least during the Reconstruction era).

This debate about the 1800s is the same debate we see today: Do more guns lead to more crime, or less? Frassetto's research suggests that the solution to violence and oppression isn't necessarily arming all people equally—it might instead be *disarming* all people equally, so long as the laws are enforced fairly. We'll talk about this more on page 179, but the data suggests this is likely true today, too.

Before we can get there, though, we still need to learn about a few more gun laws. Let's head west, to some towns with some surprising gun regulations.

THE "WILD" WEST

It's midafternoon in Tombstone, Arizona, in 1881. It's late October, so it's not too hot. The town is vibrating with tension: A group of outlaws called the Cowboys has been fighting with a group of cops for a while now, and it doesn't seem like anyone's backing down.

The Cowboys—Billy Claiborne, Ike and Billy Clanton, and Tom and Frank McLaury—are hanging out behind the O.K. Corral, a horse pen. That's when the cops—town marshal Virgil Earp and policemen Morgan Earp, Wyatt Earp, and Doc Holliday—see them.

Someone fires the first shot. No one's really sure who. It all happens so fast: Within the next thirty seconds, around thirty shots are fired.

When the bullets stop flying, the cops are fine, though some are wounded. Ike Clanton and Billy Claiborne seem to have run away. And Billy Clanton and both McLaury brothers are dead.

The McLaury brothers and Billy Clanton, worse for the wear after the gunfight.
[Wikimedia Commons]

When we think of the Wild West, we think that shoot-outs like the famous gunfight at the O.K. Corral happened all the time. But in reality, these towns were chock-full of safety-based gun laws.

In the West, guns were everywhere. But gun control laws were everywhere, too. In 1873, for example, Dodge City, Kansas, adopted a resolution that read: "Any person or persons found carrying concealed weapons in the city of Dodge or violating the laws of the State shall be dealt with according to law." In a photograph of the city from around that time, a large sign reads: THE CARRYING OF FIRE ARMS STRICTLY PROHIBITED. Visitors to other towns would exchange their guns at the police station for a token and then pick them up later.

In fact, at the time of the gunfight at the O.K. Corral, there was a law against carrying deadly weapons in Tombstone. Ordinance No. 9 said that "it is hereby declared unlawful to carry in the hand or upon the person or otherwise any deadly weapon within the limits of said city of Tombstone, without first obtaining a permit in writing."

And laws like Tombstone's and Dodge City's worked. As historian Richard Shenkman explains:

> The truth is many more people have died in Hollywood westerns than ever died on the real frontier. . . . In the real Dodge City, for instance, there were just five killings in 1878, the most homicidal year. . . . In the most violent year in Deadwood, South Dakota, only four people were killed. In the worst year in Tombstone, home of the shoot-out at the O.K. Corral, only five people were killed.

So what gives? Why is our image of the Wild West so wrong? Well, it has something to do with a man named William Frederick Cody—also known as Buffalo Bill—and other people like him. At the Chicago World's Fair of 1893, Buffalo Bill set up a show about life on the frontier in which shoot-outs were commonplace. Stories like his were popular, and so this is still the way we think of the Wild West—even though the frontier had more gun laws than many states do today.

CHAPTER 5

THE FIRST NATIONAL GUN LAWS

Around the turn of the twentieth century, America's urban population exploded; millions of people, including immigrants, moved to cities throughout the United States. The population of New York City alone jumped from 3.4 million in 1900 to more than 5.6 million in 1920, or an increase of 64 percent. For comparison, the whole country's population grew by 39 percent in the same timeframe.

Many of the people who moved to cities were following jobs: America was in the middle of its second industrial revolution, and most manufacturing jobs were located in urban areas. By the time of the 1920 census, more Americans lived in urban than in rural areas for the first time in American history. Urbanization was accompanied by a rise in violent crime, and soon states and cities—and eventually the federal government—would pass gun laws to reduce the violence. In response to the first federal gun legislation, the NRA would do some of its early lobbying, beginning to shape the gun-policy landscape we have today.

RISING CRIME RATES

Nationally, the homicide rate grew by almost 50 percent between 1900 and 1925—but it increased by much more in major cities, doubling in Baltimore, tripling in New Orleans and Chicago, and quadrupling in

Cleveland. In the early 1920s, the robbery rate in Chicago was *one hundred times* as great as London's. "A new breed of criminal seemed more calculating and more predatory," writes professor of history and criminology Jeffrey S. Adler, "as holdup men and bank robbers, armed with Thompson submachine guns and fast getaway cars, invaded business districts, targeted respectable citizens, and evaded law enforcers."

Many of the homicides during this era were attributed to Prohibition, organized crime, and bootlegging. In 1919, making and selling alcohol was outlawed by the Eighteenth Amendment, which said that "the manufacture, sale, or transportation of intoxicating liquors . . . for beverage purposes is hereby prohibited." Called Prohibition or the Noble Experiment, the Eighteenth Amendment didn't prohibit the consumption of alcohol, and it didn't actually stop people from selling it. Making alcohol illegally was called bootlegging, and it led to the creation of gangs that fought each other for turf.

Dumping out liquor during Prohibition. [Library of Congress]

While most people who committed crimes used pistols, the Thompson submachine gun—also known as the tommy gun—became bootleggers' preferred weapon. John T. Thompson, who developed the gun for World War I, patented it in 1921, and it became available to the public within a few years for $175 (more than two thousand dollars today). Manufacturers advertised that it was "for use by those on the side of law and order," but police didn't really buy the gun—mobsters did. The tommy gun made it much easier for them to kill their rivals: It was the first portable machine gun, which meant one trigger pull would fire many bullets automatically. One writer described it as a "diabolical engine of death."

The media also contributed to sensationalizing this violence. News and radio were "all filled with crime stories," Adam Winkler notes, which "only heightened the public's distress." For example, one newsreel from the era shows the damage caused by gun warfare in New York City, sensationalizing the violence by emphasizing its effect on young children. The camera pans across bullet-ridden walls, and the narrator says, "Here is Samuel Davino, only five years old, pointing to where he was shot in the leg by gangland's ruthless gunmen. But poor little Samuel is more fortunate than Michael Vengali, also five. Michael met death. And this casket will hold his tiny body, broken by machine gun bullets."

In 1921, in response to the rising homicide rate, a Chicago businessman placed newspaper notices nationwide offering a thousand dollars to "anyone who should give one good reason why the revolver manufacturing industry should be allowed to exist and enjoy the facilities of the mails." ("Enjoy the facilities of the mails" just means "ship their guns through the mail.") In September 1922, the American Bar Association, or ABA, recommended a national ban on pistols (except for police) after finding that they were the preferred weapon of almost all the country's murderers. The ABA had concluded that laws prohibiting the carrying of guns weren't effective, so any new restriction needed to go straight to the source. Gun control advocates argued that if "nobody had a gun, nobody would need a gun," and some suggested the police be disarmed. (We're used to seeing police with guns in America, but in many other countries—including Britain, Ireland, Norway, Iceland, and New Zealand—police are unarmed in most circumstances.)

STATE AND LOCAL ACTION

During this time, some states and cities took action to curb gun violence. In 1911, New York State passed the Sullivan Dangerous Weapons Act, which required people to get a permit to carry a concealable weapon such as a handgun. (New York City had passed a similar permit law in 1905, which gun control advocates hoped would be strengthened by a state law.) The Sullivan Act also made carrying an unlicensed concealed weapon outside the home a felony, which meant it was punishable by jail time. (Before the law, this act was only a misdemeanor.) Similarly, in 1913, Oregon passed a law requiring a license to purchase handguns. In 1923, Arkansas passed a law requiring that all handguns be registered with local officials, and California passed a law preventing people who had been convicted of felonies from possessing a pistol. By the mid-1920s, seventeen states had enacted laws that regulated handguns in some way.

But local action wasn't really effective. People could always get guns in more permissive states and take them to states with strict gun laws. And, as DeConde explains,

> City, state, and other laws often clashed. Chicago, for instance, issued no permits to individuals to carry pistols but a state court order compelled it to honor firearms licenses issued elsewhere in Illinois. Another court ruled the city's strict pistol ordinance invalid because

it conflicted with state law. Approximately the same thing happened to Chattanooga, which had enacted a weapons ban more severe than had the state of Tennessee.

And the criminal laws that *were* on the books weren't being enforced. Adler reports that in the 1920s "in American cities, four out of every five killers went unpunished." This was, in part, because of juror behavior; juries often refused to convict "white men who had killed to affirm masculine privilege. . . . Jurors acquitted husbands who killed their wives' lovers, and drunken brawlers who engaged in 'fair fights,' and they returned not guilty verdicts for men who participated in mob violence, including lynching" of Black people. Still, juror behavior accounted for only a small part of the problem.

Instead, the primary reason the laws weren't being enforced was because judges and prosecutors were dismissing most cases before they went to trial. In New York City, for example, almost 75 percent of homicide cases never even made it to the grand jury. In many of these cases, the reason was bias:

> Inadequate police work sometimes compelled district attorneys to dismiss charges. More often, however, even with murders, prosecutors dropped cases they deemed unimportant. Southern district attorneys, for example, routinely eliminated cases involving black-on-black violence. "So long as they [African American assailants] do not kill white men," a Louisiana African American newspaper editor explained, "everything is all right. But it is 'just another nigger gone' when a colored man is killed." In New Orleans during the early 1920s, African Americans were two-thirds of homicide victims, 86 percent of whom died at the hands of other African Americans. Yet prosecutors secured convictions in only 6 percent of African American intraracial homicide cases. Northern

prosecutors employed a similar approach with immigrant crime, anticipating intransigence from foreign-born witnesses, believing such violence inevitable, and hence casually dismissing cases.

All this—rising violent crime, media sensationalism, and reports on the failures to convict—contributed to a crime panic. In 1926, one gun control advocate warned that "unless something is done, and done soon, to check the rising tide of crime, the very foundation of the country itself will be threatened."

Gun control advocates saw that local laws were failing and began to apply pressure on Congress to pass *federal* gun legislation. They thought that "this new breed of gun wielders had become too powerful or elusive for local police to control. With ready access to telephones, automobiles, gun silencers, sawed-off shotguns, and submachine guns, desperadoes now roamed larger areas faster than in the past, sped across state lines, robbed and killed, and at times outgunned police." The gun control advocates found support from the national media, who gave the issue prominent coverage. For example, the *Christian Science Monitor* argued in 1925 "that any effective regulation prohibiting the traffic in firearms must be imposed by Federal authority."

The problem, though, was that until this time, crime was considered a local issue. Herbert Hoover, who was elected president in 1928, denounced "the gangster life" but noted that "the responsibility for the control of crime rests emphatically upon the States and local communities." He thought allowing the federal government to pass gun laws would step on the states' toes.

Then, in 1929, the economy fell to pieces. After the stock market crashed in October, the unemployment rate began to skyrocket: It hit almost 25 percent in 1933, compared with about 3 percent in 1929. This was the Great Depression.

The First National Gun Laws

FDR'S NEW DEAL FOR CRIME

In the depths of the Depression, Franklin Delano Roosevelt was elected president in a landslide. He took office in 1933. FDR had previously been governor of New York, where he'd supported strict state handgun laws. Shortly after he was elected, FDR was himself the target of gun violence, when a man at a political rally tried to shoot him and barely missed.

FDR was also an avid supporter of federal power. Under his New Deal, the federal government expanded its power to help the country recuperate from the Great Depression. It did so by passing extensive legislation and creating many new executive agencies.

These agencies took many forms. To reduce unemployment rates, for example, FDR created the Works Progress Administration, which employed millions of people to carry out projects including public construction, and the Civilian Conservation Corps, which employed young people (often men) to do forestry and fire-prevention work. And to help stabilize crop prices for farmers, he created the Agricultural Adjustment Administration.

Under FDR, the federal government also started getting involved in criminal justice in a way it hadn't in the past. FDR put his main legal adviser, Attorney General Homer Cummings, in charge of what he called a New Deal for Crime.

But here's the thing. By the time FDR became president, violent crime rates were actually *falling*; violent crime peaked around 1925 and then started to decline. Adler notes that "from the mid-1920s until 1940, the homicide rate dipped by one-third nationally"; and between 1931 and 1940, "rates of aggravated assault fell by 23 percent and robbery by 47 percent."

By this point, however, the war on crime had "assumed a life of its own, increasingly detached from actual crime." Even though the violent

A poster by the WPA promoting its construction projects.
[Library of Congress]

crime rate was dropping, the public's perception was that it was still on the rise—and politicians were leaning into citizens' fears to push forward their agendas. "Like most wars," Adler explains, the war on crime "enhanced the authority of the state and provided myriad opportunities for political leaders to pursue other agendas, often concealed within anticrime measures." Violence had become a political issue, and political leaders responded to calls for national legislation because they fit into their larger agendas. In FDR's case, he used the crime panic to further build up federal power.

The first item on FDR's New Deal for Crime agenda was ending

Prohibition. In 1933, he worked to ratify the Twenty-First Amendment, which repealed the Eighteenth.

Next, FDR pushed for the first federal gun legislation. Shortly after coming into office, he proposed a bill that would regulate a whole variety of guns, including handguns and the weapons used by mobsters. Before he was elected, FDR had served on a committee that found that federal gun control was necessary to stop the crime wave. In 1934, his attorney general, Homer Cummings, suggested the government could heavily tax guns to prevent people from buying them. Cummings also suggested that the government establish a national gun registry in order to enforce the tax. That way, Cummings thought, anyone who hadn't registered his gun or paid the tax could be arrested, even if the government couldn't prove the person had committed any other crimes.

The National Rifle Association wasn't pleased.

THE NRA'S OPPOSITION TO FDR'S PROPOSAL

The NRA didn't want *all* guns to be regulated, though the organization was okay with the regulation of the machine guns associated with mobsters. The NRA's president during this time was Karl T. Frederick, a Princeton- and Harvard-educated lawyer who had won three gold medals in pistol shooting at the 1920 Summer Olympic Games, and who was also the vice president of the National Wildlife Federation.

Frederick told Congress that he was "as much against the gangster as any man" but that he didn't "believe we should burn down the barn in order to destroy the rats." He was worried that people needed handguns in order to protect themselves: "I think we should be careful in considering the actual operation of regulatory measures to make sure that they do not hamstring the law-abiding citizen in his opposition to the crook." He noted that while he could not support "drastic" proposals, he was nevertheless in favor of "reasonable" legislation.

Karl T. Frederick
[The National Archives and Records Administration]

DeConde explains that the NRA's "political activism accompanied a deepening cooperation between it and firearms manufacturers and dealers." In other words, the NRA was getting involved politically because it had close relationships with the gun manufacturers that would be hurt by the law. The NRA and gun manufacturers had similar interests at stake. As DeConde puts it:

> Officers of the firearms companies, many of whom had been in the military, joined the shooting clubs. They often took over leadership positions, producing, in the case of the NRA, an intimacy that led critics to dub it the unofficial trade organization for the firearms industry. The gunmakers and dealers supported the association for both practical and ideological reasons. Its firearms advocacy and its extolling of gun ownership as a right contributed to sales and profits. Both groups hated the idea of regulation and both praised the nation's gun culture as a fount of patriotism.

The NRA asked its members to tell their representatives they opposed the "drastic" portions of the law—those that had to do with handguns.

The NRA wrote: "The issue is clear cut between the Attorney General and his undesirable law on the one side, and the sportsmen of America and all other law-abiding citizens of America on the other side, with the armed criminals of the country on the side lines, rooting for the Attorney General." The NRA was saying, basically, that the only thing that stops a bad guy with a gun is a good guy with a gun—the same thing it is saying today. Note, however, that the NRA's lobbying at this time had nothing to do with the Second Amendment. Indeed, Frederick himself said that protection of gun rights was "not to be found in the Constitution."

In short, the NRA during this era promoted gun ownership, but within bounds, and its leaders were willing to compromise for public safety. As Franklin L. Orth, executive vice president of the NRA from 1959 until his death in 1970, once pointed out, "The National Rifle Association has been in support of workable, enforceable gun control legislation since its very inception in 1871."

THE FIRST FEDERAL FIREARMS LEGISLATION

Congress responded to the concerns of the NRA members. The final version of the National Firearms Act of 1934 heavily taxed only machine guns and sawed-off shotguns, the weapons used most often by mobsters. The 1934 act also said that these weapons had to be registered—which meant their owners had to be fingerprinted.

The law worked, at least with regard to machine guns: Sales of the guns covered by the act dwindled among both mobsters and civilians, just as Attorney General Cummings had expected. Most people didn't want to pay the two-hundred-dollar tax, which was twenty-five dollars more than the price of these guns. While mobsters *could* afford it, they didn't want to register the guns. And if they bought a gun and didn't register it, they could be imprisoned for up to five years, even if the government couldn't prove that they'd committed any other crimes.

WHAT DOES IT MEAN TO "LOBBY"?

When the NRA asked its members to write to their representatives in Congress, they were "lobbying." Lobbying can have negative connotations—it's tied to the idea that groups might have too much power in Washington, D.C. But at its core, lobbying just means working to influence politicians. From Merriam-Webster's online dictionary:

LOBBY verb

lobbied; lobbying

intransitive verb

: to conduct activities aimed at influencing public officials and especially members of a legislative body on legislation

transitive verb

1 : to promote (something, such as a project) or secure the passage of (legislation) by influencing public officials

  // *lobby a bill through Congress*

2 : to attempt to influence or sway (someone, such as a public official) toward a desired action

  // *lobbying senators for tax reform*

Lobbying works in many ways, but it often involves organizations that believe in a particular mission, like the NRA and gun rights. Lobbyists advertise, ask for money from supporters, and get people who agree with them to sign petitions. They meet with lawmakers and try to influence legislation. If the lawmakers do things that the lobbyists don't like, the lobbyists often threaten to persuade people to vote those lawmakers out. We'll learn a lot more about lobbying in chapter 8.

A few years later, Congress passed the Federal Firearms Act of 1938. The law required gun dealers to obtain a federal license—the license cost one dollar—and it prohibited dealers from shipping guns interstate to people who had been convicted of felonies or people who didn't have licenses their state required. "The apparent aims of the 1938 legislation," law professor Franklin Zimring argues, "were to create an independent federal policy banning receipt of firearms by what must have been thought of as the criminal class of society"—in other words, another legal scholar explains, the purpose was to stop "the flow of firearms into undesirable hands." By requiring dealers to obtain a license and banning those dealers from selling guns to people considered "undesirable," the government hoped to keep an eye on who was selling guns and who was buying.

The NRA was okay with the law because it "focused on the criminal rather than the gun"; indeed, the NRA actually helped draft it. Which might explain why, as DeConde says, the "law never really worked": People unable to buy a gun under the act "easily evaded its provisions by lying." Zimring agrees, noting that the law didn't require dealers to verify that their customers were allowed to purchase guns.

Some states passed laws that went even further than the federal legislation. Delaware, for example, made it a felony to possess a sawed-off shotgun or machine gun, regardless of whether it was registered. Many years later, in 1986, machine gun laws would go even further: Congress would pass a law criminalizing civilian possession of machine guns manufactured after 1986, effectively limiting the number of machine guns civilians could own to those already in circulation. Today, machine guns are rarely used in crime, and none have been used in mass shootings.

Some people argue that the firearms that people can legally own today—including the AR-15, the military-style rifle that many mass shooters use—are just as dangerous as machine guns and should be added to

THE FBI

To help fight his war on crime, FDR granted more power and money to an agency known as the Bureau of Investigation. The bureau was founded in 1908 by a different President Roosevelt: Theodore, also known as Teddy, who was FDR's fifth cousin. Before then, presidents had used a private police force, the Pinkerton National Detective Agency, to collect secret intelligence. Teddy decided to create an investigative force that was inside the government. This group—mostly made up of former Secret Service agents—would become the Bureau of Investigation.

In 1935, FDR renamed the agency the *Federal* Bureau of Investigation, or FBI. He doubled its budget, added two hundred agents, and let those agents carry guns. He wanted FBI agents, who could cross state lines, to enforce federal laws like the National Firearms Act. But by turning the FBI into a major law-enforcement organization, FDR also helped contribute to rising incarceration rates (especially of Black people) even as crime was decreasing.

FDR also helped transform the FBI's image. Before he came to power, the bureau wasn't terribly popular with the public. In 1919 and 1920, the Bureau of Investigation had arrested people they thought were anarchists or communists in what were known as the Palmer Raids. This was all part of the Red Scare—the fear of communism that engulfed the country after World War I. Many innocent people were captured and hurt during the Palmer Raids, and soon public opinion turned against the investigative agency.

In the 1930s, the FBI rebuilt its popularity by targeting armed mobsters. Even though robbery rates were falling, Adler explains, the FBI unleashed a public relations campaign that turned bank robbers into "public enemies"— whom the FBI would then bring to justice. The FBI had some help from Hollywood in transforming its image. In these years, Hollywood made movies about FBI agents pursuing mobsters, which made FBI agents look heroic.

the National Firearms Act's list of weapons that must be registered. But as we'll see in chapter 8, the NRA—and the Republican politicians they almost exclusively support—have blocked any attempts at legislation.

In 1939, the Supreme Court heard a challenge to the National Firearms Act in a case called *United States v. Miller.* Jack Miller, a member of the O'Malley Gang, was an infamous bank robber who had been arrested for possessing an unregistered sawed-off shotgun, in violation of the National Firearms Act. Miller argued that the law violated his Second Amendment rights, but the Supreme Court rejected his argument.

In a unanimous ruling, the Supreme Court held that the law that banned sawed-off shotguns didn't violate the Second Amendment since there was no evidence that these weapons had any "reasonable relationship to the preservation or efficiency of a well-regulated militia." In other words, the state was free to regulate who could own a sawed-off shotgun.

The *Miller* opinion was confusing, to say the least. One interpretation is that the Supreme Court upheld the law because the arms in question weren't reasonably tied to militia service; another interpretation is that the Supreme Court upheld the law because the Second Amendment didn't provide an individual right to bear arms. Nevertheless, in the years that followed, lower courts went with the second of these options, and the Supreme Court never objected. That is, of course, until *District of Columbia v. Heller*, the case that defines how we understand the Second Amendment today.

Before we can get to *Heller*, though, we have to understand a few more things. We saw how cities and states responded to rising crime in the early part of the twentieth century, and how FDR took advantage of the crime panic sweeping the nation to push forward landmark federal legislation: the National Firearms Act of 1934 and the Federal Firearms Act of 1938. During this time, the NRA dipped its toes into politics, opposing the parts of the 1934 Act that it thought went too far and helping draft the 1938 law in a way that served its interests.

Still, the group's position was moderate. "In its early days," writes David Cole, legal director of the American Civil Liberties Union (the ACLU), the NRA "did not systematically oppose gun regulation." The NRA itself notes that it "did not lobby directly at this time" but rather chose to "mail out legislative facts and analyses to members, whereby they could take action on their own."

And in the years that followed the firearms acts of 1934 and 1938, the NRA began to focus less on politics and more on hunting. After World War II ended in 1945, veterans joined the NRA in droves—many of them had been exposed to guns during the war and came home interested in hunting. (They weren't interested in target shooting, journalist and historian Osha Gray Davidson hypothesizes, because it may have "reminded them too much of military life.") As Alexander DeConde explains, the influx of soldiers and sailors led the NRA's "leaders to acknowledge that the demarcations separating hunter, target shooter, and gun collector had become blurred. It also compelled them to cooperate with all kinds of gun owners and to devote more of their attention to shooting as sport, especially to hunting."

So when the NRA moved into a new headquarters building in Washington, D.C., in the late 1950s, the mission statement it decided to display next to the main entrance came as no surprise: FIREARMS SAFETY EDUCATION, MARKSMANSHIP TRAINING, SHOOTING FOR RECREATION. But that mission would begin to change in the tumultuous 1960s, when the federal government took another stab at federal gun control legislation.

CHAPTER 6

THE CIVIL RIGHTS MOVEMENT

Emmett Till was a Black kid from Chicago spending the summer in Mississippi with his family. On August 28, 1955, fourteen-year-old Till was murdered by two white men. His alleged crime? A white woman in a grocery store said that he had whistled at her.

He was just there to buy candy.

As punishment for Till's supposed crime, the woman's husband and his half brother kidnapped Till and beat him before shooting him in the head and throwing his body in the Tallahatchie River. Three days later, his body was discovered, grossly mutilated. But it wasn't until *sixty years later* that the white woman who accused Till would admit that she had lied.

Mamie Till, Emmett's mother, took his body home to Chicago and insisted on an open-casket funeral. She wanted the world to see what those men had done to her son. She wanted to show them the true nature of racism in this country.

Photos of Emmett's mutilated body were published in *Jet* magazine and the Black newspaper *Chicago Defender*. The murder trial gripped not just the country, but the world. A Belgian newspaper, for example, published an article called "Racism in the USA: A young black is lynched in Mississippi." Nevertheless, Emmett's killers—who later confessed to

Bryant's Grocery and Meat Market, where Emmett Till went to get candy.
[*The Chicago Defender*]

Look magazine that they had in fact committed the murder—went free. An all-white, all-male jury found them not guilty.

One hundred days after Emmett Till's murder, a forty-two-year-old secretary by the name of Rosa Parks was arrested for refusing to give up her seat to a white passenger on a bus in Montgomery, Alabama. Years later, she told Mamie Till that she was thinking of Emmett when she did it. The injustice of his murder had motivated her. "Rosa Parks would tell me how she felt about Emmett," Mamie Till later wrote, "how she had thought about him on that fateful day when she took that historic stand by keeping her seat."

But Parks's actions were not spontaneous, explains historian David Garrow. They were strategic, tied not only to the murder of Emmett

Till but also to the generations of injustices faced by Black Americans. Indeed, Black people in Montgomery had been strategizing for years about how to desegregate the bus system.

Parks's arrest helped broaden the visibility of the modern-day civil rights movement, which sought to secure equal rights for Black Americans. It's important to look at the civil rights movement when we're thinking about guns in America, both because guns were an integral component of the movement and because the movement would help lead to the second wave of national gun legislation in America: the Gun Control Act of 1968.

After Parks was arrested, the Black community organized a bus boycott, and they asked a little-known twenty-six-year-old preacher to help lead it. That preacher's name? Dr. Martin Luther King Jr.

Rosa Parks, with Martin Luther King Jr. in the background.
[Wikimedia Commons / National Archives and Records Administration]

Rosa Parks's arrest report. [Wikimedia Commons]

MLK would soon become one of the most important figures in the civil rights movement. He had been a pastor at a Baptist church in Montgomery for about a year before being asked to lead the bus boycotts, and he soon became well known for advancing civil rights through nonviolent resistance.

MLK giving his famous "I Have a Dream" speech. [National Archives Museum]

MLK was committed to nonviolence, but he also knew he needed to protect himself from racist violence. In 1956, after a bomb went off on the porch of his home in Montgomery, MLK applied for a concealed-carry permit, but the local sheriff denied it. At that time, local officials had discretion over who received a concealed permit. It was not surprising that MLK's application was denied; Black people were often denied permits during this era.

While he didn't have a concealed-carry permit, MLK did have guns at home, though they may not have belonged to him; his home was even described as "an arsenal." When a journalist visiting MLK tried to sit in an armchair, another nonviolent activist shouted, "Wait, wait! Couple of guns on that chair!" MLK explained: "Just for self-defense." (Later, however, MLK "evolved beyond this moment," as his daughter put it in 2019, and changed his mind on keeping guns around.)

It might seem surprising that a nonviolent activist would own guns for self-defense, but in *This Nonviolent Stuff'll Get You Killed: How Guns Made the Civil Rights Movement Possible*, civil rights scholar and journalist Charles E. Cobb Jr. explains that guns were actually integral to the civil rights movement—guns let protestors protect themselves from violence even while they themselves practiced nonviolence. There was a difference, Cobb explains, between violence as retaliation, which was off-limits, and self-defense, which was quite different. "Indeed, there were few black leaders who did *not* seek and receive armed protection from within the black community. They needed it because both local law enforcement and the federal government refused to provide it."

THE DEACONS FOR DEFENSE AND JUSTICE

One of the groups that provided this protection was called the Deacons for Defense and Justice. The group formed in 1964 in Jonesboro, Louisiana, in response to increased acts of violence by the KKK. A Black civil rights organization called the Congress of Racial Equality, or CORE, had recently arrived in town. CORE organizers were registering voters and organizing nonviolent protests in rural areas, and their efforts attracted violence from KKK members and local police.

Even though white supremacist violence against both CORE organizers and Black townspeople had increased, "Jonesboro's black community wanted the CORE activists in their town and had no intention of letting Klansmen run them off." So a few men began to guard the CORE organizers, first unarmed, then later with weapons. Many of these men were older than the activists, and had served in the military in World War II or the Korean War. They told the CORE activists: "O.K., you guys can be nonviolent if you want to . . . and we appreciate you being nonviolent. But we are not going to stand by and let these guys kill you."

Robert F. Kennedy, then attorney general, speaking to a crowd outside the Justice Department with a sign for the Congress of Racial Equality in the background.

[Library of Congress]

On January 5, 1965, the Black defenders formally incorporated their organization as the Deacons for Defense and Justice. Although there were certainly other groups and individuals who had acted in self-defense against racist violence around this time, the Deacons were the "first formally organized paramilitary organization in the modern civil rights movement," writes Lance Hill in his history of the Deacons.

CORE organizers were conflicted about the armed protection, unsure whether it could coexist with CORE's commitment to nonviolence. But slowly, as white violence increased, the organization changed its tune. "The concept that we are going to go South and through love and patience change the hearts and minds of Southern whites," a discussion paper for CORE volunteers read, "should be totally discarded." And as CORE national director James Farmer later wrote, "CORE nonviolence" was "never a way of life, but only a strategy."

While CORE accepted protection from the Deacons, MLK did not embrace the group, later denouncing what he considered their "aggressive violence." This issue came to a head during James Meredith's 220-mile March Against Fear, which began in Memphis, Tennessee, and ended in Jackson, Mississippi. Meredith, the first Black person to enroll at the University of Mississippi, intended for the march to be a solitary one, but he was nonfatally shot by a sniper not long after he started. Civil rights organizations—including CORE, MLK's Southern Christian Leadership Conference, and the Student Nonviolent Coordinating Committee—gathered in Memphis, Tennessee, to discuss continuing the march while Meredith recovered. But the groups couldn't agree on whether the Deacons should be invited as protection.

Ultimately, the Deacons were invited to accompany the march, and while there were confrontations with the Mississippi police, there were no shoot-outs. The division over the Deacons, however, reflected larger ruptures within the civil rights movement. As Cobb explains:

This was an issue not of guns or of armed self-defense but, rather, of consciousness. Black consciousness had become "blacker" by the mid-1960s, and Afro-Americans had learned to dig deeper into their shared black experience for political purpose. This change would have enormous consequences, both in the days, weeks, and months following the Meredith march and also in the decades to come.

The tenor of the civil rights movement was shifting. During the Meredith march, Stokely Carmichael, chair of the Student Nonviolent Coordinating Committee, had called for "Black Power." Many white people, even those opposed to segregation, reacted with fear and resentment, worried that these ideas were too controversial. They wanted Black people to obtain their rights slowly, not in a way that threatened white power. But Black people had been waiting for their rights for years. They were tired of it.

This shift in the civil rights movement would lead to the formation of more radical groups, like the Black Panther Party for Self-Defense. Like the Deacons, the Black Panthers would use guns for self-defense—but as Cobb explains, because the Panthers' political expression was linked to violence, this "would have the unfortunate side effects of letting white hysteria distort what guns had meant in the earlier phases of blacks' struggle for freedom." In other words, white people would begin to view guns in the civil rights movement differently with the advent of the Panthers.

THE BLACK PANTHER PARTY FOR SELF-DEFENSE

In October 1966, Bobby Seale and Huey P. Newton founded the Black Panther Party for Self-Defense in Oakland, California. In his book *Seize the Time*, Bobby Seale said that he and Huey had wanted freedom, decent housing, and "an immediate end to police brutality and murder of black people":

"Let's summarize these points. We want land, we want bread, we want housing, we want education, we want clothing, we want justice, and we want some peace."

That's the way Huey put it and I wrote it down. . . . Huey said, "This . . . is what we want and what we believe. These things did not just come out of the clear blue sky. This is what black people have been voicing all along for over 100 years since the Emancipation Proclamation and even before that. These things are directly related to the things we had before we left Africa."

At that time, many Black people felt that the civil rights movement hadn't fulfilled its promises. Though landmark antidiscrimination laws had been passed, Black people were still the victims of police brutality on a regular basis. There were widely publicized examples—like when police used attack dogs and fire hoses on Black people at peaceful protests. (In some communities, local police and the KKK were intertwined: In 1961, the Birmingham, Alabama, commissioner of public safety told KKK members they could have fifteen minutes to attack civil rights protestors with iron pipes.) But there was also pervasive, everyday police brutality, which frequently took place during routine traffic stops.

Newton and Seale suggested that they could "end police brutality in our black community by organizing black self-defense groups that are dedicated to defending our black community from racist police oppression and brutality." Like the Deacons, the Panthers believed that "black people should arm themselves for self-defense." Historian Winkler writes, "While they weren't the first civil rights activists to have guns, the Panthers took it to the extreme."

It was around this time that the Second Amendment was becoming popular in legal journals. In 1965, the first article advocating for an individual-rights interpretation of the Second Amendment was published in the *American Bar Association Journal*. The ABA had sponsored an essay contest asking what the Second Amendment meant and whether it extended "to the keeping and bearing of arms for private purposes not connected with a militia." The winning essay, which was published in the *Journal*, argued that the Second Amendment supported an individual right to bear arms and that this original meaning had been "lost." Soon the amount of legal scholarship on this issue would balloon, much of it funded by the NRA and other pro-gun groups.

Newton and Seale held the same view—they also believed the Second Amendment provided an individual right. They wrote: "The Second Amendment to the Constitution of the United States gives a right to bear arms."

When they learned that California law at the time allowed people to carry guns in public as long as they were not concealed, the Panthers made it their mission to "police the police," openly carrying guns while they drove around their neighborhoods and observed arrests. They did this because they thought it was more likely the police officers would respect the civil rights of Black people when there were witnesses—especially armed witnesses.

Newton and Seale taught the Panthers about their rights to carry firearms, how to use their guns, and how to communicate with the police. Seale tells the story of a day when the Panthers, and Huey in particular, had an encounter with the police: "Huey told everybody to remember what he'd said—that nobody in the car should say anything. Only the driver should do the talking, and Huey happened to be the driver. . . . Huey *knew* something about law, and he could use it to make it serve him." More officers arrived, and one asked whether he could see Huey's gun. Huey refused. "We have a constitutional right to carry the guns, anyway, and I don't want to *hear* it," he said.

Seale and Newton in the Panthers' signature uniform.
[Library of Congress]

At that point, a crowd had gathered, and though the police tried to shoo the bystanders away, Huey encouraged them to stay. "You have a right to observe an officer carrying out his duty," Huey said. "As long as you stand a reasonable distance away, and you *are* a reasonable distance. *Don't go anywhere.*"

There were plenty of witnesses, and Huey knew his law. There weren't any violations that the Panthers could be charged with, so the officer let them go without incident.

That very day, the Panthers got about a dozen more recruits. "And after *that*, we really began to patrol," Seale writes, "because we got righteous recruits."

Like the Deacons, the Panthers only intended to use their guns for self-defense. "We don't use our guns, we have never used our guns to go into the white community to shoot up white people," Seale writes. "We only defend ourselves against anybody, be they black, blue, green, or red, who attacks us unjustly and tries to murder us and kill us for implementing our programs."

Nevertheless, the Panthers had multiple encounters with police. In 1967, for example, founder Huey Newton was involved in the shooting death of Oakland police officer John Frey. Newton was convicted of voluntary manslaughter in 1968 but only served two years of his sentence before his conviction was overturned.

In response to the Panther police patrols, Don Mulford, a Republican state assemblyman, decided to propose a new gun control law. In a law journal article titled "California's Attempts to Disarm the Black Panthers," Cynthia Deitle Leonardatos identifies a report in Assemblyman Mulford's legislative files on the Black Panthers. This report explained the need for new legislation to disarm them:

> For police agencies to be aware of the activities of the Black Panther Party is not enough. With Black Panthers leaders, Bobby Seale and Huey Newton, stating that their prime objective is to arm the Negro community to full capacity for the purpose of backing all plays by the Negro community and to act as a deterrent to all organizations, including police departments, makes it clear that new enforceable legislation is urgent and imperative that would better control the use of weapons by any group. This is particularly true when the weapons are used as a threat to the peace of the community. Under present existing laws, the police are powerless to act.

Mulford wound up proposing a bill that would make carrying loaded weapons in public places a misdemeanor, which would effectively put an end to the Panthers' police patrols. (Later, Mulford backtracked and said his law wasn't meant to target the Panthers, but the report identified by Leonardatos, along with the text of the law itself—which said that "California has witnessed, in recent years, the increasing incidence of organized groups and individuals publicly arming themselves"— suggests otherwise.)

When Newton and Seale learned of Mulford's bill, they knew they had a job to do. They drove up to the California state legislature in Sacramento, where the bill was being debated.

They decided to storm the capitol. Legally, of course.

THE STORMING OF THE SACRAMENTO STATEHOUSE

On May 2, 1967, thirty Black Panthers arrived at the California state legislature in Sacramento, almost all of them carrying a gun.

Meanwhile, on the statehouse lawn, future president Ronald Reagan—then the governor of California—was meeting with a group of eighth graders. The politicians of California in the 1960s were primarily white (as they are today). That day, the Black Panthers approached, carrying their guns. Reagan, who supported Mulford's bill, panicked and hurried inside. The Panthers followed, guns in hand.

In the statehouse, the California legislature was debating Mulford's bill. Trailed by journalists, the Panthers walked into the statehouse, their guns pointed peaceably to the ceiling. Some even made their way into the assembly before police escorted them from the building.

Standing on the capitol steps, Seale read a statement to reporters. "The American people in general and the black people in particular," he announced, must

take careful note of the racist California legislature which is now

The Black Panthers protesting in the Sacramento statehouse. [Walt Zeboski / Associated Press]

considering legislation aimed at keeping the black people disarmed and powerless at the very same time that racist police agencies throughout the country are intensifying the terror, brutality, murder, and repression of black people. . . . Black people have begged, prayed, petitioned, demonstrated, and everything else to get the racist power structure of America to right the wrongs which have historically been perpetuated against black people. All of these efforts have been answered by more repression, deceit, and hypocrisy. As the aggression of the racist American government escalates in Vietnam, the police agencies of America escalate the repression of black people throughout the ghettoes of America. Vicious police dogs, cattle prods, and increased patrols have become familiar sights in black communities. City Hall turns a deaf ear to the pleas of black people for relief from this increasing terror.

Shortly after Seale finished reading the statement, the Panthers left the building and drove away. As they were leaving Sacramento, they stopped at a gas station, where they were approached by police. The officer asked if they were a gun club, and Seale replied: "No, we're the Black Panther Party. We're black people with guns. What about it?" Twenty-five members of the group were arrested on charges including disturbing the peace.

The Panthers wanted people to pay attention to their mission, and people did: The next day, the *New York Times* ran its first-ever story on the group. A few days later, the *Times* sent a reporter to write a profile of Newton. Other papers, too, ran front-page stories about the storming of the Sacramento statehouse.

But in some ways, the Panthers' protest backfired. Rather than soften the bill, Mulford decided to make it even stricter by adding a ban on having a loaded gun in the state capitol. This was a slap in the face to Newton, Seale, and their fellow Panthers.

Republicans in California, including Governor Reagan, supported the gun control bill. Reagan told reporters that afternoon that the Mulford Act "would work no hardship on the honest citizen" and that he saw "no reason why on the street today a citizen should be carrying loaded weapons." A few months later, he would sign the bill into California law, immediately stripping Newton, Seale, and their fellow Panthers of their right to carry firearms in public places.

Often, when a law is passed in one state or city, others will follow suit. And indeed, in 1967, Philadelphia passed a law similar to the Mulford Act. The law prohibited people from carrying "a firearm upon the public streets or upon any public property at any time unless that person is: (a) licensed by the Commonwealth of Pennsylvania to carry a firearm or licensed to hunt; (b) actively engaged in a defense of his life or property from imminent peril or threat; or (c) a police officer or member of the

An article from the Sacramento Bee *about the storming of the statehouse.*
[*The Sacramento Bee.* © 1967 McClatchy. All rights reserved. Used under license.]

State or Federal militia on active duty." The penalty for violating the law was a fine of at least three hundred dollars and imprisonment of at least ninety days.

These laws demonstrate that the right to bear arms has been limited throughout American history—at times, very limited. And soon these state and local laws would be followed by the Gun Control Act of 1968, the first federal gun control law since the 1930s. But the path to this new federal law was not without its obstacles.

THE GUN CONTROL ACT OF 1968

By the time 1968 rolled around, gun control advocates had been trying to pass gun legislation for years—particularly after President John F. Kennedy was assassinated by gun in 1963. Senator Thomas Dodd, a Democrat from Connecticut, supported restricting mail-order sales of guns like the one that had been used to assassinate JFK. "What more do we need than the death of a beloved President to arouse us to place some regulation on the traffic in guns for crime?" Dodd asked. (It's surprising that Dodd did this, since several major gun manufacturers, including Colt and the Winchester Repeating Arms Company, were located in his home state of Connecticut.)

Even though polls suggested that the public wanted some sort of gun legislation, Congress failed to pass Dodd's bill. The NRA had mobilized its membership in opposition to the bill; four NRA members even drove from Phoenix, Arizona, to Washington, D.C., to beg their senators for their "God-given right" to guns. Ultimately, the legislation simply faded away as the country's attention focused instead on the war in Vietnam and the civil rights movement.

Around this time, race riots across the country "pitted black communities against police," DeConde writes, and "involved a greater dispersal of firearms and a much more intense use of firepower than in comparable past situations." One of these riots, in 1967 in Newark, New Jersey, began in response to the brutal beating of a Black taxi driver during a traffic stop. The riot lasted four days; twenty-six people were killed and many more were injured. Newspapers published shocking photos, and the riots gripped the country.

Many people, alarmed by the Panthers and other armed Black people whom they believed to be "undermining the social order," began to call for more gun control.

Then, in 1968, Dr. Martin Luther King Jr. was assassinated by gun. "I hope that this brutal, senseless killing will shock the Congress into backing me in this fight to take the guns from the hands of assassins and murderers," Senator Dodd said. In the wake of MLK's murder, riots once again engulfed the country as people mourned the death of the civil rights leader. Much like the earlier riots, these "stoked a very particular

A photo from the New York Times *of the riots in Newark, New Jersey.*
[Don Hogan Charles / *The New York Times* / Redux]

and dramatic fear of black violence, one that could spill into the white sub-urbs"—thus further adding fuel to the gun control fire. "White America, by and large, was not mourning Dr. King," one journalist observed; "rather it was frightened by the violence which took place in the wake of the assassination, and it felt that politicians were too permissive."

Just two months later, Senator Robert F. Kennedy was also assas-sinated. On the day he died, people protested in front of the NRA with signs that read: NRA: YOUR ARMS HAVE BLOODY HANDS, THE AIR IS ALIVE WITH THE SOUND OF BULLETS, STOP VIOLENCE, STOP THE NRA, WHEN WILL WE LEARN; ABOLISH THE NRA, and READY, AIM, LOVE.

As Winkler notes, after RFK's assassination "the political will to enact gun control shifted literally overnight," and Congress passed the Omnibus Crime Control and Safe Streets Act of 1968 the next day. The Safe Streets Act outlawed the shipment of pistols and revolvers across state lines and restricted the sale of handguns to minors. President Johnson said it was "a halfway step" because it excluded other firearms, like shotguns and rifles, and hoped Congress would pass another law that would go even further.

The second law would become the Gun Control Act of 1968. On TV, Johnson explained what he hoped this law would do:

> I propose that Congress go further to give Americans the elementary protection that the people of every other civilized nation have long enjoyed.
>
> I propose the first national registration of every gun in America.
>
> Second, I propose that every individual in this country be required to obtain a license before he is entrusted with a gun.

To people who thought this was too big a step, Johnson said, "Registration and licensing have long been an accepted part of daily life in America." Cars, boats, dogs, and bikes had to be registered, and you needed a license to have a pet, to fish, and to drive a car. "Certainly no less should be required for the possession of lethal weapons that have caused so much heartbreak and horror in this country in this century. Surely, the slight inconvenience for the few is minimal when measured against the protection for all." Johnson even suggested that cities should ask their citizens to voluntarily turn in their old, unwanted guns.

The NRA went into panic mode. It told its almost one million members that they'd be faced with "stiff controls" and that the administration's aim was "now total gun registration and owner licensing," urging them to write letters to Congress opposing the Gun Control Act of 1968. Senate Majority Leader Mike Mansfield, a Democrat from Montana, reported that "mail on this subject is the heaviest to reach my office in 26 years as a Member of the Congress. . . . The division is overwhelmingly against control legislation."

The mailing campaign worked; the NRA succeeded in blocking the parts of the Gun Control Act of 1968 it disliked—namely, national licensing and registration. (As we discussed in chapter 1, the NRA dislikes licensing and registration because it thinks those requirements will lead to a national gun registry, which the federal government can then use to determine who to disarm.) "I asked for the national registration of all guns and the licensing of those who carry guns," Johnson told Congress. "The voices that blocked these safeguards were not the voices of an aroused nation. They were the voices of a powerful lobby, a gun lobby, that has prevailed for a moment in an election year."

The Gun Control Act of 1968 may not have required national licensing and registration, but it *did* ban mail-order guns, establish a federal licensing system for gun dealers, ban the sale of guns to minors, and prohibit classes of people deemed "dangerous"—like people who had committed felonies or been dishonorably discharged from the military—from purchasing or possessing guns. It also banned importation of the Saturday night special, an inexpensive, poorly made handgun that was seen as popular in minority communities. For this reason, some believed this portion of the law was targeted at Black people.

Throughout the civil rights movement, Black people took up arms in self-defense—from the Deacons for Defense and Justice to the Black Panthers. By policing the police and storming the Sacramento statehouse, the Panthers brought attention to the police brutality Black people had been enduring for years. Their protests also led to the passage of California's Mulford Act and the Gun Control Act of 1968, the first federal gun control law since the 1930s. But while these laws may have been passed to disarm groups like the Panthers, they'd soon have a surprising effect: Within a decade, they would help transform the NRA into the no-compromises lobbying machine we know today.

CHAPTER 7

A REVOLUTION AT THE NRA

T he leadership of the NRA may not have been thrilled by the Gun Control Act of 1968, but it wasn't too upset either. Franklin Orth, then the NRA's executive vice president, wrote that once the national registration and licensing provisions had been removed, the law appeared "to be one that the sportsmen of America can live with."

But a divide was growing in the NRA. For a group of gun hard-liners, the Gun Control Act of 1968 was *not* something they could live with, even after the more restrictive provisions had been removed. It wasn't any specific section of the law that bothered these hard-liners; as journalist and historian Osha Gray Davidson explains, "it was the concept of *gun control itself* that they disliked, even hated." Eventually, this group would rise up against the organization's leadership in 1977's Cincinnati revolt.

THREE STRIKES AND THE OLD GUARD IS OUT

In the 1960s and 1970s, the hard-liners kept getting more and more worried about the direction in which the NRA was headed. In the 1960s, "gun violence began to assume the status of a public controversy," and the hard-liners within the NRA worried that "even minor measures would open the door to a flood of legislation designed

Harlon Carter (left), the leader of the hard-liners, and Franklin Orth testifying before Congress in 1965. Awkward! [Getty Images / Bettman]

to deprive gun owners of all claimed rights." They felt that the organization's leaders—the "Old Guard"—weren't taking their concerns seriously and wouldn't fight back against government regulation of guns.

The first strike was the Gun Control Act of 1968; the second was the fear of local handgun bans. And the third and final strike was the Old Guard's threat to leave Washington, D.C.—and politics—altogether.

STRIKE 1: THE GUN CONTROL ACT OF 1968

"The advent of the modern-day NRA," writes David Cole, "can be traced to 1968." The NRA's leadership may have considered the Gun Control Act of 1968 a law "that the sportsmen of America can live with," but most of the hard-liners in the NRA weren't "sportsmen." As professor and historian Scott Melzer explains, they were "Second Amendment fundamentalists who believed that any form of gun control was illegal under the Constitution."

While there had always been people in the organization who viewed guns this way, the divide never really came to the forefront until the 1960s; gun control had been a nonissue for more than thirty years. In the years after the firearms acts of 1934 and 1938 passed, Congress and the NRA "went back to their respective corners and more or less left each other alone," as Osha Gray Davidson puts it. But starting in the 1960s, that began to change.

The activities of the Panthers, along with those of other armed Black people, had led to the passage of the Gun Control Act of 1968—which was "aimed largely at disarming urban black leftist radicals" but, ironically, "led to a backlash by rural white conservatives." For this reason, Adam Winkler notes, the hard-liners "can trace their roots to, of all people, the Black Panthers." Though the groups had very different histories and motivations, they both believed that guns were about self-defense and that the Second Amendment protected an individual right to bear arms.

On that basis, the hard-liners argued their gun rights shouldn't be limited to hunting and sporting—in fact, they didn't want their gun rights to be limited at all.

STRIKE 2: LOCAL HANDGUN BANS

Then, in 1974, the National Council to Control Handguns—which would later become Handgun Control Inc. and then the Brady Campaign—was formed. The group's leader explained that his goals were to "slow down the number of handguns being produced and sold in this country," to "get all handguns registered," and then, eventually, to "make possession of all handguns and all handgun ammunition—except for the military, police, licensed security guards, licensed sporting clubs, and licensed gun collectors—totally illegal." (The group would later expand its mission to regulating other types of gun as well.) The emergence of groups like this made NRA members worry that they'd no longer be able to own handguns.

And indeed, a year later, the Washington, D.C., City Council banned handguns altogether as part of the Firearms Control Regulations Act of 1975. The law was passed in reaction to the high levels of violent crime in D.C.: The chair of the council at the time explained that "handgun crimes were just getting out of sight" and that the council "had to isolate and contain the problem. We thought a handgun law would do that." The D.C. Council passed the law in a 12–1 vote, and a poll conducted the year after the law was passed found that three-quarters of city residents supported the ban. The law's supporters hoped it would lead to handgun bans across the country, and the NRA hard-liners were worried that the Old Guard wouldn't do enough to fight against them.

LONG GUNS VS. HANDGUNS

There are two types of guns: long guns, which include rifles and shotguns, and handguns. Handguns are smaller and can be held in one hand, whereas long guns are, well, longer, and they're usually fired with two hands. People most often say they need handguns for self-defense, while they say they need long guns for hunting or target shooting. Handguns are the gun most often used in crime: Today, they are used in 70 to 80 percent of firearm murders.

STRIKE 3: MOVING TO COLORADO

In 1976, Maxwell Rich, then the head of the NRA and part of the Old Guard, decided that the NRA was going to move to Colorado, where it would refocus on hunting and outdoor activities and leave politics behind. The group wanted to "distance itself," Scott Melzer explains, "literally and figuratively, from the political lobbying scene in Washington, D.C." Rumor had it that at least one board member wanted to take the rifle out of the NRA by changing its name to the National Outdoor Organization.

That was the last straw for the die-hard gun lovers in the NRA. As Melzer summarizes, the hard-liners' worries had piled up:

> More politicians have been shot and two assassination attempts were made on President Ford; gun crimes are increasing; public support for gun control (including registration) is strong; the Gun Control Act of 1968 passed and many increasingly restrictive bills continue to be presented in Congress; the Republican administration is proposing some gun control; . . . gun control groups seeking bans or strict controls have formed; some Democrats are pursuing what amounts to virtual handgun bans; and the Old Guard is trying to move the NRA out West and get out of politics.

The hard-liners knew they had to do something. Otherwise, they might lose their gun rights forever.

THE REVOLT AT CINCINNATI

The leader of the hard-liners, Harlon Carter, was born in 1913 in a small Texas town and spent most of his life working for the U.S. Border Patrol. There was nothing Carter liked less than gun control. "The very idea of the government coming between a law-abiding citizen and his or her choice of firearms sent Carter into fits," writes Osha Gray Davidson. "Sweat would break out on his already glassy dome, and his face would turn as red as freshly butchered game."

In 1975, Carter became the leader of the lobbying branch of the NRA, known as the Institute for Legislative Action, or ILA. At that time, the ILA was more radical than the Old Guard, who were still the folks in charge. Because of these philosophical differences, Carter complained, the Old Guard wasn't giving his branch of the organization enough resources.

In November 1976, Rich fired dozens of employees associated with the hard-liners. Carter resigned in protest, and he started scheming with the fired hard-liners about how they'd get their organization back from the Old Guard. Together, they formed the Federation of the NRA.

The goals of the federation were simple: As hard-liner Neal Knox later told the *Washington Post*, the idea was to quit "the general outdoor sports and conservation projects," and instead stick to what he considered the NRA's "traditional purpose of fighting government intrusion in the right to bear arms." As we've seen, however, that was not the NRA's traditional purpose—it was founded initially for military preparedness.

In May 1977, the NRA held its annual members meeting in Cincinnati. (It was supposed to have been in D.C., but the NRA boycotted the city after the handgun ban passed.) Over a thousand hard-liners arrived at that meeting with a mission: to take control of the organization. And the Old Guard, writes Winkler, "had no idea what was coming."

The federation members walked in, wearing orange hats and carrying walkie-talkies. Though they weren't employees of the NRA anymore, they were still members of the organization, and they knew that all members were allowed to suggest changes at the annual meeting to the NRA's governing structure.

The convention hall was sweaty—the federation thought the NRA's current leaders might've turned off the air-conditioning to make the meeting end sooner. But it lasted through the night, and by four in the morning, the federation had voted out almost all the Old Guard and replaced them with hard-liners. They canceled the move to Colorado, and they secured an increased budget for the ILA.

The Old Guard was no longer in charge—Harlon Carter was. He had just been voted the new head of the NRA.

In a letter to the NRA membership, Carter wrote that in the new NRA, there would be "no compromise. No gun legislation." The NRA would become an organization "so strong," he told a crowd in 1983, "that no politician in America mindful of his political career would want to challenge our legitimate goals."

This new NRA, writes Melzer, had been transformed into the "primary defender of the Second Amendment." Before the revolt, the Second Amendment had not been a focus for the group. As Adam Winkler points out, even in 1975 the NRA described the Second Amendment as being "of limited practical utility" as an argument against gun laws in its *NRA Fact Book on Firearms Control.*

After the revolt, however, the NRA's bylaws were changed to say that the NRA's purpose was "to protect and defend the U.S. Constitution, especially the political, civil and inalienable rights of the American

A New York Times article on the Cincinnati revolt, with a photo of Harlon Carter speaking at the convention.

people to keep and bear arms as a common law and Constitutional right both of the individual citizen and of the collective militia." And soon the NRA would replace the old motto on the wall of its headquarters with a new one: THE RIGHT OF THE PEOPLE TO KEEP AND BEAR ARMS SHALL NOT BE INFRINGED.

Notice anything missing here? That's right, the entire first half of the Second Amendment: "A well regulated Militia, being necessary to the security of a free State." After the Cincinnati revolt, the NRA's focus would be on the second half of the Second Amendment, and the second half alone.

CHAPTER 8

THE NEW NRA

fter the revolt at Cincinnati, the NRA embraced the idea that the Second Amendment protected an individual right to own guns—a view the Supreme Court would eventually adopt in 2008 in *District of Columbia v. Heller*. But what happened in those forty years between the revolt and *Heller*? How did the individual-rights interpretation of the Second Amendment make it from the Black Panthers and the NRA to the Supreme Court? For two hundred years, courts viewed the Second Amendment as a militia right. What changed?

The new NRA, defender of the Second Amendment, spent forty years changing the legal landscape so that the Supreme Court could rule in its favor. By 2008, the prevailing view of the Second Amendment would be theirs.

PLAYING OFFENSE: THE NRA LAYS THE GROUNDWORK FOR *HELLER*

To change constitutional law, advocates often employ tactics that don't actually involve the Supreme Court at all. As David Cole explains, that's exactly what the NRA did to lay the groundwork for *Heller*. First, the NRA made sure to get influential people on its side, including legal scholars and politicians. And second, it focused on state gun laws before moving to the national level. Let's take a look at these strategies one by one.

INFLUENTIAL SUPPORTERS

As you can see in the chart that follows, the amount of legal scholarship that supported an individual-rights interpretation of the Second Amendment ballooned after the late 1960s, much of it paid for by the NRA. While legal scholarship doesn't technically have authority in the Supreme Court, legal scholars' expertise and opinions on particular topics can go a long way toward persuading the justices.

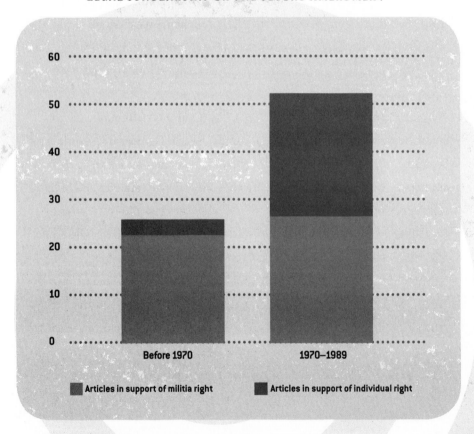

LEGAL SCHOLARSHIP ON THE SECOND AMENDMENT

Before 1970 | 1970–1989

■ Articles in support of militia right   ■ Articles in support of individual right

The new NRA also found a friend in President Ronald Reagan, a Republican whom the organization had endorsed when he was running for president. (In fact, Reagan was the first presidential candidate ever to be endorsed by the NRA.) If you remember, President Reagan had supported Don Mulford's bill to disarm the Black Panthers back in 1967, when he was the governor of California. But Reagan's views had changed a lot since then; he was now firmly in the camp of the NRA.

Why? Guns had become a partisan issue—in other words, support for gun rights was divided along political lines. Indeed, 1968 was the first year in which the Democratic and Republican platforms included the parties' respective positions on gun control. That year, Republicans said they wanted to enact laws to "control indiscriminate availability of firearms" while "safeguarding the right of responsible citizens to collect, own and use firearms." Democrats, on the other hand, endorsed "the passage and enforcement of effective federal, state and local gun control legislation."

After 1968, these positions split even further—Republican politicians became more and more pro-gun, while Democratic politicians became more and more pro–gun control. Democrats found most of their support in urban areas, where rates of gun violence tended to be higher, and from women and racial minorities, who were less likely to own guns. Republicans, on the other hand, found most of their support in the South and rural areas, where the rate of gun ownership was higher.

In 1983, President Reagan became the first sitting president to speak at an NRA gathering. Addressing the group, he expressed his "great respect for your fine, effective leaders in Washington," including Harlon Carter, and promised that he would "never disarm any American who seeks to protect his or her family from fear or harm."

"And by the way," President Reagan said, "the Constitution does not say government shall *decree* the right to keep and bear arms. The Constitution says 'the right of the people to keep and bear arms shall not be infringed.'" The audience burst into applause and rose to their feet.

After President Reagan was elected, Senator Orrin Hatch of Utah—a longtime member of the NRA—became the chair of the Senate Judiciary Committee's Subcommittee on the Constitution. As chair, Hatch helped produce a report on the Second Amendment that advocated for the NRA's individual-rights view. Hatch said the committee discovered "clear— and long lost—proof that the second amendment to our Constitution was intended as an individual right of the American citizen." When Hatch's next election rolled around, the NRA donated more than $20,000 to his campaign. There's no way to know for sure whether the NRA was repaying Hatch for the report, but the timing is suspect.

Of course, not everyone was on board with the NRA's reading of the Second Amendment. In a 1991 interview with PBS, the former chief justice Warren Burger said that the individual-rights interpretation was baloney:

> This has been the subject of one of the greatest pieces of fraud, I repeat the word "fraud," on the American public by special interest groups that I have ever seen in my lifetime. Now just look at those words. There are only three lines to that amendment. A well regulated militia—if the militia, which was going to be the state army, was going to be well regulated, why shouldn't 16 and 17 and 18 or any other age persons be regulated in the use of arms the way an automobile is regulated? It's got to be registered, that you can't just deal with at will.

Soon that "fraud" would be accepted by the Supreme Court. But first, the NRA would turn to the states.

STATE-BY-STATE STRATEGY

The NRA also helped lay the groundwork for *Heller* by supporting politicians who worked to change state laws and constitutions to protect
an individual right to bear arms. Most gun laws are passed at the state
level, so if the NRA could get states to recognize the individual right to
bear arms, most gun owners would be protected. And when many states
pass similar laws, or start amending their constitutions in the same
way, the Supreme Court is more likely to interpret the federal constitution in that way as well. (But keep this in mind for chapter 9, where
we'll learn that the Supreme Court in *Heller* said it was interpreting
the Constitution as the founders—not present-day Americans—would
have wanted.)

The NRA pushed for five main initiatives at the state level. First, it
supported amending state constitutions to protect gun owners. In the
1980s and 1990s, ten states changed their constitutions so that they
explicitly protected an individual right to bear arms—New Hampshire,
Nevada, North Dakota, Utah, New Mexico, Maine, Nebraska, Alaska,
Delaware, and Wisconsin.

For example, in 1987, Maine changed its constitutional protection for
gun ownership to read: "Every citizen has a right to keep and bear arms;
and this right shall never be questioned." Before then, the provision had
said: "Every citizen has a right to keep and bear arms *for the common
defense*; and this right shall never be questioned" (italics added). By
deleting the phrase "for the common defense," Maine clarified that the
right to bear arms belonged to the individual. Today, forty-four state
constitutions guarantee the right to bear arms. Almost all of these guarantee an *individual* right.

Second, starting in the mid-1980s, the NRA helped pass what are
known as preemption laws. Remember the handgun ban in Washington,
D.C., and how proponents of the law hoped it would start a trend

throughout the country? Well, thanks to the NRA, it didn't. When other cities tried to pass handgun bans, the NRA encouraged state governments to preempt local gun regulation.

Preemption happens when a higher level of government (like a state) takes power away from a lower level of government (like a city). At the urging of the NRA, many states in the 1980s and 1990s said that local governments couldn't regulate guns and ammunition. Some of these preemption laws were full (meaning a local government couldn't regulate guns at all), while others were partial (meaning some but not all local gun regulation was preempted).

The NRA pushed for these laws because it knew it could be more effective at the state, not city, level. Gun violence tends to be more of an issue in cities than in rural areas, and people who live in cities tend to be more liberal. City governments would therefore be more likely to pass gun laws, while the NRA would have more sway in state legislatures, where rural interests are often disproportionately represented. Preemption laws mean that cities can't pass gun control laws by themselves—they need to persuade the state government to go along with them.

The NRA worked on getting preemption laws passed throughout the 1980s and 1990s. Before 1980, only seven states had either full or partial preemption laws, but by early 2005, that number had jumped to *forty-five states*. The NRA was able to use these preemption laws to get local gun restrictions overturned in state courts, arguing that local governments weren't allowed to pass the restrictions in the first place.

Third, the NRA focused on loosening concealed-carry laws. If you recall, these laws require a license to carry a hidden weapon, and they allow local officials to approve who gets a license. Most states had these laws. But starting in the 1980s, the NRA pushed for "shall issue" licensing, which basically said that if you weren't disqualified for one of a

PREEMPTION LAWS IN THE STATES

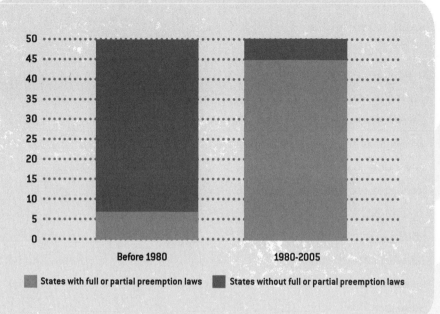

Before 1980 **1980-2005**

■ States with full or partial preemption laws   ■ States without full or partial preemption laws

few very limited reasons—like a prior criminal conviction or a mental health issue—local officials *had* to give you a concealed-carry license. In 1987, the first "shall issue" law passed in Florida; as of 2019, twenty-seven states (of the thirty-five that require a permit for concealed weapons) have similar laws.

Fourth, the NRA helped pass what are known as stand-your-ground laws. These laws say that if you are attacked and reasonably fear serious injury, you have no duty to retreat and can use deadly force in self-defense. Stand-your-ground laws extend the "castle doctrine"—which says you can use deadly force in self-defense if you're attacked in your home—to public places. (The doctrine's name comes from the saying "A man's home is his castle.") At the NRA's urging, Florida became the first state to pass a stand-your-ground law in 2005, and since then twenty-five other states have followed.

TRAYVON MARTIN, THE NRA & RACE

In 2012, an unarmed Black teenager named Trayvon Martin was shot to death in a gated community in Florida while walking home from the store. His killer, a white man named George Zimmerman, went free. Why? Zimmerman claimed he was acting in self-defense, even though Martin was unarmed and even though Zimmerman—who thought of himself as a "community watchman"—had tracked Martin down to shoot him.

While Zimmerman didn't explicitly cite the stand-your-ground defense, the instructions to the jury sounded a lot like it: "If George Zimmerman was not engaged in an unlawful activity, and was attacked in any place where he had a right to be, he had no duty to retreat and had the right to stand his ground and meet force with force, including deadly force if he reasonably believed that it was necessary to do so to prevent death or great bodily harm to himself or another."

Reacting to Martin's murder, NRA celebrity spokesperson and board member Ted Nugent made various racist remarks to the media. He said that "Trayvon got justice" and that Martin was a "gangsta wannabe" who had a "bloodthirst" and was eager to "get into fights with people." Nugent is still on the NRA's board today.

In response to other instances in which unarmed Black people have been shot by the police, the NRA has argued that those individuals should have been armed and used their guns against the officers. For example, after an unarmed Black man named Botham Jean was shot to death in his own apartment by an off-duty police officer—she later claimed she thought she was in her own apartment—the NRA suggested that Jean wouldn't have been killed if he had a gun.

In an article for the *Atlantic*, staff writer Adam Serwer points out that the NRA's reaction in these instances contrasts sharply with its "conspicuous lack of outrage after the shootings of Philando Castile, Jason Washington, and Alton Sterling, all black men killed by police while in possession of a firearm." Serwer continues: "When armed black men are shot by the police, the NRA says nothing about the rights of gun owners; when unarmed black men are shot, its spokesperson says they should have been armed."

While the circumstances surrounding each of these gun deaths vary, the NRA's responses demonstrate its support of the use of guns by police officers and its tendency to blame Black people for their own deaths. These instances suggest NRA advocacy isn't strictly about advocacy for *all* citizens.

And fifth, the NRA went to bat to protect gun manufacturers. In the 1990s, dozens of cities and counties sued gun manufacturers for injuries and deaths caused by guns, arguing that the manufacturers should've taken reasonable steps to prevent the weapons' misuse. In the New York case *Hamilton v. Accu-tek*, for example, the plaintiffs argued that nine gun manufacturers should be held responsible for a shooting because the "companies knew or should have known that oversupplying guns to southern states with weak gun laws led to 'the iron pipeline'—the shipping of guns up [Interstate] 95 for illegal use in strong gun control states like New York." Though these suits were often unsuccessful or overturned on appeal, the gun industry couldn't afford to lose even one of them. The city of Chicago alone was asking for $433 million in its 1998 lawsuit against certain gun dealers, and the gun industry's total annual sales around this time were only about $1.4 billion.

That's where the NRA came in. In 1999, Charlton Heston, who was then the organization's president, told a group of gun industry executives, "Your fight has become our fight." After that, the NRA worked to lobby state legislatures to pass immunity laws for the gun industry—in other words, laws saying that "manufacturers could not be held liable when the injuries were caused by criminals or others who misused their guns, rather than by a defective product." By 2005, thirty-three states had passed laws that protect the gun industry from such suits. That same year, Congress passed the Protection of Lawful Commerce in Arms Act, providing immunity at the national level with only a few exceptions.

Nonetheless, some people have been successful in challenging gun manufacturers under state law (as long as their states don't provide immunity to gun manufacturers). In March 2019, for example, the Connecticut Supreme Court ruled that the families of nine victims of a shooting at Sandy Hook Elementary School could sue Remington

Arms, the company that manufactured the rifle used in the shooting. The families had sued Remington over its marketing practices, arguing that the gun manufacturer violated the Connecticut Unfair Trade Practices Act—which prohibits advertisements that promote or encourage violent, criminal behavior—by marketing a military-style weapon to civilians. Remington countered by arguing that the 2005 Protection of Lawful Commerce in Arms Act provided manufacturers with immunity. The Connecticut Supreme Court ruled in favor of the families, holding that Congress did not intend for the federal immunity law to get in the way of state law. In August 2019, Remington asked the U.S. Supreme Court to review the Connecticut decision. In November 2019, the Supreme Court denied that petition, allowing the state court decision to stand and the case to proceed. At the time of this writing, the case is still ongoing in state court.

Why did the NRA go to bat for gun manufacturers? Robert Spitzer explains that since the early 1900s, there has been a "revolving door" between NRA personnel and gun manufacturers. In other words, people from gun manufacturers would go work at the NRA, and people from the NRA would go work at gun manufacturers. Indeed, there are currently several gun industry execs on the NRA's board.

The groups have a shared interest: When there are fewer laws restricting gun use, gun manufacturers can sell more of their products. So the NRA does the lobbying, and gun manufacturers, in turn, contribute to the NRA financially. From 2005 to 2011, manufacturers donated between $15 million and $39 million to the NRA, or about $2.5 million to $6 million per year. Manufacturers also support the NRA by placing advertisements in the NRA's many publications, including *American Rifleman*, *America's 1st Freedom*, and *Shooting Illustrated* magazines. In 2017, the NRA made around $26.9 million by selling advertisements in its publications. That's a substantial chunk of the organization's annual revenue, which was about $312 million that same year.

This arrangement—the NRA lobbies, the manufacturers contribute—is beneficial to gun manufacturers because it lets them stay out of the public debates. As the *New York Times* explains, "Many firearms manufacturers have chosen to remain in the background of the raging debate over tighter restrictions on the sale and possession of guns, preferring to leave their public talking to the National Rifle Association." The NRA does all the talking, and it gets all the negative attention from gun control advocates. Manufacturers, meanwhile, can continue making guns quietly in the background.

But the NRA hasn't been shy about turning on manufacturers who step out of line. After fifteen people died during the Columbine High School shooting in Littleton, Colorado, in 1999, Smith & Wesson—then the country's largest gun manufacturer—voluntarily agreed to reform its practices. These reforms included adding child-safe triggers, developing "smart guns" (which can only be fired by their rightful owner), and preventing sales to gun dealers linked to crimes. "Would I put locks on our guns if it might save one child? The answer was yes," Smith & Wesson's former chief executive said later. In response, the NRA issued a statement called "The Smith & Wesson Sellout," and other gun rights advocates organized a boycott that lasted months. Smith & Wesson nearly went bankrupt.

Eventually, Smith & Wesson recovered from the boycott and went on producing weapons. And when on February 14, 2018, a young man killed seventeen students at Marjory Stoneman Douglas High School in Parkland, Florida, he used a gun manufactured by Smith & Wesson.

WHY IS THE NRA SO EFFECTIVE?

In the 1980s and 1990s, the NRA changed gun laws across the country

CHARLTON HESTON AND THE RETURN OF THE MILITIA

Before Charlton Heston was president of the NRA, he was an Academy Award–winning actor. Sort of a random choice to lead the NRA? Not really. Heston's fame and widespread appeal, NRA leaders thought, would help the group recover from a *major* public relations error—its response to the Oklahoma City bombing in 1995.

Charlton Heston and actress Janet Leigh in the 1958 movie Touch of Evil.
[Wikimedia Commons]

In the 1990s, groups that called themselves militias started sprouting up across the country. These groups armed themselves and conducted training exercises because they believed they might one day need to fight off the federal government. They also feared—without any evidence—that the United Nations was planning to invade the United States, a conspiracy theory promoted by NRA executive Wayne LaPierre. Though these groups weren't formed by the NRA, the NRA did nothing to discourage them.

The militia movement really exploded after Congress passed the Brady Bill (enacted as the Brady Handgun Violence Prevention Act), a gun control law we'll learn about later in this chapter. By 1996, there were more than eight hundred militia groups, many of them formed in reaction to what they saw as governmental overreach. One man interested in this militia activity would later become known as the Oklahoma City bomber.

The Oklahoma City bomber was a gun rights fanatic. He stamped his letters with the logo I'M THE NRA (a phrase based on one of the NRA's ad campaigns), though he actually thought the NRA wasn't fanatical *enough*. The bomber also hated the federal government, and on April 19, 1995, he killed 168 people by bombing a federal building in Oklahoma City.

The NRA disavowed the bomber's activity, but critics weren't buying it—they noted that the NRA had done nothing to discourage this sort of behavior. Some people, including former president George H. W. Bush, resigned from the group to protest the way its leaders spoke about these issues. To rebuild its public image, the NRA brought Heston on board in 1998—and membership numbers skyrocketed, as the following graph demonstrates.

NRA MEMBERSHIP LEVELS, 1940–2006

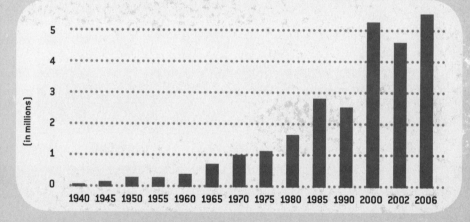

Today, these anti-government groups of armed citizens still exist and still call themselves militias. There were almost three hundred of them as of 2017, though their numbers were much higher under President Obama. Likewise, anti-government rhetoric "went into overdrive" when President Obama was elected. "It's no coincidence that this coincided with the election of America's first black president," argues Adam Serwer, a staff writer at the *Atlantic*. During Reconstruction, Serwer notes, white terrorist groups came together because of their fear of Black political power. Today, many militias align themselves with far right-wing politics, as when in 2017, several militia groups joined the white supremacist Unite the Right rally in Charlottesville, Virginia.

and got influential people to support the group's views. But how'd they do it? What makes the NRA so powerful?

Well, part of it is a numbers game. The NRA has about five million members spread across all fifty states. While there may be that many people (or more) who support gun control, fewer join gun control organizations; in 2010, for example, the Brady Campaign had only about 600,000 members. The NRA provides its members with community, offering a whole bunch of incentives and activities that don't have to do with advocacy—like shooting competitions, magazines, and gun shows—something gun control organizations don't do. Money matters too: historically, gun rights groups, including the NRA, have spent far more money on lobbying than have gun control organizations.

Lobbying Expenditures

YEAR	GUN CONTROL	GUN RIGHTS
2018	$2,009,212	$11,850,845
2017	$1,942,415	$11,440,684
2016	$1,657,992	$11,181,199
2015	$1,678,956	$11,406,347
2014	$1,942,396	$12,013,482
2013	$2,217,765	$15,292,052
2012	$250,000	$6,129,911
2011	$280,000	$5,580,651
2010	$290,000	$5,847,597
2009	$251,425	$5,209,870
2008	$150,000	$4,128,771

But "the real source of the NRA's influence," David Cole explains, "is its remarkable ability to mobilize its members and supporters at the ballot box." It's not that gun control supporters care less. As Philip Cook and Kristin Goss put it, "the more significant gap is not in intensity, but in action." NRA members are more likely than their gun control counterparts to vote, donate money, and call their members of Congress.

Why? Gun owners are terrified of losing their guns—and are willing to fight to keep them. The NRA uses this fear to motivate its members, arguing that any gun regulation will eventually lead to total confiscation. As Scott Melzer, author of the book *Gun Crusaders*, explains:

> My conversations with committed NRA members reveal their profound love of the United States and their belief that gun rights are one of many that free citizens enjoy. But love is not the emotion that drives the NRA. . . . Listening to NRA leaders and speaking with members, their most palpable emotion is *fear*.
>
> They feel threatened by a gun culture on the decline, gun control organizations, "anti-gun" politicians, and any gun control legislation. They fear the government having the power to tell them how many and which kinds of guns they can own, if any, when and where they can shoot them or carry them, how and from whom they can buy them, and even under what circumstances they can be used for self-defense. They fear losing their guns, and they fear losing their freedoms.

Indeed, as mentioned in chapter 1, gun sales rise most when gun owners are afraid of regulation. The biggest jump in sales in the last decade occurred after Sandy Hook, when gun owners thought Congress would pass gun regulations. Historically, sales also spiked in 1968 and 1993, the years the Gun Control Act and the Brady Act were enacted.

ESTIMATED NATIONAL GUN SALES, 2000–2014

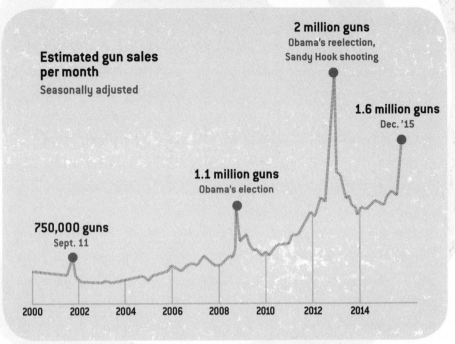

2 million guns
Obama's reelection,
Sandy Hook shooting

Estimated gun sales per month
Seasonally adjusted

1.6 million guns
Dec. '15

1.1 million guns
Obama's election

750,000 guns
Sept. 11

2000   2002   2004   2006   2008   2010   2012   2014

The right to bear arms is often gun rights supporters' number one issue when it comes to voting. People usually consider lots of issues when they vote—things like the environment, health care, and civil rights. But for some people, one issue is more important than all the others, so they'll vote for politicians that match their feelings on that issue. This is what's known as being a "single issue" voter, and for many NRA members, that single issue is guns.

"Yeah, I'm like a lot of people," one member explains. "I mean, I think most Americans have a single primary issue, political primary issue . . . and I think I'm not different in that I'm a single-issue voter as well, and my single issue is the Second Amendment rights."

The NRA's motivated members are what prevent legislators from passing gun regulations. As President Bill Clinton explained to *Rolling Stone* magazine in 2000:

The truth is that when legislation time comes, a lot of the people in Congress are still frightened of the NRA. . . . The NRA can muster an enormous percentage of the vote—maybe 15 percent, even 20 percent in some districts, because for those people guns are a primary voting issue. So if you've got a race where you're ahead 60 to 30, but in your 60 percent, gun control is a primary voting issue for 10 percent of the people, and in their 30 it's a primary voting issue for 20 percent of their people—the truth is, you're a net loser by 10 percent. That's what happens in Congress and state legislatures. They're genuinely afraid.

Scholars agree that elected officials often support the NRA because of their "desire to avoid potentially nasty confrontations with NRA supporters"—a phenomenon that's been referred to as the "hassle factor." The NRA, one politician explains, "can put fifteen thousand letters in your district overnight and have people in your town hall meetings interrupting you." As an aide to a former senator put it: "I don't think [politicians] care about the contributions they get from the NRA. They care about the piles of mail, these nasty calls, and people picketing their state offices. Politicians are risk averse."

In 2012, for example, the NRA targeted Debra Maggart, a Tennessee Republican who had postponed consideration of a bill supported by the NRA. The bill would've allowed people to keep guns in locked cars. Maggart had had an A+ rating from the NRA for years, but soon after she decided to table the bill, the NRA put up billboards in her district that compared her to President Barack Obama, a Democrat who supported gun control. DEFEND FREEDOM—DEFEAT MAGGART, the billboards read.

"I went out and looked, and I couldn't believe it," she said. "The billboards said I was just like Obama, and where I'm from, that's deadly." In the next election, the NRA supported her Republican rival, and she

Billboard comparing Debra Maggart to Barack Obama. [Jessica Hill / Associated Press]

lost the Republican primary by 15 percentage points. (A primary is the first step in an election, in which voters choose among candidates from their own party. The winners of the Republican and Democratic primaries then compete against each other in the general election.) All she'd done to deserve this was postpone consideration of an NRA-supported bill—she didn't even vote against it.

In a confidential 1993 memo, the NRA itself explained that its aim is to make "it exceedingly expensive, difficult and unpleasant" for politicians to oppose gun rights: "Victory springs from imparting excruciating political pain in unrelenting political attacks on a single politician as an example to others." Put another way, the NRA's strategy is to make it too politically costly for politicians to support gun control. And that's why it succeeds.

PLAYING DEFENSE: FEDERAL GUN CONTROL IN THE 1990S

While the NRA was tallying up all these smaller, incremental victories, the gun control movement was pushing for sweeping national reform that went nowhere. In the 1980s, however, gun control advocates changed their approach, advocating for smaller-scale policy changes. That led to two victories in the early 1990s, the Brady Act and the ban on assault weapons. The impact of both these victories, however, was minimal, and even after the massacre at Columbine, no stricter national gun laws passed in Congress.

THE BRADY ACT

In 1993, Congress passed the Brady Bill, which President Clinton signed into law. The law imposed a waiting period on handgun purchases, in which time law enforcement would conduct a background check. Supporters also thought the waiting period would be useful as a cooling-off period—in other words, it might prevent people from buying guns when they were angry and using them to hurt someone. It was named after President Ronald Reagan's press secretary, James Brady, who had been shot and permanently paralyzed during an assassination attempt on the president. James's wife, Sarah, soon became a gun control activist, joining the board of Handgun Control Inc., which was later renamed the Brady Campaign to Prevent Gun Violence in Jim and Sarah's honor.

The Brady Act was supposed to fill a gap left by the Gun Control Act of 1968. Though the 1968 law prohibited the sale of firearms to certain groups of people, including those convicted of felonies and those with mental illness, it basically worked on the honor system. Potential buyers could just lie about their criminal record or history of mental illness, and the gun would be theirs. The Brady Act, however, required police to make a "reasonable effort" to conduct the background check, which advocates hoped would prevent people from flat-out lying.

The law's supporters described it as "a *minor* step forward," stressing, as Osha Gray Davidson says, "the word *minor*." In fact, before the

Police surrounding President Reagan's would-be assassin moments after the shooting.
[Wikimedia Commons]

Cincinnati revolt, the NRA itself had supported waiting periods, noting in the mid-1970s that a "waiting period could help in reducing crimes of passion and in preventing people with criminal records or dangerous mental illness from acquiring guns." But the new NRA was opposed to *any* gun control. As noted in chapter 1, Wayne LaPierre once explained that "the anti-gunner's formula for surrendering our Second Amendment freedoms is clear: First, enact a nationwide firearms waiting period; second, after the waiting period fails to reduce crime, enact a nationwide licensing and registration law; and the final step, confiscate all registered firearms."

Bipartisan support, however, helped push the bill through Congress. Even Ronald Reagan, who was no longer president at the time (and so no longer beholden to the NRA), supported the bill. "You do know that I'm a member of the National Rifle Association," Reagan said, "and my position on the right to bear arms is well known. But I want you to know something else, and I am going to say it in clear, unmistakable language: I support the Brady Bill and I urge the Congress to enact it without further delay."

In 1993, the Brady Bill passed both houses of Congress, was signed by President Clinton, and became the Brady Act. Five years later, the waiting period was eliminated and replaced by an "instantaneous" background check. (In reality, the process takes a few minutes.) Today, to conduct a background check, a gun dealer asks a potential buyer for personal information—like age, address, and whether they've ever been convicted of a felony—and then submits that information to the FBI by phone or online. The FBI checks the information against its databases of individuals disqualified from owning a gun, then approves or denies the sale.

Nevertheless, today ten states and the District of Columbia still require waiting periods before a handgun purchase. Even though background checks can be completed quickly, these states believe that a cooling-off period may be useful to prevent crimes of passion.

One study suggests that the Brady Act helped stopped the flow of guns from states with relaxed gun laws to states with strict gun laws. Before the act passed, some states required background checks, but not all. That meant that people trying to get around a background check could drive to a nearby state and purchase a gun there. One result of the Brady Act "was to shut down much of the pipeline from those unregulated states into Chicago," Professors Cook and Goss write. "Before Brady, one-third of the handguns confiscated in Chicago originated in Mississippi, Alabama, and other loosely regulated states—starting in 1994, that fraction was cut in half, to just 16%."

But other studies found that the Brady Act had little impact on homicide rates, likely because of a loophole that allowed many gun purchases to go unregulated. That loophole was created by the Firearm Owners' Protection Act of 1986 (or FOPA), a law that the NRA had pushed for in the 1980s. While the Gun Control Act of 1968 imposed restrictions on all licensed dealers "engaged in the business" of selling firearms, FOPA changed the definition of what it meant to be "engaged in the business" of selling guns. FOPA said that if you were a "person who makes occasional sales, exchanges, or purchases of firearms for the enhancement of a personal collection or for a hobby, or who sells all or part of his personal collection of firearms" (regardless of its size), you weren't subject to regulation by the government. (FOPA did other things, too, like ban the sale of new machine guns—discussed in chapter 5.)

As one legal scholar explained, the "central thrust of the FOPA definition [was] toward limiting the term 'engaged in the business' to those who treat firearm sales as a business." This was supposed to help one-time gun sellers—like a friend who sells you a gun—avoid the burden of filling out paperwork and running a background check. But today, 30 to 40 percent of all gun purchases occur through private sales like this, often at gun shows—which means 30 to 40 percent of gun sales don't include a background check. And as a study reported in the *Journal of the American Medical Association* argued, this is likely why the Brady Act didn't really work:

> Secondary-market sales account for about 40% of the approximately 10 million gun transfers in the United States each year and are the source for the large majority of guns obtained by juveniles and criminals. The secondary market in guns, which is currently almost completely unregulated, is thus an enormous loophole that limits the effectiveness of primary-market regulations.

The Brady Act's ineffectiveness, the study concluded, was likely because of FOPA—which revised the Gun Control Act of 1968 to allow many, many gun sales to go unregulated.

THE ASSAULT WEAPONS BAN

In 1994, Congress passed a law that banned the manufacture, transfer, or possession of assault weapons. Several years prior, in 1989, a man had used a semiautomatic AK-47 assault rifle to kill five children and wound dozens more at an elementary school in Stockton, California. But there was one small problem in crafting the legislation: It was hard to define "assault weapon."

Assault weapons include fully automatic weapons, like machine guns, but they also include semiautomatic weapons. Fully automatic weapons reload automatically and fire bullets continuously when the trigger is pulled. Semiautomatic weapons reload automatically as well, but they require one trigger pull per fire, which means they shoot bullets more slowly than do fully automatic weapons. Here's the thing, though: Today, the majority of guns in America are semiautomatic.

Lawmakers knew they wouldn't be able to pass a law banning *all* those guns, so they set criteria that many considered arbitrary: The law banned only those weapons with "military-style design characteristics." In other words, it banned guns that looked deadly, regardless of how deadly they actually were. Congress banned nineteen specific guns and any guns that looked like them, but it also explicitly said 661 other guns were *not* banned. Even so, gun manufacturers were able to get around the ban by making small changes to the guns' design, producing weapons that were just as lethal as those Congress tried to outlaw. The ban was also only set to last for ten years, and when it expired in 2004, Congress chose not to renew it.

COLUMBINE

In the 1999 mass shooting at Columbine High School in Colorado, two seventeen-year-old boys killed twelve of their fellow students and a teacher before taking their own lives. Three of the four guns used in the shooting were purchased at a gun show by another student—an eighteen-year-old friend of theirs who bought the guns for the under-age boys. The friend later testified that she wished there had been background checks at the gun show:

> [The shooters] had gone to the Tanner gun show on Saturday and they took me back with them on Sunday. . . . While we were walking around, [the shooters] kept asking sellers if they were private or licensed. They wanted to buy their guns from someone who was private—and not licensed—because there would be no paperwork or background check. . . . It was too easy. I wish it had been more difficult. I wouldn't have helped them buy the guns if I had faced a background check.

Less than two weeks after the shooting, the NRA held its national convention in Denver, Colorado. Dave Cullen, author of *Columbine*, explains that it "was a ghastly coincidence. Mayor Wellington Webb begged the group to cancel its annual convention, scheduled long before. Angry barbs had flown back and forth all week. 'We don't want you here,' Mayor Webb finally said."

The NRA refused to budge. They showed up in Denver anyway, where they were met by thousands of protestors. Protest signs said: SHAME ON THE NRA, THANKS NRA FOR MAKING THE COLUMBINE MASSACRE SO POSSI-BLE, and HEY, HEY, NRA, HOW MANY KIDS DID YOU KILL TODAY!! Some teens wore signs that read I DON'T WANT TO DIE.

One man, Tom Mauser, had a sign that said, MY SON DANIEL DIED AT

Tom Mauser lifting his hands in the American Sign Language gesture for "love."
[Getty Images / Kevin Moloney]

COLUMBINE. HE'D EXPECT ME TO BE HERE TODAY. Normally a reserved man, Tom told the crowd, "When a child can grab a gun so easily and shoot a bullet into the middle of a child's face, as my son experienced, something is wrong."

"It is time for change," he said, before bursting into tears.

Two weeks before the tragedy, Tom's son Daniel had learned about the Brady Act. He came home and asked his father whether he knew that loopholes in the law allowed purchases at gun shows to evade the background-check requirement. Tom later saw this as a sign: Daniel would be murdered by one such gun.

Wayne LaPierre, the executive vice president of the NRA, said the organization would consider supporting background checks at gun shows as long as they didn't impose extra costs on gun buyers. LaPierre also spoke in favor of "absolutely gun-free, zero-tolerance, totally safe schools.

That means no guns in America's schools, period . . . with the rare exception of law enforcement officers or trained security personnel." (Keep this in mind for later—we'll learn about how the NRA changed its tune on these issues after *District of Columbia v. Heller*.)

After Columbine, both Colorado and Oregon passed laws that required private sellers at gun shows to conduct background checks on their customers. A similar law that would apply nationwide was proposed in Congress, but it failed to pass: Democrats and Republicans couldn't agree on what would happen if the FBI didn't quickly approve or deny a sale after a dealer submitted a background-check request. Republicans wanted the sale to automatically proceed after twenty-four hours, and Democrats wanted to delay the sale for up to three days. The two sides, at an impasse, passed no law at all.

Because of Columbine, gun control became a big issue in the 2000 presidential campaign. The NRA spent more than $2.2 million to help George W. Bush, a Republican who supported gun rights, win against his Democratic opponent, Al Gore. Republicans and the NRA focused their messaging on Gore's support of gun control, which former president Bill Clinton suggests may have cost Democrats the presidency: "I believe Al lost Arkansas because of the National Rifle Association . . . and maybe Missouri, and maybe Tennessee, and maybe New Hampshire. . . . I don't think the NRA got near as much credit as they deserve for Bush's election. They hurt us bad."

And after the NRA helped get him elected in 2000, President Bush nominated two U.S. Supreme Court justices who supported gun rights: John Roberts and Samuel Alito. "In retrospect," writes David Cole, "had Bush not received the NRA's support in 2000 and 2004, he might have lost either election, a Democratic president would have elected the court's two replacements, and the court's decision in *Heller* might well have turned out differently."

In the 1980s and 1990s, the NRA got influential opinions on its side in the Second Amendment debate, and it lobbied for more protections for gun owners, including explicit state constitutional provisions, state preemption laws, "shall issue" laws, stand-your-ground laws, and immunity for gun manufacturers. While gun control laws like the Brady Act and the assault weapons ban passed in the 1990s, neither had a very large impact. The NRA was also able to prevent Congress from passing federal gun regulations in the wake of Columbine and, indeed, used the fear of gun regulations to help get George Bush elected. In short, "the NRA worked tirelessly for decades, in every state in the Union and [Washington, D.C.], to advance recognition of an individual right to bear arms," which would help make a victory in *Heller* more likely.

But when Dick Heller and his lawyer Alan Gura decided to bring their case to the Supreme Court, the NRA thought it was too soon—they didn't think the Supreme Court would rule in their favor yet.

Alan Gura, however, had other ideas.

CHAPTER 9

DISTRICT OF COLUMBIA v. HELLER

O

ne can argue that our right to own guns was given to us by . . . can you guess?

Nope, not the founders.

Grizzly bears.

Let me explain. It all started on March 18, 2008, when *District of Columbia v. Heller* was argued at the U.S. Supreme Court.

When a case gets to the U.S. Supreme Court, you know it's serious. That's because there are three levels of courts in the federal system: ninety-four district courts, thirteen courts of appeal, and the one and only Supreme Court. Typically, you have to get through your local district court and court of appeals before the Supreme Court even knows about your case. And if you start out in state court, you have to go through similar hoops to get to your state's supreme court before you can even think about taking your case to the U.S. Supreme Court.

To bring a federal lawsuit, you first file your case in a district court. If you lose your case in the district court and want to challenge the decision, you file a brief with the court of appeals explaining where the district court went wrong.

If you lose in the court of appeals, you might then ask the Supreme Court to hear your case. This is called filing a petition for a writ of certiorari, or a "cert petition." Try saying that ten times fast.

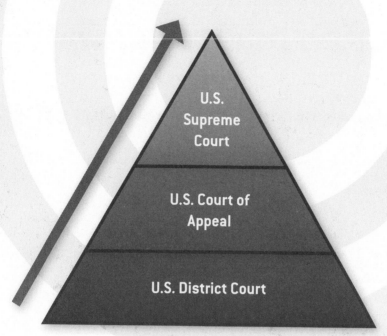

Court levels in the federal system.

In most situations, the Supreme Court doesn't *have* to take your case—it can decide whether or not it wants to. In fact, of the seven thousand to eight thousand cert petitions filed each year, the Supreme Court takes only about eighty.

That's a 1 percent chance. In other words, it barely happens.

So it's a big deal to have the Supreme Court consider your case, and then you have to head to Washington, D.C., to present an oral argument to the nine Supreme Court justices. People are usually pretty nervous. But not Alan Gura—or so he said.

On the morning of March 18, 2008, the young, relatively inexperienced lawyer Alan Gura walked to the Supreme Court from his nearby hotel. This was his first time arguing in front of the Supreme Court, and the whole country was watching.

Gura was there to challenge a D.C. law banning handguns, which was part of the Firearms Control Regulations Act of 1975. As discussed

DID D.C.'S HANDGUN BAN WORK?

Initially, research suggested that D.C.'s handgun ban was effective. A 1980 study by the U.S. Conference of Mayors noted that robberies, assaults, and homicides using handguns plummeted in D.C. after the ban was enacted, concluding that "the Firearms Control Act, and not chance alone or other extraneous factors, has been responsible for the significant reduction in both firearm and handgun crime."

Other studies, however, called these findings into question. They suggested that the decline in crime was caused not by the handgun ban but by increases in law enforcement activity more generally. Similarly, the NRA suggested that because crime was "cyclical," it would've gone down anyway.

In the late 1980s and early 1990s, rising drug use led to an increase in violent crime in the city, including murder. In 1991, D.C. became known as the nation's murder capital, with 81 homicides per 100,000 people. (The national average at that time, by contrast, was just 9.8 homicides per 100,000 people.) That same year, the *New England Journal of Medicine* published a study suggesting that deaths would have been *even higher* without the gun ban—that without the ban there would have been 47 more deaths (both suicides and murders) in the city each year.

At the end of the day, the problem with the law was just what its supporters had identified: People intent on committing crimes could always get their guns in neighboring Virginia or Maryland. Indeed, many of the firearms seized by police in D.C. while the ban was in effect could be traced to dealers across state lines.

in chapter 7, the D.C. Council had passed the law because there was so much gun violence in the city; the council hoped reducing the number of guns would reduce the amount of violence. But even some of the law's supporters worried that it wouldn't have much of an impact, since people could always get guns from the nearby states of Maryland and Virginia. The idea, though, was that the law might lead to similar handgun bans across the country.

Gura didn't like D.C.'s law. He wasn't associated with the NRA, but he was a libertarian, which meant he believed that government should stay out of his business. If he wanted a gun, why should the government care?

He also knew that winning a case like this would be a huge break for him—he could become a well-known lawyer. After years of extensive lobbying by the NRA, the gun control debate had become a central topic in American politics. Gura knew that if he could take a case to the Supreme Court, he would make history by settling the question raised by the Black Panthers in the 1960s and carried into the new millennium by the NRA: Did *every* Joe and Jane have the right to bear arms?

This all goes back to that age-old question about the Second Amendment:

A well regulated Militia, being necessary to the security of a free State, the right of the people to keep and bear Arms, shall not be infringed.

Whose right *is* it? The militia's or the people's?

For over two hundred years the Second Amendment had been interpreted as a militia right—but the NRA had waged a decades-long campaign to change that interpretation. The leaders of the NRA, however, still thought it was too early to bring a Supreme Court case. They were worried they didn't have enough votes on the Supreme Court in support of the view that the Second Amendment protected an individual right. (To win a case at the Supreme Court, you need to convince a majority of the nine justices—in other words, at least five.)

Indeed, they tried to convince Gura to drop the case, and when that didn't work, they lobbied to get D.C.'s handgun ban repealed so the case would be moot. ("Moot" means that the person bringing the claim doesn't have anything left to challenge; here, if the law had been repealed, there would've been nothing for Heller to sue about.)

Then, in 2007, thirty-two people died in a mass shooting at Virginia Tech. The NRA released a brief statement on its website sending "thoughts and prayers" to "the families and friends who lost loved ones to this senseless act," but claiming it was "not a time for political discussions or public policy debates." Nevertheless, the political winds shifted against the NRA's efforts to get D.C.'s gun law repealed. Gura's case lived to see another day.

Initially, Gura's team had put together a group of six plaintiffs—in other words, six people the lawyers would represent. Sometimes clients come to lawyers, but other times lawyers find the clients themselves—particularly when the lawyers have ideological goals they're trying to achieve.

Three of the plaintiffs were women and three were men, including a seventy-five-year-old white man named Dick Heller. Heller was a security guard who used a gun at work, and he wanted to use one for self-defense at home, too—he lived in a part of town where there were plenty of shootings. Heller thought a gun was necessary to protect himself, but he couldn't have one because of D.C.'s ban.

Heller wasn't the perfect plaintiff. He thought guns were necessary to combat government tyranny, a view his lawyers worried would make him unsympathetic to the court and the general public. But in the end, Heller was the only one of these plaintiffs who could bring the lawsuit.

In order to sue someone, you have to prove that you've been harmed by them—this is what's called "standing." Heller had standing because he didn't just *want* a gun—he actually filled out an application to register a gun he already possessed. That petition was denied, and he had the denial slip. He wasn't harmed in the way we usually think of the word, but he had a piece of paper that proved he was unhappy with the government's decision to deny him a gun. And for that reason, he had standing to sue.

Heller, represented by Gura, lost his case in the district court. He appealed to the U.S. Court of Appeals for the District of Columbia Circuit, where he won. His opponents then decided to appeal that decision to the U.S. Supreme Court.

The Supreme Court agreed to hear the case. In the court's gilded halls, the justices would host a case that would define America's relationship to guns for posterity: *District of Columbia v. Heller.*

While Alan Gura walked to the Supreme Court on that March morning, Walter Dellinger rode there on his bike. His white hair was tucked under his helmet, and he wore a puffy jacket over his suit. He had been to the court many times when he was solicitor general, the federal government's lawyer, before he took a job near the top of a fancy law firm. He would represent D.C. in Dick Heller's case against the city.

After passing through security, Dellinger and Gura walked into the courtroom. The gallery was full of spectators, many of whom had waited all night to get a seat. This was set to be one of the biggest battles in all gun history. The country was riveted by this case that was set to decide, once and for all, the meaning of the Second Amendment.

People waiting in the cold to hear arguments in District of Columbia v. Heller.
[Getty Images / *The Washington Post*]

Outside the courtroom, demonstrators on both sides of the issue held signs. Pro-gun advocates shouted, "More guns! Less crime!" Anti-gun advocates responded, "More guns! More death!"

Pro-and anti-gun demonstrators outside the U.S. Supreme Court.
[Pablo Martínez Monsiváis / Associated Press]

Inside, the marshal loudly banged the gavel and all nine justices walked in. "Oyez! Oyez! Oyez!" the marshal shouted. "All persons having business before the Honorable, the Supreme Court of the United States, are admonished to draw near and give their attention, for the Court is now sitting. God save the United States and this Honorable Court!"

Even though the justices are supposed to stay out of politics, they often have political views that come out in their opinions. Indeed, in 2008, the Supreme Court was neatly divided into two camps—liberal and conservative—with just one defector: Justice Anthony Kennedy.

"Swing Justice" Kennedy, the justice whom Gura and Dellinger couldn't peg.
[Wikimedia Commons]

Because Justice Kennedy sometimes voted conservatively, sometimes liberally, he'd earned the nickname of the "swing justice." Born in Sacramento, California, in 1936, Justice Kennedy had worked in private practice, as a professor, and as an appeals court judge before he was nominated to the Supreme Court by President Ronald Reagan in 1988. Interestingly, Justice Kennedy was President Reagan's third choice for the job. Robert Bork, the president's first choice, failed to receive enough votes from Senate Democrats, who thought he was too conservative. Douglas Ginsburg, President Reagan's second choice, withdrew from consideration after it was discovered that his wife had provided abortions when she was a medical resident. Ultimately, Justice Kennedy was nominated by President Reagan and confirmed by the Senate with a 97–0 vote.

The Supreme Court in 2008 (top row, from left to right: Breyer, Thomas, Ginsburg, Alito; bottom row, from left to right: Kennedy, Stevens, Roberts, Scalia, Souter).
[Wikimedia Commons]

But Justice Kennedy was only one of the nine justices on the Supreme Court in 2008. The other eight were Stephen Breyer, Clarence Thomas, Ruth Bader Ginsburg, Samuel Alito, John Paul Stevens, John Roberts, Antonin Scalia, and David Souter. And they each had their quirks, too.

THE LIBERALS

STEPHEN BREYER · **RUTH BADER GINSBURG** · **DAVID SOUTER** · **JOHN PAUL STEVENS**

[Wikimedia Commons]

★ Playing for the liberals, there's **Stephen Breyer**, who was appointed by President Bill Clinton and is well known for his practicality. When he makes decisions, he thinks a lot about their real-world consequences. Justice Breyer is also known for his determination. In 1994, when President Clinton was considering him for a spot on the Supreme Court, Justice Breyer was involved in a bike accident. Even though he had several broken ribs and a punctured lung, Justice Breyer still attended his meeting with the president—and eventually secured his position on the bench.

★ Next up is **John Paul Stevens**, who passed away in July 2019. A Chicago native, Justice Stevens served in the navy during World War II and went to Northwestern Law School after the war. Justice Stevens clerked for a Supreme Court justice after he graduated from law school, then went on to become a law firm partner and a law professor at University of Chicago and Northwestern University. He was appointed to the Supreme Court in 1975 by President Gerald Ford, a Republican, but over time he came to vote consistently with the liberal wing of the court. He retired from the Supreme Court in 2010 at the age of ninety.

★ **David Souter** was born in Massachusetts but moved to New Hampshire when he was eleven. After graduating from Harvard College and Harvard Law School, he went back to New Hampshire to work first in private practice, then in the New Hampshire attorney general's office, then as a state court judge. Like Justice Stevens, Justice Souter was appointed by a Republican—President George H. W. Bush—but eventually started playing for the liberals. In 2009, Justice Souter retired and moved back to (you guessed it) New Hampshire, where he currently lives.

★ And last but not least for the liberals, there's **Ruth Bader Ginsburg**, who was appointed by President Bill Clinton. Justice Ginsburg earned the nickname "the Notorious RBG" with her fiery dissents and steadfast commitment to women's rights. In the 1970s, she directed the Women's Rights Project of the ACLU, where she argued six gender-discrimination cases before the Supreme Court. In her own life, Justice Ginsburg herself experienced gender discrimination. As a student at Harvard Law School, for example, she was told she'd taken "a man's spot." Later, as a professor, she hid the fact that she was pregnant from her coworkers so as to avoid discrimination.

THE CONSERVATIVES

[Wikimedia Commons]

★ First up for the conservatives is **John Roberts**, who was appointed by President George W. Bush. Chief Justice Roberts grew up in Indiana, which might explain his midwestern personality. He believes that courts should be umpires: They should apply the rules, not create them. In particular, he thinks the Supreme Court should stay out of political questions, since those are better handled by Congress. This means that Chief Justice Roberts might abandon his conservative beliefs if he thinks the law doesn't support them. And as the chief justice, he can choose who writes the majority opinion when he sides with the majority. This gives him a lot of influence over the ruling.

★ **Antonin Scalia**, who passed away in 2016, was appointed by President Ronald Reagan. Justice Scalia was well known for his flowery writing style—one particularly famous dissent included the phrases "pure applesauce" and "jiggery-pokery." He was a die-hard originalist, which meant he interpreted the Constitution as he thought the founders would. In this way, he disagreed with Justices Ginsburg and Breyer, who believe in a "living Constitution" that evolves with society. But Justices Scalia and Ginsburg would never let politics get in the way of their friendship. They were both big opera fans and would often go to performances together.

★ **Clarence Thomas**, the third justice for the conservatives, is known for his reticence—he almost never asks questions during oral argument. But because he's arguably the most conservative member of the court, his colleagues usually know what he's thinking anyway. When President George H. W. Bush nominated him to the Supreme Court in 1991, Justice Thomas's former employee, Anita Hill, came forward to allege that she had been sexually harassed by him. Nevertheless, the Senate confirmed Justice Thomas in October 1991.

★ Finally, there's **Samuel Alito**, who was appointed by President George W. Bush. Justice Alito has always had Supreme Court dreams—he wrote in his college yearbook that he wanted to be a Supreme Court justice. Even though he has strong conservative beliefs, Justice Alito tends to take each case on its own terms—and when he identifies with the parties, he'll often show sympathy. In a 2011 freedom-of-speech case, for example, the other eight justices said that the First Amendment allowed the Westboro Baptist Church to protest at military funerals. Justice Alito dissented, arguing that the church's "outrageous conduct caused" the family "great injury" and should not be protected by the First Amendment.

As they prepared for oral argument before the Supreme Court, Walter Dellinger and Alan Gura expected that the liberal and the conservative justices would stick to their political leanings.

The four liberal justices would likely agree with the militia interpretation, while the four conservative justices would likely go with the individual-rights interpretation. Liberals typically favor gun control, for the reasons explored previously: Many liberals live in urban areas, where rates of gun violence tend to be higher, and many liberals are women and racial minorities, who are less likely to own guns. By arguing that the right to bear arms was meant to be a collective militia right, liberals seek to prevent individual people from asserting that they've got a constitutional right to own a weapon. In this way, they allow the government to regulate guns more freely.

Most conservatives, on the other hand, believe in gun rights, in part because they often live in rural areas where gun ownership is more common. They argue that the Second Amendment protects an individual right, not a militia right and that every Joe and Jane has a right to challenge gun control laws in court as unconstitutional. The more court challenges there are, the more opportunities there are for courts to strike those laws down—which is exactly what gun rights supporters want.

STARE DECISIS

Every year, for about two weeks around the holidays, most students get a winter break. Now, let's say one year your school announced there would be no time off—no Christmas, no New Year's, nothing, even though you'd always had two weeks off in the past. The school officials just changed their minds without explanation. Wouldn't that feel unfair?

Law is similar. When a court makes a decision, that opinion is binding law. And when other cases are put before that court, the lawyers look to rulings from the past, which are called precedent. That's why lawyers are always explaining how their case is similar to or different from prior cases—courts have to abide by precedent. This is known as stare decisis, Latin for "to stand by things decided."

Now, it's not quite that simple. As discussed, there are multiple levels of courts in the federal system: district courts, circuit courts, and the Supreme Court. An opinion is binding only on the court that issued it and those beneath it; for example, while Supreme Court opinions bind all three levels of courts, a circuit court opinion only binds that circuit and the district courts that fall within its geographic boundaries. But! Even if an opinion isn't binding precedent, it can still be persuasive.

Think about it this way: If you're a circuit court, your boss is the Supreme Court. You've gotta do what the Supreme Court says. But as a circuit court, you're the boss of the district courts that are in your region. If they say you should do something, you can think about it and see whether it makes sense to you, but you don't necessarily have to do it. The district courts' opinions are persuasive, not mandatory.

But if you're the boss—ahem, the Supreme Court—can you ever change your mind? Or do you have to stick with what you said before? Well . . . it depends. If you want to change your mind, you need a *really* good reason—for example, you could say that a lot of things have changed in society since the time the earlier case was decided.

This all makes sense if you think back to your winter break from school. It would seem really unfair if your school canceled winter break for no reason, but less unfair if you learned that this was because there would be a new standardized test in January, and the teachers needed all the time they could get to prepare. In other words, your school had a reason to reverse its own precedent.

But just when you thought you had it down . . . it gets even more complicated, since there are state courts in addition to federal courts. As noted in chapter 2, federal courts take only a few types of cases—those that are about federal laws and those that are between citizens of different states. State courts, on the other hand, take all sorts of cases.

Like federal courts, there are three levels of state courts: state trial courts, state appellate courts, and state supreme courts. And just like in the federal system, a state court opinion is only binding on the court that issued it and those beneath it.

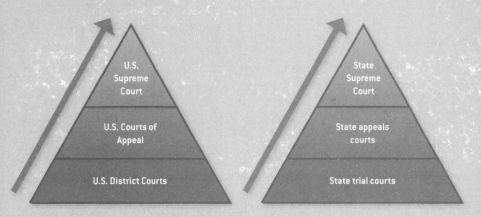

Court levels in the federal and state systems.

But here's where it gets *really* messy. Does a state court ever bind a federal court? And does a federal court ever bind a state court?

The answer is: sometimes. State supreme court opinions can be binding on federal courts if the federal court is interpreting state law. And *all* courts—state courts included—are bound by the decisions of the U.S. Supreme Court on issues of federal law.

Confusing as all this is, what it means at the end of the day is that Supreme Court decisions are really important and that it's very hard for the Supreme Court to change its mind. Which is why *Heller* was such a big deal.

That morning Walter Dellinger planned to focus on what James Madison had been thinking when he wrote the Second Amendment. Based on the historical evidence, Dellinger would argue, the right to bear arms was always meant to be a militia right—not an individual right that could protect people like Dick Heller. In other words, Dellinger was planning to use originalism to support his argument.

LIVING CONSTITUTIONALISM vs. ORIGINALISM

Living constitutionalism is the idea that the Constitution should grow and change with society—that it should adapt to fit its time period. In the 1950s and 1960s, the Supreme Court applied this doctrine to interpret the Constitution broadly, in part by giving more protections to criminal defendants and expanding the right to privacy. Because it provides more people with more rights, liberals tend to support living constitutionalism.

Living constitutionalism stands in contrast to another judicial philosophy, originalism, which is the idea that we should interpret the Constitution according to how the founders thought about it. In other words, originalism asks us to get into early Americans' heads and understand what they thought. Originalism became popular in the 1970s, when conservatives decided they needed a way to interpret the Constitution that aligned with their political beliefs. They developed a methodology, originalism, that would allow them to interpret the Constitution with what they called judicial restraint.

Originalism's biggest proponent was none other than conservative Supreme Court Justice Antonin Scalia—which makes it pretty ironic that Dellinger was using originalism to support the liberal position in *Heller*.

Alan Gura also planned to use originalism, but differently: He intended to argue that the amendment was always about the issue of individual self-defense, which supported the individual-rights interpretation. In his view, this interpretation of the Second Amendment wasn't new—it had just been lost.

At that point, history had been on Dellinger's side. Almost every federal court to consider the matter had ruled that the right to bear arms was not an individual one—and that included the Supreme Court. (Remember how hard it is for the Supreme Court to overturn its own precedent.) In 1939, the Supreme Court upheld a federal gun law that banned sawed-off shotguns in *United States v. Miller*. As discussed in chapter 5, the Supreme Court held that the National Firearms Act of 1934 didn't violate the Second Amendment because there was no evidence that a sawed-off shotgun had any "reasonable relationship to the preservation or efficiency of a well regulated militia." Even though the *Miller* opinion was pretty confusing, lower courts interpreted it to mean that the Second Amendment didn't provide an individual right to bear arms.

But in 2000, George W. Bush became president with the support of the NRA, and he soon nominated two pro-gun justices to the Supreme Court: Samuel Alito and John Roberts. Around the same time, a federal court in Texas ruled for the first time that the Second Amendment protected the individual right to bear arms.

The political tides were shifting. Would the Supreme Court follow suit?

It all depended on the justice they couldn't peg—the wild card, Justice Kennedy. Sitting in the courthouse that morning, both Gura and Dellinger wondered what Justice Kennedy was thinking.

The only case on the docket that morning was *District of Columbia v. Heller*. Dellinger strolled up to the podium. "Good morning, Mr. Chief Justice, and may it please the Court," he said.

Dellinger began by arguing that when the Second Amendment was written, the phrase "bear arms" was always tied to the militia. "Every person who used the phrase 'bear arms,'" he said, "used it to refer to the use of arms in connection with militia service." Back when the Constitution was written, Dellinger posited, guns were definitely *not* an individual right.

But Chief Justice Roberts cut him off. He wanted to know why the amendment said "the right of the people" if it just meant that state militias had the right to bear arms. "If you're right, Mr. Dellinger," he said, "it's certainly an odd way in the Second Amendment to phrase the operative provision" (the most important part, the chief justice meant).

Dellinger groaned inwardly and reiterated his point. He explained that in that day and age, the words "people" and "militia" were often used synonymously: "The people are the militia, the militia are the people."

Chief Justice Roberts wasn't buying it. "If the militia included all the people, doesn't the preamble that you rely on not really restrict the right much at all?" Basically, Chief Justice Roberts told Dellinger that his argument contradicted itself: If the people really are the same thing as the militia, then the right should be considered an individual one.

Hmm. That was a fine point.

Meanwhile, Justice Thomas looked on silently.

Justice Scalia jumped in next. He disagreed with Dellinger, noting that the "two clauses go together beautifully: Since we need a militia, the right of the people to keep and bear arms shall not be infringed." He thought the militia clause explained *one* reason why we have the right to bear arms—but that it wasn't the *only* reason.

It seemed as though Justice Scalia really wanted Gura to win. Justice Scalia frequently went hunting, and as a child, he would carry his rifle to school with him on the New York City subway system.

Dellinger began to respond, but then Swing Justice Kennedy interrupted. He had a question about—you guessed it!—grizzly bears.

Might the Second Amendment have something to do with "the concern of the remote settler to defend himself and his family against hostile Indian tribes and outlaws, wolves and bears and grizzlies and things like that?"

Crap, Dellinger thought. "That is not the discourse that is part of the Second Amendment."

It was then that Gura knew he had won.

To backtrack, this is why: Justice Kennedy's opinion here was crucial because it would more or less determine who won the case. His comment about grizzlies meant that he thought the right to bear arms was about personal self-defense against threats like bears. And if the right was about self-defense, it meant that the amendment pertained to an individual right—*not* state militias. And if Justice Kennedy, the swing justice, believed that the Second Amendment was about the individual, then the case was closed. The conservatives would win.

And that they did.

On June 26, 2008, the Supreme Court issued a groundbreaking opinion in *Heller*. The four conservative justices were joined by Swing Justice Kennedy in the majority, winning the case for Dick Heller and Alan Gura. Walter Dellinger and his militia argument had lost, and unprecedented gun rights were granted to the individual.

The majority opinion, written by Justice Scalia, minimized the militia clause and instead put the emphasis on the "right of the people" clause. Applying originalism, Justice Scalia analyzed how people in the eighteenth century would have understood the phrases "right of the people," "keep and bear Arms," "well regulated Militia," and "security of a free State." Justice Scalia concluded that the first half of the Amendment didn't limit the right to bear arms to militia service, but rather "announce[d] a purpose": preventing elimination of the militia by preventing disarmament. The Second Amendment, he wrote, "could be rephrased" as follows: "Because a well regulated Militia is necessary to the security of a free State, the right of the people to keep and bear Arms shall not be infringed." In other words, Justice Scalia wrote, the Second Amendment was intended to "guarantee the individual right to possess and carry weapons in case of confrontation."

Wait, what? What about all the gun regulations that have existed since the earliest days of this country? And wasn't it the NRA that spent decades trying to reshape the popular understanding of the Second Amendment? After the *Heller* opinion came out, J. Harvie Wilkinson III, a conservative federal judge in Virginia, condemned what he saw as the majority's overreach: "In *Heller*, the majority read an ambiguous constitutional provision as creating a substantive right that the Court had never acknowledged in more than two hundred years since the amendment's enactment." Though Justice Scalia purported to be applying originalism, Judge Wilkinson stated, it was the NRA he was responding to instead.

Other scholars agreed. In a piece in the *Harvard Law Review*, law professor Reva Siegel argued that even though the majority in *Heller* said it was being originalist, it had actually "interpreted the Second Amendment in accordance with the convictions of the twentieth-century gun-rights movement" and so "demonstrated the ascendancy of the living Constitution." In other words, Justice Scalia, the foremost proponent of originalism, had applied living constitutionalism instead, Siegel said.

Both Justice Stevens and Justice Breyer wrote long dissents in *Heller*. (A dissent is an opinion written by a judge who disagrees with the majority. It explains the dissenting judge's reasoning and how that judge would've decided the case.) Justice Stevens's dissent also applied originalism (and even cited some of the same sources) to argue that the Second Amendment was originally only about militias. This shows us one of originalism's limitations: Since we can't ever really know what the founders were thinking, people can come to totally opposite conclusions even when looking at the same sources.

In *Heller*, Justice Scalia didn't say he was overruling *Miller*, the 1939 case. As discussed earlier, overruling precedent is a big deal, and courts often try to avoid it by distinguishing their case in some way. So in *Heller*, Justice Scalia explained that *Miller* didn't actually say whether the individual-rights interpretation or the militia interpretation was the right one. Instead, Justice Scalia wrote, *Miller* was just a case about sawed-off shotguns, a type of weapon that was "not eligible for Second Amendment protection." For that reason, *Miller* didn't prevent the court from coming to a different conclusion in *Heller*.

Justice Scalia's majority opinion also acknowledged that "the right secured by the Second Amendment is *not unlimited*"—in other words, even though the Second Amendment gave every individual the right to bear arms, some restrictions were still okay. Justice Scalia clarified that mentally ill people and people convicted of felonies could be prevented from owning guns and that laws could prohibit people from carrying guns to school or other sensitive areas. Some people think Scalia may have included this paragraph as a compromise, in order to persuade Swing Justice Kennedy to join the majority.

Even though it hadn't wanted to bring the case, the NRA came out on top. It got what it had wanted for decades—the individual right to bear arms was now officially part of the Constitution. "The Second Amendment as an individual right now becomes a real permanent part of American constitutional law," Wayne LaPierre proclaimed.

In a statement, President George W. Bush said, "As a longstanding advocate of the rights of gun owners in America, I applaud the Supreme Court's historic decision today confirming what has always been clear in the Constitution: The Second Amendment protects an individual right to keep and bear firearms."

Newspapers around the world reported on the decision. The *New York Times* called Justice Scalia's majority opinion "his most important in his 22 years on the court." And those words were right. In the years that followed, *Heller* revolutionized how we view gun control in America.

WOULD MORE GUN LAWS REDUCE GUN DEATHS?

As we saw in chapter 1, there were 39,773 firearms deaths in the United States in 2017, the highest number in fifty years. Can we blame these deaths on lax gun laws and the sheer number of guns in the country? In other words, would more gun control cut down on gun deaths?

To answer this question, let's look at how the United States compares with other countries, then at the differences between states with strong gun laws and states with weaker gun laws, and finally at some of the NRA's arguments against gun control.

INTERNATIONAL COMPARISONS

When we look at other countries' gun policies and gun death rates, we learn that they have far fewer guns, much stricter gun laws, and much fewer gun deaths.

THE UNITED STATES

The United States is now the country with the most guns per person in the world—about 120 guns for every 100 people. That means there are more guns than people in the United States, the only country in the world where that is the case.

COUNTRIES AND TERRITORIES WITH HIGHEST NUMBER OF CIVILIAN GUNS PER 100 RESIDENTS

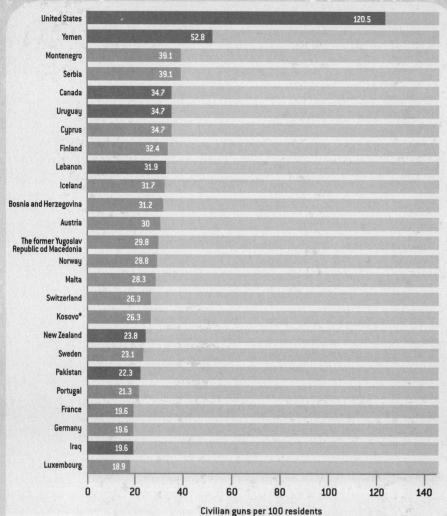

Country	Civilian guns per 100 residents
United States	120.5
Yemen	52.8
Montenegro	39.1
Serbia	39.1
Canada	34.7
Uruguay	34.7
Cyprus	34.7
Finland	32.4
Lebanon	31.9
Iceland	31.7
Bosnia and Herzegovina	31.2
Austria	30
The former Yugoslav Republic od Macedonia	29.8
Norway	28.8
Malta	28.3
Switzerland	26.3
Kosovo*	26.3
New Zealand	23.8
Sweden	23.1
Pakistan	22.3
Portugal	21.3
France	19.6
Germany	19.6
Iraq	19.6
Luxembourg	18.9

Civilian guns per 100 residents

* The designation of Kosovo is without prejudice to positions on status and is in line with UN Security Council Resolution 1244 and the International Court of Justice Opinion on the Kosovo declaration of independence.

Getting a gun in the United States is not hard. Most sales through a licensed dealer involve an instant background check, and that's it. In a 2016 test, for example, a columnist for the *Philadelphia Daily News* was able to purchase an AR-15, the same weapon used in the Parkland shooting, in seven minutes at a gun shop in Philadelphia. (Of course, the steps vary from state to state, and some states require waiting periods of several days before purchasing a gun.)

As the following chart demonstrates, the United States has the highest number of guns and the highest gun death rate compared with other countries with similar income levels. The shape of this graph demonstrates what's called a correlation between these variables. In other words, as the number of guns increases, so too does the number of gun deaths.

RELATION BETWEEN GUN-RELATED DEATHS AND NUMBER OF GUNS PER COUNTRY

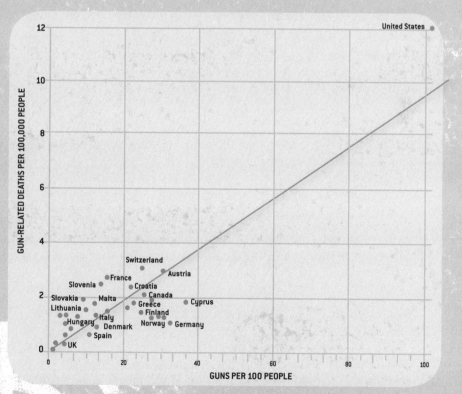

But while the gun death rate in the United States is an outlier, its overall crime rate is fairly average among countries with similar incomes. We'll see later that more guns may lead to more gun deaths, but they don't necessarily lead to more crime.

NONVIOLENT AND VIOLENT CRIME RATES OF 15 INDUSTRIALIZED COUNTRIES IN 2000

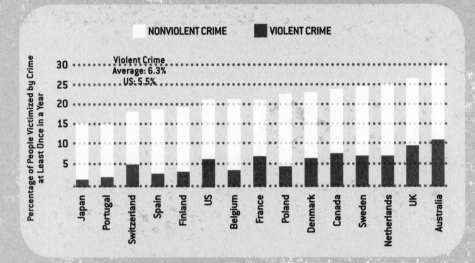

To be sure, gun deaths listed in the preceding chart include both homicides and suicides, and gun rights supporters often argue that this is the incorrect figure to be using; they say people who want to die by suicide will find a way to do so no matter what. But as you read in chapter 1, guns are the deadliest method of suicide, which makes it easier to translate impulse into action.

What's more, in the graph that follows, the *New York Times* demonstrates that the United States is also an outlier when it comes to mass shootings.

NUMBER OF MASS SHOOTERS VS. NUMBER OF GUNS PER COUNTRY IN 2016

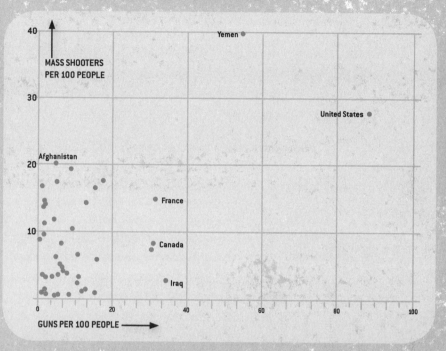

MASS SHOOTERS PER 100 PEOPLE

40

Yemen

30

United States

20 Afghanistan

France

10

Canada

Iraq

0   20   40   60   80   100

GUNS PER 100 PEOPLE

THE UNITED KINGDOM

Compared with the United States, gun regulations in the United Kingdom are much stricter. The United Kingdom has long had stringent gun regulations, but after a mass shooting at a school in Dunblane, Scotland, in 1998—in which sixteen children and one teacher were killed by a shooter carrying four handguns—the country banned handguns altogether. In the years after the shooting, the number of gun suicides declined from 136 in 1998 to 101 in 2015. (The overall number of suicides went down, too, from 6,354 in 1998 to 4,910 in 2015.) At least in part due to the scarcity of guns, there are only a few dozen gun homicides a year in the United Kingdom. The United Kingdom had only 0.06 violent gun deaths per 100,000 people as of 2017, compared with 4.43 in the United States.

AUSTRALIA

Similarly, Australia passed major gun law reforms in response to a mass shooting in 1996. These reforms included a ban on automatic and semi-automatic long guns, a twenty-eight-day waiting period, and a national firearm licensing and registration system. To buy a gun, you have to have a "genuine reason," like recreational hunting—personal protection doesn't count. The government also promised to buy back all weapons that did not comply with the new laws. In the years since these laws were introduced, there have been no mass shootings in Australia, and there has been a reduction in the rates of gun-related homicides, suicides, and accidents.

Gun-Related Deaths in Australia		
YEAR	GUN HOMICIDE RATE (PER 100,000)	GUN SUICIDE RATE (PER 100,000)	GUN ACCIDENT RATE (PER 100,000)
1996	0.57	2.09	0.16
2016	0.18	0.80	0.02

NEW ZEALAND

After a shooting claimed the life of fifty Muslims in an attack on two mosques in Christchurch, New Zealand, on March 15, 2019, Prime Minister Jacinda Ardern, the world's youngest female head of government at the time, promised change. Less than a month later, the New Zealand Parliament passed a law banning military-style semiautomatic weapons and assault rifles, including all the weapons used by the Christchurch gunman. The law was passed almost unanimously. Though it's too soon to know the effect of the law, New Zealand's homicide rates were low and mass shootings were very rare even before the legislation was passed. In 2016, for example, New Zealand's gun homicide rate was two in a million.

JAPAN

In Japan, gun licenses are issued only for specific purposes, like hunting, professional necessity, or gun competitions. Prospective gun buyers must not only pass a background check but also attend a daylong class, pass a written test, a shooting test, and mental health and drug tests. Police then inspect the gun annually, and gun owners must retake the class and exam every three years. In Japan—a country of 126 million people— there were three gun homicides in 2015, and twenty-three gun deaths in total.

STATE-BY-STATE COMPARISONS

Much like the international comparisons, state-by-state studies have concluded that states with higher gun ownership rates and weaker gun laws tend to have more gun deaths (including both homicides and suicides).

Other studies have shown that states with weaker gun laws and higher gun ownership rates also have more mass shootings, a statistic that doesn't include suicide. The graphs that follow demonstrate the relationships between restrictiveness of gun laws, gun ownership rates, and mass shooting rates. To assess gun law restrictiveness, researchers used ratings from a report published by legal professionals, which scores states from 0 (completely restrictive) to 100 (completely permissive) based on more than thirteen factors.

In the first graph, the upward-sloping line shows a correlation between gun ownership rates and mass shooting rates. The second graph shows that states with more permissive gun laws also have more mass shootings. The third graph shows that states with more permissive gun laws have higher gun ownership rates.

RATE OF MASS SHOOTINGS COMPARED TO GUN OWNERSHIP AND SEVERITY OF STATE GUN LAWS PER STATE

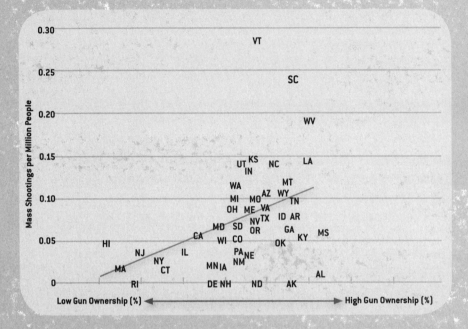

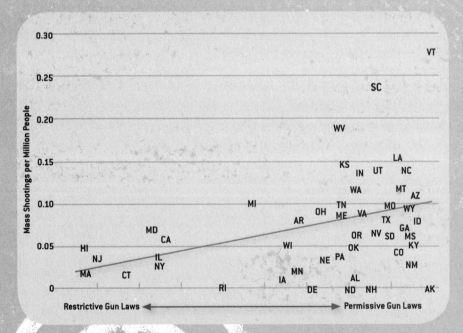

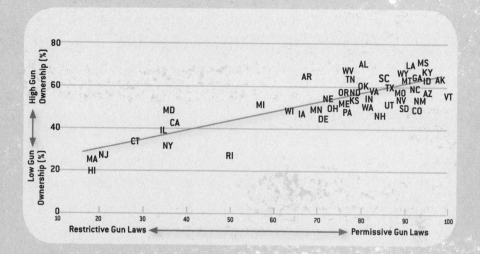

THE NRA'S COUNTERARGUMENTS

In the face of all this evidence, the NRA nevertheless argues that more gun laws would make the United States less safe. In the NRA's view, gun laws only disarm law-abiding people, and "good guys" need guns to fight "bad guys." But this isn't really the case.

Laws that limit guns' availability affect *everyone*, including people who commit crimes. Most people who commit crimes get their guns from family, friends, and street sources, and it's easier to set up these sales in states where more people have guns. As Robert Spitzer explains, whether people who commit crimes will have access to guns is directly related to the prevalence of guns in that area; if fewer guns are available, fewer crimes are committed with guns. Indeed, one study found that after local gun ownership fell by 10 percent, gun robbery fell by 5 percent and robbery murder fell by 4 percent, even though the overall rate of robbery stayed the same.

Similarly, other scholars have concluded that while assaults and robberies are not more common in the United States than in other countries, they are more deadly because in the United States these crimes are more often committed with guns. The NRA likes to say that "guns don't kill people, people kill people," but as Philip Cook and Kristin Goss explain, "guns *intensify* violence"; when someone uses a gun rather than a knife or a pair of fists, it's far more likely that the encounter will end in death. Rather than "more guns, more crime," Cook and Goss suggest, the better phrasing might be "more guns, more deaths."

Another argument the NRA makes is that people need guns to protect themselves—either because they live in a dangerous area or because they think the police can't protect them. The truth, though, is that defensive gun uses are pretty rare. While the numbers vary, one study of twenty-seven thousand crimes of personal contact (including assaults, robberies, rapes, and home invasions) found that the victim used a gun in self-defense in less than 1 percent of cases. This is likely because it's hard for a victim to shoot first when the person committing the crime is the one who acts first. That's part of why the NRA's favorite saying—"The only thing that stops a bad guy with a gun is a good guy with a gun"—doesn't make much sense.

Another major problem with this saying is that it's not always clear who is "bad" and who is "good." In 1992, for example, an exchange student from Japan and his friend were looking for a Halloween party in a New Orleans neighborhood that they didn't know very well. They walked up to the wrong house and the owner pulled out his gun and told them to get back. The students, who weren't familiar with Halloween, thought the homeowner might just be playacting, but the owner—who later said he felt threatened—shot and killed both of them. Because of Louisiana's stand-your-ground law, which says you have no duty to retreat when you feel threatened, he was acquitted of charges for what many people would consider to be murder but what he considered to be self-defense. (This is similar to the case of Trayvon Martin in chapter 8.) In a study conducted by three researchers at the Harvard School of Public Health, a group of five criminal court judges reviewed gun uses that the shooters believed had been in self-defense. For a majority of these gun uses, most judges concluded that the shootings should've been considered illegal.

The idea behind stand-your-ground laws is that people would commit fewer crimes if they knew their victims were allowed to kill them. However, studies show that when states pass stand-your-ground laws, rates of assault, robbery, and crime don't go down, but homicide rates do go up. In his 1998 book *More Guns, Less Crime*, John R. Lott made an argument similar to the one used by supporters of stand-your-ground laws; he suggested that states that adopted "shall issue" concealed-carry laws—in other words, states that made guns easier to get—saw violent crime drop. (Again, the theory here is that that people would commit fewer crimes if they thought their victims were carrying weapons.) But other scholars, along with the National Research Council, a government body tasked with providing accurate and reliable policy advice, found Lott's conclusions "unreliable."

GUNS IN SCHOOLS

What does all this information about gun prevalence and gun death teach us about arming teachers and administrators? First, when you introduce guns into schools, you make it more likely that a gun will be stolen, that there will be an accident, or that someone may use it to die by suicide. For example, in an Ohio school, two first graders picked up a gun that was part of a program meant to keep the school safe but that had been left unattended. No one was hurt, but the chance of incidents like this happening increases as more guns are brought into schools. Plus, there's no guarantee that an armed security guard will be able to prevent an attack—in fact, Columbine had an armed guard who was unable to prevent the massacre.

So . . . we've seen that defensive gun uses are pretty rare, and that while more guns may not lead to more crime, they will certainly lead to more death. We've also seen that other countries have stricter gun laws, fewer guns, and fewer gun deaths. In spite of the NRA's arguments, the evidence strongly suggests that more guns lead to more gun deaths, even if they don't increase the crime rate, and that more restrictions on guns could help reduce these numbers.

CHAPTER 10

#NEVERAGAIN

On December 14, 2012, six-year-old Jessica Rekos was chatting with her mom about Girl Scout cookies while they sat in the car, waiting for the school bus to arrive. Jessica had never sold the cookies before—she was excited for it. The bus pulled up, and Jessica hopped out of the car and climbed up the bus steps. "She sat in the front seat, looked at me through the window, and smiled and waved as the bus pulled up the hill," her mom later wrote. "That was the last time I saw Jessica alive."

Later that day, a twenty-year-old man took three of his mother's guns—a semiautomatic AR-15 assault rifle and two pistols—and headed toward the nearby Sandy Hook Elementary School. After shooting his way into the building, the gunman killed twenty elementary school children, including Jessica, and six staff members.

The nation was horrified by the tragedy at Sandy Hook. That day, President Barack Obama gave a tearful speech from the White House:

> The majority of those who died today were children—beautiful little
> kids between the ages of five and ten years old. They had their entire
> lives ahead of them—birthdays, graduations, weddings, kids of their
> own. Among the fallen were also teachers—men and women who

devoted their lives to helping our children fulfill their dreams. So our hearts are broken today for the parents and grandparents, sisters and brothers of these little children, and for the families of the adults who were lost.

Two days later, when President Obama visited the families of the children who had been killed at Sandy Hook, he looked over at his Secret Service agents, usually calm and collected. They were crying.

The parents of six-year-old Ana Marquez-Greene, who was killed in the massacre at Sandy Hook. [Jessica Hill / Associated Press]

After the Sandy Hook tragedy, gun reform seemed inevitable. A few months later, Democrats and Republicans came together to support a bill to close the loophole that had been created by the Firearm Owners' Protection Act of 1986. The bill would require background checks for private gun sales, including sales at gun shows and online. A 2013 poll suggested that 86 percent of Americans supported universal background checks after the Sandy Hook shooting. Even a majority of NRA members supported the bill. The bill's sponsors were Joe Manchin, a Democrat from West Virginia, and Patrick Toomey, a Republican from Pennsylvania—both of whom had A-grade ratings from the NRA.

But the NRA—which had considered supporting universal background checks and gun-free school zones after Columbine—had changed its tune. Wayne LaPierre said background checks would lead to a gun registry, which would in turn lead to the confiscation of all guns in the country. He said the existing background-check system was broken because states weren't good at keeping track of who was ineligible.He also mocked the idea of a gun-free zone, saying it was an invitation to the "monsters" who "walk among us every single day."

In fact, Sandy Hook was when LaPierre first began giving his "good guy with a gun" response, stating at a Washington press event: "The only thing that stops a bad guy with a gun is a good guy with a gun. . . . With all the money in the federal budget, can't we afford to put a police officer in every single school?"

By persuading four Democrats and almost all Republicans not to vote for the bill, the NRA managed to block Congress's bipartisan efforts to pass a background-check law after Sandy Hook. One of those Democrats was Senator Mark Begich of Alaska. After the shooting, Begich said he wouldn't "shy away" from taking on the NRA. But then NRA members and other gun rights activists called and e-mailed to warn him not to vote for the bill; they said he needed to stop violating their gun rights or he wouldn't be reelected. Responding to their lobbying, he voted against the legislation.

What changed in the NRA's position between Columbine in 1999 and Sandy Hook in 2012? You know the answer: the 2008 Supreme Court case *District of Columbia v. Heller.*

CONSTITUTIONAL RIGHTS AND POLARIZATION

Because of *Heller*, the NRA has an additional tool in its belt: its members have evidence that the right they believe in is firmly grounded in America's most sacred text—the Constitution. "The ability to point to the right's protection in the Constitution," writes David Cole, "gives the NRA a legitimacy and power that it might not otherwise have."

Lawyer and historian Michael Waldman agrees. "When the Supreme Court declares something a constitutional right, it rocks not only the legal world. It enshrines an idea with legitimacy," he notes. "Whereas once gun debates turned on hunting or street crime, now it almost instantly reverts to evocations of hallowed constitutional rights." Indeed, shortly after *Heller* was decided, one of the NRA's lobbyists called it a "monumental decision" that "has put politicians on notice that this is a fundamental right. It can't be rationed. It can't be unduly restricted on the whims of local officials."

What this does is "deepen polarization," Waldman explains—in other words, it makes pro-gun people more pro-gun, and anti-gun people more anti-gun. Examples of this deepening polarization are everywhere. For instance, in 2013, a man named Dick Metcalf was fired from his job at *Guns & Ammo* magazine after writing an article that criticized the absolutist view of gun ownership—that is, the view that any form of gun control, no matter how small, is unacceptable. All he said was that "way too many gun owners seem to believe any regulation of the right to keep and bear arms is an infringement" and that "all constitutional rights are regulated, always have been, and need to be." For this, he was called a "gun control collaborator" and a "decrepit, mentally defunct self-important old fart."

Deepening polarization is also evident in the response by gun rights supporters to what are known as smart guns. Smart guns use technology to prevent them from firing unless they are used by their rightful owner, which helps prevent gun theft and accident. No reason the gun rights supporters would have a problem with that, right?

Wrong. In 2014, when a Maryland gun store owner considered selling smart guns, gun rights activists responded by calling for a boycott of his store and even sending him death threats. These activists disagree with any gun limitations at all, and they worry that if smart guns become popular, that might lead to bans on *non*-smart guns. The gun store owner responded:

> How can the NRA or people want to prohibit a gun when we are supposed to be pro-gun? We are supposed to say that any gun is good in the right person's hands. How can they say that a gun should be prohibited? How hypocritical is that? . . . If you're pro-gun does it matter what kind of gun the person has?

Of course, as we've seen, there have always been people who've viewed gun rights in this absolutist way. But "the right to keep and bear arms has reached new heights" after *Heller*, historian Patrick Charles explains. "No longer is the Second Amendment seen as just another political issue, nor can politicians flat out ignore the gun control–gun rights debate. It is center stage, and a politician's stance on the Second Amendment can affect everything from campaign contributions, to political endorsements, to winning a primary election."

As Charles explains, this polarization is perhaps most apparent in the deepening divides between Democrats and Republicans on gun control. Before *Heller*, politicians from both parties supported gun control measures such as waiting periods, background checks, and assault weapon bans. After *Heller*, Republicans started opposing enhanced background checks, which they worried would become a gun registry.

(As we discussed before, a gun registry is a list of all people who have guns, which the NRA thinks would lead to total gun confiscation.)

To win endorsements from the NRA, politicians such as Senator Ted Cruz, a Republican from Texas, passionately proclaim their support of gun rights. For example, on September 1, 2019, he tweeted that the Second Amendment right to keep and bear arms is a God-given right that "SHALL NOT be infringed."

POST-*HELLER* GUN CONTROL ADVOCACY

But that's not the end of the story. Remember that paragraph in Justice Scalia's opinion that said "the right secured by the Second Amendment is *not unlimited*"? Because of this paragraph, courts have upheld all sorts of gun control laws after *Heller*. These include bans on firearm possession by people who have been convicted of felonies, who use drugs, and who have been convicted of domestic violence misdemeanors. Courts have also upheld the constitutionality of concealed-carry laws, laws prohibiting certain types of weapons, such as machine guns or sawed-off shotguns, and location-based laws prohibiting the possession of guns in post offices and near schools. On the few occasions when federal courts struck down gun regulations, the regulations were particularly unusual.

Gun control advocates have also been taking on the NRA through grassroots action. Of course, there have always been groups and individuals who have helped push for gun reform—both after mass shootings and in response to more frequent community gun violence. As we learned in chapter 1, gun violence disproportionately affects students of color. Black and Brown communities have been expressing concerns over the violence for years through the Newark Anti-Violence Coalition, the Crown Heights Community Mediation Center, the Wear Orange Campaign, Mothers in Charge, Mothers Against Senseless Killings,

Black Lives Matter, and the Community Justice Reform Coalition. But in part because many recent shootings have occurred in suburban areas with largely white populations, gun control groups have been gaining national attention.

After Sandy Hook, mothers who were horrified by what they saw came together to form Moms Demand Action for Gun Sense in America, which started as a Facebook group but blossomed into a grassroots organization of moms, now with a chapter in every state. The group challenged, for example, Starbucks's decision to allow customers to carry loaded guns in its stores: "As mothers," they said, "we wonder why the company is willing to put children and families in so much danger. Nobody needs to be armed to get a cup of coffee." Harnessing the power of social media, they created Facebook posts that reached more than five million people, and a petition that received forty thousand signatures. In response, the Starbucks CEO said guns would no longer be welcome in its stores. Moms next targeted Chili's, Chipotle, Sonic, and Target, all of which changed their policies to reject firearms.

In 2014, Moms Demand Action merged with Mayors Against Illegal Guns, an organization led by former New York City mayor Michael Bloomberg. Together, they formed a new group: Everytown for Gun Safety. In the 2018 midterm elections, Everytown and another gun control organization, Giffords, spent more than $37 million to support candidates who favored gun control (and to oppose candidates who didn't) at both the state and federal levels—almost twice as much as the NRA spent during the same election cycle. (Giffords was founded by Gabrielle Giffords, a congresswoman from Arizona who was shot while speaking with constituents outside a supermarket in January 2011. She survived, but six people died and twelve others were also wounded.)

Giffords focused its efforts on Mike Coffman, Barbara Comstock, John Culberson, and Jason Lewis, four members of the House of

Representatives who had A-grade ratings from the NRA. By funding these politicians' opponents, Giffords helped ensure that all four lost. Similarly, Everytown focused on sixteen districts where the incumbent (the person currently in office) supported gun rights. In fifteen of those sixteen districts, the candidate whom Everytown preferred—that is, the candidate who supported gun control—won the election.

Gun control groups have also been fighting at the state level, taking a cue from the NRA. In the year after the Sandy Hook school shooting, hundreds of state bills that tightened restrictions on guns were introduced across the nation. Of those, thirty-nine eventually became law. (Note, however, that at the same time, some states were passing laws that *weakened* gun regulations.)

Students fought for change after the Parkland shooting, too. A few days after the shooting, Emma González gave an impassioned speech at an anti-gun rally in Fort Lauderdale, Florida:

> Companies trying to make caricatures of the teenagers these days, saying that all we are is self-involved and trend-obsessed and they hush us into submission when our message doesn't reach the ears of the nation, we are prepared to call BS. Politicians who sit in their gilded House and Senate seats funded by the NRA telling us nothing could have been done to prevent this, we call BS. They say tougher guns laws do not decrease gun violence. We call BS. They say a good guy with a gun stops a bad guy with a gun. We call BS. They say guns are just tools like knives and are as dangerous as cars. We call BS. They say no laws could have prevented the hundreds of senseless tragedies that have occurred. We call BS. That us kids don't know what we're talking about, that we're too young to understand how the government works. We call BS.

The Parkland students used tools like Snapchat and Twitter along with editorials and TV appearances to amplify their message. They started the #NeverAgain hashtag, and they raised $3.7 million in the three days after the shooting. Parkland student Emma González gathered over one million Twitter followers in a week. Since then, that number has swelled to over 1.62 million followers—more than double the NRA's followers.

The Parkland students also joined forces with students from Chicago schools, who had been suffering from gun violence in their community for years. These Chicago students, who were predominantly Black, were part of an organization called Peace Warriors that had been formed a decade prior to fight gun violence, but many of their efforts went unnoticed by the national media. The Parkland students were quick to acknowledge that the reason their own voices had been heard—and the Peace Warriors' had been ignored—was white privilege.

"Parkland is one of the safest cities in Florida," Arieyanna Williams, one of the Peace Warriors explained. "It's a different moment for them to realize that just because they had that title that it wouldn't happen to them. The students in Chicago see it every day. The difference is the amount of violence going on, the similarity is the hurt." The students recognized that they were "fighting for the same thing," but that national attention only reached the issue when gun violence began to affect white communities.

Together, the students from Parkland and Chicago planned the March for Our Lives. On March 24, 2018, hundreds of thousands of marchers turned out for more than eight hundred protests on every continent except Antarctica.

Shortly after the shooting at Parkland, the NRA was also dropped by a series of corporate sponsors and supporters. Dick's Sporting Goods and Walmart, for example, decided to stop selling assault-style weapons in all stores and stop selling guns or ammunition to anyone under twenty-one. Other companies, including United Airlines and the First National Bank of Omaha, ended corporate discounts to NRA members.

Delta
@Delta

Delta is reaching out to the NRA to let them know we will be ending their contract for discounted rates through our group travel program. We will be requesting that the NRA remove our information from their website.

473K   9:32 AM - Feb 24, 2018

124K people are talking about this

kaky @kakymc · Feb 22, 2018
Replying to @fnbo and 2 others
Please END your relationship with the @NRA.
#NRABloodOnYourHands

First National Bank of Omaha
@fnbo

Customer feedback has caused us to review our relationship with the NRA. As a result, First National Bank of Omaha will not renew its contract with the National Rifle Association to issue the NRA Visa Card.

3,627   3:05 PM - Feb 22, 2018

1,423 people are talking about this

United Airlines
@united

United is notifying the NRA that we will no longer offer a discounted rate to their annual meeting and we are asking that the NRA remove our information from their website.

355K   11:26 AM - Feb 24, 2018

82.3K people are talking about this

Tim Peacock @TimAPeacock · Feb 22, 2018
@Hertz @AVIS @Budget @Enterprise @alamo @NationalPro

This is what the #NRA stands for. Are you going to continue sponsoring their efforts to stall legislation that could save children's lives?peacock-panache.com/2018/02/nra-me…

Alamo Rent A Car
@alamocares

Thanks for contacting us. We ended the program – effective March 26. twitter.com/messages/compo…

999   8:29 PM - Feb 22, 2018

277 people are talking about this

Corporate sponsors dropped NRA discounts after the Parkland shooting. [Twitter]

The Parkland students also fought for change in state legislatures. The first on their list was Florida, a state so hospitable to the NRA that it's been called the "Gunshine State." Florida is often used as the NRA's testing ground; it's where the gun lobbyists bring legislation to see whether it will work, before trying to pass it in other states.

It was in this context that the Florida legislature considered a law that would respond to the Parkland shooting, the Marjory Stoneman Public Safety Act. Among other things, the proposed law raised the minimum age for gun ownership from eighteen to twenty-one (the shooter was nineteen) and banned bump stocks, devices that allow rifles to fire more rapidly. (The federal government would ban bump stocks the year after the shooting at Marjory Stoneman Douglas, in 2019.) The proposed law also authorized extreme risk protection orders, which allow for the temporary confiscation of guns from individuals deemed to be a risk to themselves or others—what's known as a red flag law.

But the bill was a compromise: It armed teachers—a provision that the Republicans in the state legislature supported but many gun control advocates opposed—and it did not ban assault weapons. Emma González explained her perspective on why teachers shouldn't be armed:

> Teachers do not need to be armed with guns to protect their classes, they need to be armed with a solid education in order to teach their classes. That's the only thing that needs to be in their job description. People say metal detectors would help. Tell that to the kids who already have metal detectors at school and are still victims of gun violence. If you want to help arm the schools, arm them with school supplies, books, therapists, things they actually need and can make use of.

Nevertheless, lawmakers on both sides of the aisle supported the bill—something, they thought, was better than nothing. Representative Jared Moskowitz gave an emotional speech on behalf of it. He explained that when the shooting happened, his four-year-old son, Sam, was at school around the corner from the high school. Sam's school also went into lockdown. Sam's teacher, Jen Guttenberg, had a daughter who died at Marjory Stoneman Douglas High School.

"She put my kid in a closet when her daughter died. I wanted to say thank you at the funeral," Moskowitz said. "I didn't know how to do that." Moskowitz hoped that his vote to pass the bill would show her all his appreciation. He encouraged his fellow representatives to vote yes "to stand with the families."

Ultimately, his plea was successful: The law passed. And it started a trend. Before Parkland, five states had red flag laws; after Parkland, that number grew to seventeen states and the District of Columbia. A red flag law could have kept guns out of the hands of the Parkland shooter, whose troubling behavior had been reported to authorities repeatedly. Indeed, in the two years after the Parkland shooting, Florida's red flag law was applied more than 3,500 times.

Within a year of the Parkland shooting, eleven states passed laws to restrict access to firearms for domestic abusers; nine states passed restrictions on bump stocks; seven passed additional background-check requirements for gun purchasers; five states made concealed-carry laws stricter; and four changed the minimum age from 18 to 21 for possession of a gun. Florida voter registration for those under twenty-nine years old spiked by nearly eight percentage points, while nationwide the share of youth registrants grew by more than 2 percent.

For all of their incredible achievements, the students who organized the March for Our Lives would undoubtedly say more needs to happen— much more. Gun violence still claims the lives of thousands of people per year. Mass shootings keep happening, and they show no signs of slowing down. And as D'Angelo McDade, the nineteen-year-old executive director of the Peace Warriors, explains:

> Just institutionalizing gun regulation in itself would not stop gun violence within the city of Chicago. Due to the impacts of school-to-prison pipelines, due to the impact of low unemployment rates, when we notice [an improvement] in those areas, we'll notice a decrease in the amount of gun violence occurring. Now, don't get me wrong. I am an

advocate, right alongside my "March For Our Lives" partners. But we have a lot more work to do than just gun regulation.

These grassroots movements, however, demonstrate that even after *Heller*, gun control advocacy is possible.

EPILOGUE

Manuel and Patricia Oliver had come to El Paso, Texas, to celebrate the memory of their son, Joaquin, who had been killed a year and a half earlier in the shooting at Parkland. Joaquin had cared deeply about immigrant rights. His parents planned to paint a mural to honor him on the border, where immigrant children were being held apart from their families. It was August 3, 2019—what would've been Joaquin's nineteenth birthday.

Then they heard the news. A few miles away, at a Walmart outside El Paso, there had been a shooting. Twenty-two people were dead. Police later reported that the killer had purchased his AK-47-style assault rifle legally.

"Joaquin brought us here for a reason," Joaquin's mom, Patricia, told a reporter in El Paso. "Joaquin is a very demanding kid. He was always, always—he keeps pushing us, pushing us, pushing us. We are not here by mistake. How can you explain that we were here?"

The gunman, a white nationalist, had targeted the retail store because many of its customers were Latinos. He said he was reacting to an "invasion of Hispanics," echoing language that President Trump has used in the immigration debate and in ads promoting his reelection. The NRA, too, has for years falsely suggested that Americans should purchase guns to protect themselves from immigrants from Mexico. In interviews with the *New York Times*, Latinos across the country explained that the shooting in El Paso "felt like a turning point, calling into question everything they thought they knew about their place in American society." As Mexican-American lawyer Dario Aguirre explained: "At least for Latinos, in some way, it's the death of the American dream."

Thirteen hours after the shooting in El Paso, a gunman in Dayton, Ohio, killed nine people and injured twenty-seven others with an assault rifle that he had purchased legally. The numbers could have been much higher: The police were able to stop the shooter within thirty seconds, just before he walked into a crowded bar.

In other words, in a single weekend in August 2019, thirty-one people died in two massacres on different sides of the country.

But the violence of those two days was not limited to mass shootings. That same weekend, an infant was killed in a drive-by shooting in Louisiana, and a man shot and killed his in-laws in Maryland. Indeed, three people died and thirty-seven were injured in shootings in Chicago alone.

After the shooting in Dayton, Ohio's Republican governor gave a speech offering his condolences for the losses suffered by the victims and their families. From the back of the room, however, shouts rang out: "Do something!"

"What do we want? Gun control!" people began to chant. "When do we want it? Now!"

Two days later, the governor suggested adopting a red flag law like those many other states had passed after the Parkland shooting. As discussed in chapter 10, red flag gun laws authorize courts to issue an order allowing police to confiscate weapons from anyone considered dangerous. These individuals are usually brought to the court's attention by friends or relatives who are concerned about a particular person's gun use. And soon after the governor made the announcement, congressional Republicans followed suit, saying they too would consider red flag laws—a major shift in policy by the Republican Party. (As of this writing, no such laws have passed.)

Of course, these red flag laws may not be effective since they rely on a friend or relative to take the initiative to remove guns from someone who they think is dangerous. "Most often," the *New York Times* explains, "guns have been removed from people who were seen as threats to themselves or to their families, or who were suffering from judgment-impairing illnesses like dementia or alcoholism, rather than posing a threat to large groups or public gatherings." Studies suggest, however, that these laws are effective in reducing suicide deaths.

So what does the future look like for gun regulation? Some gun control advocates—including the late Supreme Court justice John Paul Stevens, who dissented in *Heller*—have suggested that we repeal the Second Amendment altogether. As Justice Stevens explained, *Heller* "has provided the N.R.A. with a propaganda weapon of immense power. Overturning that decision via a constitutional amendment to get rid of the Second Amendment would be simple and would do more to weaken the N.R.A.'s ability to stymie legislative debate and block constructive gun control legislation than any other available option."

Gun control advocates support repeal because they think it could lead to more gun control laws. The mere possibility of being sued under the Second Amendment prevents states from passing gun control laws in the first place, since defending yourself against a lawsuit is expensive and difficult. State legislators know that if they pass gun control laws—especially innovative gun control laws, like requiring all guns to be smart guns—they'll be the targets of lawsuits. Rather than deal with that, they often decide to pass no laws at all. If we were to repeal the Second Amendment, gun control advocates argue, people would be less likely to challenge gun control laws in court, which could lead to more states passing restrictions on gun ownership and use.

To repeal the Second Amendment, two-thirds of the House and the Senate would have to vote for another amendment that says "the Second Amendment is repealed." Then, three-fourths of the fifty states—thirty-eight of them—would have to sign on. Given the widespread support for the Second Amendment, this seems nearly impossible. In the history of the United States, the only amendment that has ever been repealed is Prohibition.

Alternatively, we could hold another constitutional convention. In that case, two-thirds of state legislatures would need to call for such a convention, and states would write amendments that would then need to be ratified by three-fourths of the states. While it's theoretically possible to change the Constitution this way, it's never happened since the Constitution was ratified.

Given how impossible this seems, some gun control advocates suggest smaller changes. These include closing the background-check loophole we've discussed throughout this text, which allows all private gun sales to go unregulated. "I think the top of the agenda should be mandatory universal background checks for every gun purchase," historian and law professor Adam Winkler noted in an interview. "Everyone agrees that criminals should not be able to buy a gun. Why are we making it easy for them by allowing people to sell guns without doing a background check?" Indeed, after the shootings in El Paso and Dayton, President Trump and other Republican leaders suggested that they might be willing to support expanded background checks—a huge departure from the Republican platform.

There's also the issue of making these background checks more effective. As we learned, background checks work by running a gun purchaser's information through the FBI's database. However, this database is in many ways incomplete and doesn't include relevant records on severe mental illness or drug abuse. In the April 2007 shooting at Virginia Tech, for example, the killer used semiautomatic handguns that he had purchased legally. Just two years prior, a judge had declared him mentally ill and a danger to himself—but because he wasn't institutionalized, he wasn't put on a state list barring him from buying a gun. And in most states, when people are disqualified from owning a gun because of mental illness, they aren't required to give up guns they already own.

Of course, while it's important to identify at-risk individuals who shouldn't have access to guns, it's also important not to stigmatize those with mental illness. "People with mental illness commit only a small fraction of violent crime," explain Philip Cook and Kristin Goss—one estimate says it's only 5 percent—and "the vast majority of people with such disorders will never run afoul of the law." Instead, advocates suggest focusing on "dangerousness" by passing red flag laws that allow removal of guns from individuals who make specific threats or who are considered dangerous to themselves or others.

Alternative potential policies include mandatory gun training before someone can get a license to own a gun, like in Japan. In some states, it's much easier to carry a concealed handgun than it is to get a hunting license. For example, in Vermont and Wyoming, hunters are required to enroll in a training course and obtain a license, but there are no similar requirements for carrying concealed weapons. As Congressman Mike Thompson, a Democrat from California, put it, "Federal law provides more protection for the ducks than it does for citizens."

The history of gun laws in America shows us that gun control coexisted with gun rights for over two hundred years. From the earliest days of this country, through the Civil War and Reconstruction, and up until the twentieth century, states, cities, and even the federal government were passing gun control laws. During this time, most people thought the right to bear arms belonged to the "well regulated Militia." And since militias weren't really in use anymore, they thought the Second Amendment was an artifact of the past.

That only started to change in the 1960s, particularly when the Black Panther Party got involved. The Panthers wanted to carry guns to defend themselves from police brutality, so they returned to the language of the Second Amendment to say that the right to bear arms was an individual right that belonged to all people. Reacting to the Panthers' armed police patrols, California and later the federal government passed major gun control legislation—the Mulford Act of 1967 and the Gun Control Act of 1968.

This inspired a group of hard-liners within the NRA to revolt against their leadership, who they worried wouldn't do enough to fight back against laws like the Gun Control Act of 1968. The new NRA that emerged from this revolt agreed with the Black Panthers' reading of the Second Amendment, but that wasn't the official interpretation in the courts of law. So for forty years, the NRA worked to lay the groundwork for a Supreme Court case that would declare once and for all that the Second Amendment was an individual right belonging to all people. That day came in 2008, when the Supreme Court decided *District of Columbia v. Heller*. And it's because of *Heller* that we are where we are—a world of increased polarization about gun control, in which it can feel almost impossible to get gun legislation past the NRA.

In recent years, we've heard a lot about mass shootings from the media and the consequent fight between gun control advocates and the NRA.

And we've heard time and time again that no federal legislation has passed. But we don't hear too much about the extremely restrictive gun laws that have existed since our country's founding. Nor do we hear about the NRA's forty-year campaign to change the popular understanding of gun rights, conducted largely at the state level. Nor do we hear about all the gun laws that have been upheld under *Heller* because of the paragraph Justice Scalia included that explained that the right to bear arms could be limited.

And while federal legislation has yet to pass, grassroots activists have helped increase engagement with gun control issues, persuade corporate sponsors to drop the NRA, elect lawmakers who support gun control, and push for gun control laws at the state level. In January 2020, Congress reached an agreement to give two federal agencies—the CDC and the National Institutes of Health—$12.5 million each to research gun violence.

And federal legislation may be on the horizon: Democrats hoping to win the 2020 presidential election have been calling for major reforms, including red flag laws, an assault weapon ban, and expanded background checks. Some go even further. Cory Booker, senator for New Jersey, for example, proposed a national firearm licensing system that would require fingerprinting, a background check, and a gun safety course. As President Lyndon B. Johnson said back in the 1960s: Cars, boats, dogs, and bikes have to be registered, and you need a license to have a pet, to fish, and to drive a car—why should we require less for lethal weapons?

What all this shows is that *Heller* does not close the door to gun control advocacy. If you support gun control, you can call, write to, or tweet at your politicians to voice your opinion. (Remember, as an aide to a former senator put it: "I don't think [politicians] care about the contributions they get from the NRA. They care about the piles of mail, these nasty calls, and people picketing their state offices. Politicians are risk averse.") And when you turn eighteen, you can vote for the candidates you support. (As David Cole explained, "the real source of the NRA's influence is its remarkable ability to mobilize its members and support-ers at the ballot box.")

Heller was decided in 2008—it is sometimes hard to remember how new our current view of gun rights is. But armed with all this history, you can make the change you want to see.

"We are going to be the kids you read about in textbooks," Emma González said a few days after the shooting in Parkland. "Not because we're going to be another statistic about mass shooting in America"—but because "we are going to change the law."

AS OF THIS WRITING

T he Supreme Court will decide whether to expand the rights granted in Heller. In *Heller*, the Supreme Court affirmed an individual right to bear arms, but it also left a lot of questions unanswered: Does the Second Amendment protect an individual's right to carry a gun outside the home, or just within it? What kind of guns are protected? How should gun laws be analyzed by courts? Right now, there's a case at the Supreme Court that could answer those questions: *New York State Rifle & Pistol Association v. New York*. It's the first major gun case in a decade, and gun control advocates worry the majority-conservative Supreme Court might use it to expand the rights granted in *Heller*. At the time the case was filed, there was a law in New York City that prevented people with a particular type of gun license from taking their guns out of the city. The New York State Rifle & Pistol Association thought this law was unconstitutional and sued the city. As of this writing, the Supreme Court has yet to decide the case.

The fate of 3D-printed guns will be determined. In a case called *State of Washington v. United States Department of State*, nineteen states and the District of Columbia sued to prevent plans for 3D-printed guns from being uploaded to the internet. Opponents of 3D-printed guns worry that because the guns are made of plastic, they can pass through metal detectors without notice. They also worry that people will evade background checks by printing their guns at home—you don't need to pass a background check to buy a 3D printer. Before 2018, publishing plans for 3D guns online was prohibited by a law called the Arms Export Control Act, but the Trump Administration lifted the ban in a settlement agreement in July 2018. Plaintiffs hurried to court, and a federal judge prevented the plans from being uploaded until the case could be permanently decided—what's called a "preliminary injunction." In November 2019, a federal district court in Washington again ruled in favor of plaintiffs, permanently preventing the plans from being uploaded (a "permanent injunction"). The government appealed this decision to the Ninth Circuit in January 2020.

Families of Sandy Hook victims will go head to head with Remington Arms. In March 2019, the families of nine victims of the shooting at Sandy Hook Elementary School sued Remington Arms, the company that manufactured the rifle used, arguing that the gun manufacturer violated the Connecticut Unfair Trade Practices Act—which prohibits advertisements that promote or encourage violent, criminal behavior—by marketing a military-style weapon to civilians. As explored in chapter 8, the Connecticut Supreme Court held that the federal immunity law wasn't meant to get in the way of state law, and the U.S. Supreme Court chose not to review this decision, thus allowing the case to proceed. This case will go to trial in 2021.

WEBSITES TO VISIT TO LEARN MORE

★ **THE TRACE,** "an independent, nonpartisan, nonprofit news-room dedicated to shining a light on America's gun violence crisis." Learn more at thetrace.org.

★ **EVERYTOWN FOR GUN SAFETY,** "a movement of Americans working together to end gun violence and build safer communities." Learn more at everytown.org.

★ **GIFFORDS LAW CENTER,** "the nation's leading policy organization dedicated to researching, writing, enacting, and defending proven laws and programs . . . on a mission to save lives from gun violence by shifting culture, changing policies, and challenging injustice." Learn more at lawcenter.giffords.org.

★ **SINCE PARKLAND,** a storytelling project spearheaded by "more than 200 teen reporters from across the country [who] began working together to document the children, ages zero to 18, killed in shootings during one year in America." Learn more at sinceparkland.org.

ACKNOWLEDGMENTS

Thank you to Christian Trimmer, Mark Podesta, and Wendi Gu for their thoughtful questions and guidance throughout this project. Thanks also to the friends and colleagues who offered their suggestions, including Hannah Joy Habte, Nancy J. Johnson, Tara Kuruvilla, Mac McAnulty, Scott Riley, Zayn Siddique, Rachel Stark, Angela Su, Julius Taranto, Jansen Thurmer, Dr. Erin Watley, and Nora Wilkinson. Thanks to my parents, Rudy and Sania, and my sister, Alisa, for their support. And thanks, of course, to Gabriel Botelho, without whom this book would not exist.

DISCUSSION GUIDE

1. "Gun rights and gun control coexisted peacefully during the birth of America" (p. 20). What evidence does the author provide to support this statement? What do you think needs to happen to return to this peaceful coexistence?

2. How is the current debate over gun rights similar to the 1920s debate over the tommy gun (p. 85)? What can we learn from this?

3. Throughout *Whose Right Is It?*, the author calls out smart gun reform alongside legislation meant to oppress specific minorities. How does the interpretation of the Second Amendment reveal America's racist beliefs, historically and perhaps also today?

4. Briefly discuss the philosophies of originalism and living constitutionalism (pp. 172–76). How do you think the courts (including the Supreme Court) should interpret the Second Amendment? Why?

5. Do you believe all U.S. citizens have a constitutional right to own a gun? Any gun? Why or why not?

6. Should gun laws be enacted by state or federal legislation? What are the advantages and disadvantages of each?

7. Do you think restrictions placed on the types of guns available in the U.S. will make us safer? If so, what restrictions do you recommend? If not, why not?

8. What incident or event related to gun violence or gun control has had the biggest influence on your community? Your state? The country as a whole? Explain.

9. How have other countries responded to mass shootings (pp. 183–84)? What have been the results? How does the United States compare?

10. It has been argued that gun owners should adhere to requirements similar to those imposed on hunters or drivers (age
limit, training classes, licenses, registration, etc.). Do you
think that's a valid argument? Why or why not?

11. In recent years, teens have become vocal activists in response
to the increase in school shootings. What have they accom-
plished? What else do you think they could do?

12. What do you think it will take to reduce (or even eliminate)
mass school shootings? Some have suggested that teachers
should be armed. Do you agree? Why or why not?

13. Some people feel the NRA has too much power and influence
on politics (and politicians) when it comes to gun rights.
What is your stance on its influence?

14. If you had an opportunity to address the NRA, what would
you say?

15. *Whose Right Is It?* ends with a discussion about the Second
Amendment and whether or not it should be repealed
(pp. 207–8). What do *you* think should happen to the Second
Amendment? Defend your position.

Discussion guide prepared by Nancy J. Johnson, professor emeritus,
Western Washington University.

SELECTED BIBLIOGRAPHY

LAWS AND COURT CASES

Boston City Council. *Charter of the City of Boston and Ordinances Made and Established by the Mayor, Aldermen, and Common Council, with Such Acts of the Legislature of Massachusetts, as Relate to the Government of Said City.* Boston, 1827. hdl.handle.net/2027/hvd.32044050955657.

District of Columbia Council. Firearms Control Regulations Act of 1975. July 23, 1976. archive.org/details/firearmscontrol00colugoog/page/n12.

District of Columbia v. Heller. 554 U.S. 570 (2008). supremecourt.gov/opinions /07pdf/07-290.pdf.

District of Columbia v. Heller. Oral argument, March 18, 2008. Transcript. supremecourt.gov/oral_arguments/argument_transcripts/2007/07-290.pdf.

Florida Legislative Council. An Act to Govern Patrols 1825. *Acts of the Legislative Council of the Territory of Florida Passed at Their Fourth Session.* Tallahassee, 1826. edocs.dlis.state.fl.us/fldocs/leg/actterritory/1825.pdf.

Hamilton v. Accu-tek. 935 F. Su 1307 E.D.N.Y. (1996). casetext.com/case/hamilton-v -accu-tek.

Maine Legislature. Constitutional Resolutions of the State of Maine. 113th Legislature, 1st Session, 1987. Chapter 2. lldc.mainelegislature.org/Open/Laws/1987/1987_CR_ c002.pdf.

New Hampshire Constitutional Convention. "Ratification of the Constitution by the State of New Hampshire," June 21, 1788. In *Documentary History of the Constitution.* Vol. 2. Washington, DC, 1894. hdl.handle.net/2027/mdp.39015053273523.

New Jersey General Assembly. An Act Against Wearing Swords, &c. 1686. *The Grants, Concessions, and Original Constitutions of the Province of New Jersey.* Edited by Aaron Leaming and Jacob Spicer. Reprint. Somerville, NJ, 1881. hdl.handle .net/2027/mdp.35112103318665.

New Jersey General Assembly. An Act for the Preservation of Deer, and Other Game, and to Prevent Trespassing with Guns 1771. *Laws of the State of New-Jersey.* Trenton, NJ, 1821. archive.org/details/lawsstatenewjer00penngoog.

Pennsylvania General Assembly. An Act for the Tryal of Negroes 1705. *The Laws of the Province of Pennsilvania Collected into One Volumn.* Philadelphia, 1714. hdl .handle.net/2027/mdp.35112203944147.

People v. Newton. 8 Cal.App.3d 359, 87 Cal. Rptr. 394 (Cal. Ct. App. 1970). casetext.com /case/people-v-newton-72.

Scott v. Emerson. 15 Mo. 576 (1852). cite.case.law/mo/15/576/.

Scott v. Sandford. 60 U.S. 393 (1856). cdn.loc.gov/service/ll/usrep/usrep060/usrep060393a /usrep060393a.pdf.

Snyder v. Phelps. 562 U.S. 443 (2011). supremecourt.gov/opinions/10pdf/09-751.pdf.

South Carolina Legislature. An Act for the Better Ordering and Governing of Negroes and Slaves 1712. *The Statutes at Large of South Carolina.* Vol. 7. Edited by David J. McCord. Columbia, 1840. hdl.handle.net/2027/nyp.33433090745146.

Texas Legislature. An Act to Regulate the Keeping and Bearing of Deadly Weapons. April 12, 1871. *General Laws of Texas,* ch. 34, p. 25. lrl.texas.gov/scanned/session Laws/12-0/CH_XXXIV.pdf.

United States v. Cruikshank. 92 U.S. 542 (1875). cdn.loc.gov/service/ll/usrep/usrep092 /usrep092542/usrep092542.pdf.

United States v. Miller. 307 U.S. 174 (1939). cdn.loc.gov/service/ll/usrep/usrep307/us
rep307174/usrep307174.pdf.

U.S. Congress. An Act to Protect All Persons in the United States in Their Civil Rights,
and Furnish the Means of Their Vindication. April 9, 1866. 14 *U.S. Statutes at
Large* 27. loc.gov/law/help/statutes-at-large/39th-congress/session-1/c39s1ch31.pdf.

U.S. Congress. Firearms Owners' Protection Act. May 19, 1986. Public Law 99-308, 100
U.S. Statutes at Large 449. govinfo.gov/content/pkg/STATUTE-100/pdf/STATUTE
-100-Pg449.pdf.

U.S. Congress. Investigative Assistance for Violent Crimes Act of 2012. January 14,
2013. Public Law112–265, 126 *U.S. Statutes at Large* 2435. congress.gov/112/plaws/
publ265/PLAW-112publ265.pdf.

U.S. Congress. Public Safety and Recreational Firearms Use Protection Act. September
13, 1994. Public Law 103–322, 108 *U.S. Statutes at Large* 1996. www.govinfo.gov/
content/pkg/STATUTE-108/pdf/STATUTE-108-Pg1796.pdf.

Virginia General Assembly. *The Statutes at Large: Being a Collection of All the Laws
of Virginia, from the First Session of the Legislature, in the Year 1619.* Vol. 4.
Edited by William Waller Hening. Richmond, 1814. https://books.google.com/
books?id=wvRGAQAAMAAJ.

Wyoming Legislative Assembly. An Act to Prevent the Carrying of Fire Arms and Other
Deadly Weapons. December 2, 1875. *Compiled Laws of Wyoming 1876*, ch. 52,
p. 352. hdl.handle.net/2027/nyp.33433007185477.

HISTORICAL DOCUMENTS

Blount, Charles. *An Appeal from the Country to the City for the Preservation of His
Majesties Person, Liberty, Property, and the Protestant Religion.* London, 1679. hdl
.handle.net/2027/uc1.31822035067651.

Burlington Free Press. "The Press on Nebraska." June 2, 1854. chroniclingamerica.loc
.gov/lccn/sn84023127/1854-06-02/ed-1/seq-1.

Butler, A. P. Speech in U.S. Senate, March 5, 1856. *Congressional Globe.* 34th Congress,
1st Session, pp. 584–87. memory.loc.gov/cgi-bin/ampage?collId=llcg&fileName=039/
llcg039.db&recNum=586.

Caldwell, C., G. W. Whitmore, F. W. Sumner, A. J. Evans, A. Bledsoe, D. W. Cole, and
John G. Bell. "Report of the Committee of Lawlessness and Violence." June 30,
1868. In *Journal of the Reconstruction Convention: Which Met at Austin, Texas,
1868–1869*, pp. 193–208. Austin, TX, 1870. tarltonapps.law.utexas.edu/constitu
tions/files/journals1868/1868_07_02_jnl.pdf.

Johnson, Lyndon B. *Public Papers of the Presidents: Lyndon B. Johnson, 1968–69.*
2 vols. Washington, D.C.: U.S. Government Printing Office, 1970. quod.lib.umich
.edu/p/ppotpus/4731573.1968.

Lincoln, Abraham. *Collected Works.* Vol. 3. Edited by Roy Basler. New Brunswick, NJ:
Rutgers University Press, 1953. archive.org/details/collectedworksof0003linc.

Madison, James. "Notes on Ancient and Modern Confederacies." [April–June?] 1786.
Founders Online, National Archives. founders.archives.gov/documents/Madison
/01-09-02-0001.

McKee, George. Speech in U.S. House of Representatives, April 3, 1871. *Congressional Globe*, 42nd Congress, 1st Session. memory.loc.gov/cgi-bin
/ampage?collId=llcg&fileName=099/llcg099.db&recNum=541.

National Rifle Association. *Annual Report 1873.* New York, 1874. books.google.com
/books?id=OMECAAAAYAAJ.

New York Times. "Bar Hidden Weapons on Sullivan's Plea." May 11, 1911. nyti.ms
/2Psnhuh.

Russell, Albert N. "Ilion and the Remingtons." September 14, 1897. In *Papers Read*

Before the Herkimer County Historical Society During the Years 1896, 1897 and 1898.
Vol. 1. Edited by Arthur T. Smith. Herkimer and Ilion, NY, 1899. archive.org
/details/papersreadbefore04herkpage/76.

Sumner, Charles. Speech in U.S. Senate, May 19–20, 1856. Published as *The Crime
Against Kansas.* Boston, 1856. www.senate.gov/artandhistory/history/resources/pdf
/CrimeAgainstKSSpeech.pdf.

*The United States Army and Navy Journal and Gazette of the Regular and Volunteer
Forces.* "The Army and the Nation." August 29, 1863. hdl.handle.net/2027
/coo.31924015232758.

*The United States Army and Navy Journal and Gazette of the Regular and Volunteer
Forces.* "Rifle-Shooting Association." August 12, 1871. hdl.handle.net/2027
/coo.31924069759904.

U.S. House of Representatives. *National Firearms Act: Hearings Before the Committee
on Ways and Means, House of Representatives, Seventy-Third Congress, Second
Session, on H.R. 9066.* Washington, D.C.: U.S. Government Printing Office, 1934.
books.google.com/books?id=8AsvAAAAMAAJ.

U.S. House of Representatives. Reconstruction debate, April 7, 1866. *Congressional
Globe,* 39th Congress, 1st Session, pp. 1837–42. memory.loc.gov/cgi-bin
/ampage?collId=llcg&fileName=071/llcg071.db&recNum=879.

Whipple, E. P. "The Johnson Party." *Atlantic.* September 1866. theatlantic.com/magazine
/archive/1866/09/the-johnson-party/518748.

BOOKS

Amar, Akhil Reed. *The Bill of Rights.* New Haven, CT: Yale University Press, 1998.

Barone, Michael. *Our First Revolution: The Remarkable British Upheaval That Inspired
America's Founding Fathers.* New York: Crown, 2007.

Cobb, Charles E., Jr. *This Nonviolent Stuff'll Get You Killed: How Guns Made the Civil
Rights Movement Possible.* New York: Basic Books, 2014.

Cole, David. *Engines of Liberty: How Citizen Movements Succeed.* New York: Basic
Books, 2016.

Cook, Philip J., and Kristin A. Goss. *The Gun Debate.* New York: Oxford University
Press, 2014.

Cornell, Saul. *A Well-Regulated Militia: The Founding Fathers and the Origins of Gun
Control in America.* New York: Oxford University Press, 2006.

Crosby, Alfred W. *Throwing Fire: A History of Projectile Technology.* New York: Cambridge University Press, 2002.

Cullen, Dave. *Columbine.* New York: Hachette, 2009.

Cullen, Dave. *Parkland: Birth of a Movement.* New York: HarperCollins, 2019.

Davidson, Osha Gray. *Under Fire: The NRA and the Battle for Gun Control.* 2nd ed.
Iowa City: University of Iowa Press, 1998.

DeConde, Alexander. *Gun Violence in America: The Struggle for Control.* Boston:
Northeastern University Press, 2001.

Dunbar-Ortiz, Roxanne. *Loaded: A Disarming History of the Second Amendment.*
San Francisco: City Lights, 2018.

Etcheson, Nicole. *Bleeding Kansas: Contested Liberty in the Civil War Era.* Lawrence:
University Press of Kansas, 2004.

Finkelman, Paul. *Dred Scott v. Sandford: A Brief History with Documents.* 2nd ed. Boston: Bedford/St. Martin's, 2017.

Foner, Eric. *The Fiery Trial: Abraham Lincoln and American Slavery.* New York: W. W.
Norton, 2010.

Foner, Eric. *Reconstruction: America's Unfinished Revolution, 1863–1877.* Updated ed.
New York: HarperPerennial, 2014.

Giffords, Gabrielle, Mark Kelly, and Harry Jaffe. *Enough: Our Fight to Keep America Safe from Gun Violence*. New York: Scribner, 2014.

Girard, Jolyon P., Darryl Mace, and Courtney Michelle Smith, eds. *American History Through Its Greatest Speeches: A Documentary History of the United States*. Vol. 1. Santa Barbara, CA: ABC-CLIO, 2017.

Haag, Pamela. *The Gunning of America: Business and the Making of American Gun Culture*. New York: Basic Books, 2016.

Henshaw, Thomas, ed. *The History of Winchester Firearms 1866–1992*. Clinton, NJ: Winchester Press, 1993.

Johnson, Nicholas J., David B. Kopel, George A. Mocsary, and Michael P. O'Shea. *Firearms Law and the Second Amendment: Regulation, Rights, and Policy*. New York: Wolters Kluwer, 2012.

Kennett, Lee, and James LaVerne Anderson. *The Gun in America: The Origins of a National Dilemma*. Westport, CT: Greenwood Press, 1975.

Kinard, Jeff. *Pistols: An Illustrated History of Their Impact*. Santa Barbara, CA: ABC-CLIO, 2003.

Marcot, Roy. *History of Remington Firearms: The History of One of the World's Most Famous Gun Makers*. Guilford, CT: Lyons Press, 2005.

Melzer, Scott. *Gun Crusaders: The NRA's Culture War*. New York: NYU Press, 2009.

Miller, John. *The Glorious Revolution*. 2nd ed. London: Routledge, 1997.

Pearson, Hugh. *Shadow of the Panther: Huey Newton and the Price of Black Power in America*. Cambridge, MA: Addison-Wesley, 1995.

Pincus, Steven C. A. *England's Glorious Revolution, 1688–1689: A Brief History with Documents*. New York: Macmillan, 2006.

Rasmussen, Daniel. *American Uprising: The Untold Story of America's Largest Slave Revolt* New York, NY: HarperCollins Publishers, 2011.

Reynolds, David S. *John Brown, Abolitionist: The Man Who Killed Slavery, Sparked the Civil War, and Seeded Civil Rights*. New York: Knopf, 2005.

Seale, Bobby. *Seize the Time: The Story of the Black Panther Party and Huey P. Newton*. Baltimore: Black Classic Press, 1991.

Spitzer, Robert J. *The Politics of Gun Control*. New York: Routledge, 2017.

Taylor, Alan. *American Revolutions: A Continental History, 1750–1804*. New York: W. W. Norton, 2016.

Till-Mobley, Mamie, and Christopher Benson. *Death of Innocence: The Story of the Hate Crime That Changed America*. New York: Random House, 2003.

Waldman, Michael. *Second Amendment: A Biography*. New York: Simon & Schuster, 2014.

Weiner, Tim. *Enemies: A History of the FBI*. New York: Random House, 2012.

Wells, Ida B. *Southern Horrors and Other Writings: The Anti-Lynching Campaign of Ida B. Wells, 1892–1900*. Edited by Jacqueline Jones Royster. Boston: Bedford Books, 1997.

Wills, Chuck. *The Illustrated History of Guns: From First Firearms to Semiautomatic Weapons*. New York: Skyhorse, 2017.

Winkler, Adam. *Gunfight: The Battle Over the Right to Bear Arms in America*. New York: W. W. Norton, 2011.

Wood, Gordon S. *American Revolution: A History*. New York: Random House, 2002.

ARTICLES AND REPORTS

Adler, Jeffrey S. "Less Crime, More Punishment: Violence, Race, and Criminal Justice in Early Twentieth-Century America." *Journal of American History* 102, no. 1 (June 2015): 34–46. doi.org/10.1093/jahist/jav173.

American Psychological Association. *Stress in America: Generation Z*, October 2018. apa .org/news/press/releases/stress/2018/stress-gen-z.pdf.

Ascione, Alfred M. "The Federal Firearms Act." *St. John's Law Review* 13, no. 2 (April 1939): 437–46. scholarship.law.stjohns.edu/lawreview/vol13/iss2/27/.

Barbaro, Michael. "Two Days, Two Cities, Two Massacres." *The Daily* podcast, August 5, 2019. Transcript. *New York Times*. nyti.ms/2yGtOta.

Benjamin, Rich. "Gun Control, White Paranoia, and the Death of Martin Luther King, Jr." *New Yorker*, April 3, 2018. newyorker.com/news/news-desk/gun-control-white -paranoia-and-the-death-of-martin-luther-king-jr.

CBS News. "Has DC's Handgun Ban Prevented Bloodshed?" March 4, 2008, cbsnews .com/news/has-dcs-handgun-ban-prevented-bloodshed/.

Centers for Disease Control and Prevention. "2017 United States Firearm Deaths and Rates per 100,000." WISQARS Fatal Injury Reports 1981–2017. webappa.cdc.gov /sasweb/ncipc/mortrate.html.

Chan, Melissa. "'They Are Lifting Us Up.' How Parkland Students Are Using Their Moment to Help Minority Anti-Violence Groups." *Time*, March 24, 2018. time .com/5201562/parkland-students-minority-groups/.

Charles, Patrick J. "Second Amendment in the Twenty-First Century: What Hath *Heller* Wrought?" *William and Mary Bill of Rights Journal* 23 no. 4 (2015): 1143–83. scholarship.law.wm.edu/wmborj/vol23/iss4/6.

Cottrol, Robert J., and Raymond T. Diamond. "'Never Intended to Be Applied to the White Population': Firearms Regulation and Racial Disparity—The Redeemed South's Legacy to a National Jurisprudence?" *Chicago-Kent Law Review* 70, no. 3 (April 1995): 1307–35. constitution.famguardian.org/2ll/2ndschol/11cd-reg.pdf.

Equal Justice Initiative. "Slavery in America: The Montgomery Slave Trade." 2018. eji .org/reports/slavery-in-america.

Fisher, Max. "A Land Without Guns: How Japan Has Virtually Eliminated Shooting Deaths." *Atlantic*, July 23, 2012. theatlantic.com/international/archive/2012/07/a- land-without-guns-how-japan-has-virtually-eliminated-shooting-deaths/260189/.

Follman, Mark. "These Women Are the NRA's Worst Nightmare." *Mother Jones*, September-October 2014. motherjones.com/politics/2014/09/moms-demand-action -guns-madd-shannon-watts-nra/.

Frassetto, Mark. "Firearms and Weapons Legislation up to the Early 20th Century." January 15, 2013. ssrn.com/abstract=2200991.

Frassetto, Mark Anthony. "The Law and Politics of Firearms Regulation in Reconstruc- tion Texas." *Texas A&M Law Review* 4, no. 1 (2016): 95–122. scholarship.law.tamu .edu/cgi/viewcontent.cgi?article=1106&context=lawreview.

Goldstein, Dana. "20 Years After Columbine, Schools Have Gotten Safer. But Fears Have Only Grown." *New York Times*, April 20, 2019. nyti.ms/2vabW8u.

Gramlich, John. "What the Data Says About Gun Deaths in the U.S." Pew Research Center, August 16, 2019. pewrsr.ch/2KPjZii.

Hall, Kevin G. "12 Months, Nearly 1,200 Deaths: The Year in Youth Gun Violence Since Parkland." *Miami Herald*, February 12, 2019. miamiherald.com/news/nation-world /national/article224680840.html.

Hannah-Jones, Nikole. "Our Democracy's Founding Ideals Were False When They Were Written. Black Americans Have Fought to Make Them True." *New York Times Magazine*, August 14, 2019. nyti.ms/2H63ygp.

Hardy, David T. "The Firearms Owners' Protection Act: A Historical and Legal Perspective." *Cumberland Law Review* 17 (1986): 585–682. constitution .org/2ll/2ndschol/46hard.pdf.

Higham, Scott, and Sari Horwitz. "NRA Tactics: Take No Prisoners." *Washington Post*, May 18, 2013, wapo.st/10F9TA9.

Jones, Edward D., III. "The District of Columbia's 'Firearms Control Regulations Act of 1975': The Toughest Handgun Control Law in the United States—Or Is It?" *Annals of the American Academy of Political and Social Science* 455 (May 1981): 138–49 .jstor.org/stable/1044076.

Leonardatos, Cynthia Deitle. "California's Attempts to Disarm the Black Panthers." *San Diego Law Review* 36, no. 4 (1999): 947–96.

Long, Emma. "Why So Silent? The Supreme Court and the Second Amendment Debate After *DC v. Heller*." *European Journal of American Studies* 12, no. 2 (Summer 2017). journals.openedition.org/ejas/11874.

Mazzei, Patricia. "Parkland: A Year After the School Shooting That Was Supposed to Change Everything." *New York Times*, February 13, 2019. nyti.ms/2E6x9oR.

Metcalf, Dick. "Target: Me." *Politico*, January 14, 2014. politico.com/magazine /story/2014/01/guns-second-amendment-target-me-102133.

Mitchell, Yolanda T., and Tiffany L. Bromfield. "Gun Violence and the Minority Experience." National Council on Family Relations, January 10, 2019. ncfr.org/ncfr-report /winter-2018/gun-violence-and-minority-experience.

Parker, Kim, Juliana Menasce Horowitz, Ruth Igielnik, J. Baxter Oliphant, and Anna Brown. "The Demographics of Gun Ownership." Pew Research Center, June 22, 2017. pewsocialtrends.org/2017/06/22/the-demographics-of-gun-ownership.

Peterson, Jillian, and James Densley. "How Columbine Became a Blueprint for School Shooters." Conversation, April 17, 2019. theconversation.com/how-columbine -became-a-blueprint-for-school-shooters-115115.

Seglin, Jeffrey L. "When Good Ethics Aren't Good Business." The Right Thing. *New York Times*, March 18, 2001, nyti.ms/34lLsQF.

Serwer, Adam. "The NRA's Catch-22 for Black Men Shot by Police." *Atlantic*, September 13, 2018. theatlantic.com/ideas/archive/2018/09/the-nras-catch-22-for-black-men -shot-by-police/570124/.

Siegel, Reva B. "Dead or Alive: Originalism as Popular Constitutionalism in *Heller*." *Harvard Law Review* 122 (November 1, 2008): 191–245. harvardlawreview .org/2008/11/dead-or-alive-originalism-as-popular-constitutionalism-in-heller/.

Spitzer, Robert J. "Gun Law History in the United States and Second Amendment Rights." *Law and Contemporary Problems* 80, no. 2 (2017): 55–83. scholarship.law .duke.edu/lcp/vol80/iss2/3.

Stevens, John Paul. "Repeal the Second Amendment." *New York Times*, March 27, 2018. nyti.ms/2pIaPuh.

Turner, Wallace. "A Gun Is Power, Black Panther Says." *New York Times*, May 21, 1967. nyti.ms/1VZf5RT.

Volokh, Eugene. "Necessary to the Security of a Free State." *Notre Dame Law Review* 83, no. 1 (November 2007). scholarship.law.nd.edu/ndlr/vol83/iss1/1.

Walker, Christina. "10 Years. 180 School Shootings. 356 Victims," CNN, cnn.com/inter active/2019/07/us/ten-years-of-school-shootings-trnd.

Webber, Alan C. "Where the NRA Stands on Gun Legislation: 97-Year Record Shows Positive Approach to Workable Gun Laws." *American Rifleman*, March 1968. www .keepandbeararms.com/images/NRA_AR_03-1968_p22.jpg.

Winkler, Adam. "Gun Control Is 'Racist'? The NRA Would Know." *New Republic*, February 4, 2013. newrepublic.com/article/112322.

Zimring, Franklin E. "Firearms and Federal Law: The Gun Control Act of 1968." *Journal of Legal Studies* 4, no. 1 (January 1975): 133–98. jstor.org/stable/724104.

ENDNOTES

ix. A Note on Language: For more information on the trend to avoid naming shooters, see Lisa Marie Pane, "Should Media Avoid Naming the Gunmen in Mass Shootings?," AP, March 17, 2019, apnews.com/00f5376066b8473fa4e0a0 63d963e89e; Adam K. Raymond, "The Push to Not Name Mass Shooters Is Catching On," *New York Magazine*, May 9, 2019, nymag.com/intelligencer/2019/05/the-push-to -not-name-mass-shooters-is-catching-on.html; Jillian Peterson and James Densley, "How Columbine Became a Blueprint for School Shooters," Conversation, April 17, 2019, theconversation.com/how-columbine-became-a -blueprint-for-school-shooters-115115.

INTRODUCTION

xi. It was Valentine's Day . . . "You're my soul mate": Patricia Mazzei, "Parkland: A Year After the School Shooting That Was Supposed to Change Everything, *New York Times*, February 13, 2019, nyti.ms/2E6x9oR.

xi. The shooter . . . a mental health question: Skyler Swisher and Paula McMahon, "Nikolas Cruz Passed Background Check, Including Mental Health Question, to Get AR-15 Rifle," *South Florida Sun Sentinel*, February 15, 2018, sun-sentinel.com/local/broward/parkland/florida -school-shooting/fl-florida-school-shooting-guns-20180215 -story.html.

xi. "I know I'm just a kid" . . . "I don't do anything": Mazzei, "Parkland."

xii. The average length . . . three and a half hours: Dave Cullen, *Parkland: Birth of a Movement* (New York: HarperCollins, 2019), pp. 3, 7.

xii. "So, the first thing . . . to step up": Fox News, "Student Says Heroic Janitor Saved Many Lives During Shooting," transcript, February 14, 2018, fxn.ws/2E5QYxM.

CHAPTER 1

1. Columbine became a blueprint . . . become known: Peterson and Densley, "Columbine a Blueprint."

2. For years the FBI . . . Sandy Hook Elementary: William J. Krouse and Daniel J. Richardson, "Mass Murder with Firearms: Incidents and Victims, 1999–2013," July 30, 2015, Congressional Research Service, no. R44126, p. 2, fas.org/sgp/crs/misc/R44126.pdf; Investigative Assistance for Violent Crimes Act of 2012, Public Law No. 112–265, 126 *U.S. Statutes at Large* 2435.

2. Other researchers . . . every day: Mark Follman, "How Many Mass Shootings Are There, Really?," *New York Times*, December 4, 2015, nyti.ms/1PBL4Ej.

2. One thing . . . greater degree: Dana Goldstein, "20 Years After Columbine, Schools Have Gotten Safer. But Fears Have Only Grown," *New York Times*, April 20, 2019, nyti.ms/2vabW8u.

2. There are . . . "school shooting since 2009": Christina Walker, "10 Years. 180 School Shootings. 356 Victims," CNN, cnn.com/interactive/2019/07/us/ten-years-of-school -shootings-trnd.

3. A recent Pew Research . . . at their schools: A. W. Geiger, "18 Striking Findings from 2018," Pew Research Center, December 13, 2018, pewrsr.ch/2ErUjHI.

3. "Those mass shootings . . . large numbers": Walker, "10 years. 180 School Shootings."

3. "In some ways . . . been living under": Goldstein, "20 Years After Columbine."

3. In a recent school . . . from Connecticut: Tim Dickinson, "Mock Executions? Real Screams and Blood? Just Another School Shooter Drill," *Rolling Stone*, March 21, 2019, rollingstone.com/politics/politics-news/teachers-injured -active-shooter-drill-811383.

3. Indeed, in a recent study . . . less stressed (34 percent): American Psychological Association, *Stress in America: Generation Z*, October 2018, p. 2, apa.org/news/press /releases/stress/2018/stress-gen-z.pdf.

4. The threat . . . "possibility of them occurring": American Psychological Association, "Stress in America," p. 2.

6. A recent Pew . . . on the East or West Coast: The following statistics come from Kim Parker et al., "The Demographics of Gun Ownership," Pew Research Center, June 22, 2017, pewsocialtrends.org/2017/06/22/the -demographics-of-gun-ownership; Christopher Ingraham, "Gun Sales Hit New Record Ahead of New Obama Gun Restrictions," *Washington Post*, January 5, 2016, washingtonpost.com/news/wonk/wp/2016/01/05/gun-sales -hit-new-record-ahead-of-new-obama-gun-restrictions; Philip J. Cook and Kristin A. Goss, *The Gun Debate* (New York: Oxford University Press, 2014), pp. 4–5; Violence Policy Center, "States with Weak Gun Laws and Higher Gun Ownership Lead Nation in Gun Deaths, New Data for 2017 Confirms," news release, January 23, 2019, vpc .org/press/states-with-weak-gun-laws-and-higher-gun -ownership-lead-nation-in-gun-deaths-new-data-for-2017 -confirms.

6. The Centers for Disease Control . . . in fifty years: Sarah Mervosh, "Nearly 40,000 People Died from Guns in U.S. Last Year, Highest in 50 Years," *New York Times*, December 18, 2018, nyti.ms/2R3h4I5; Centers for Disease Control and Prevention, "2017 United States Firearm Deaths and Rates per 100,000," WISQARS Fatal Injury Reports 1981–2017, webappa.cdc.gov/sasweb/ncipc /mortrate.html; John Gramlich, "What the Data Says About Gun Deaths in the U.S.," Pew Research Center, August 16, 2019, pewrsr.ch/2KPjZii.

6. And there are . . . every gun death: Robert J. Spitzer, *The Politics of Gun Control* (New York: Routledge, 2017), p. 78.

6. Of these deaths . . . military combined: Alexandra Rubenstein et al., "Alarming Trends in Mortality from Firearms Among United States Schoolchildren," *American Journal of Medicine* 132, no. 8 (August 2019): pp. 992–94, doi.org/10.1016/j.amjmed.2019.02.012.

6. While policymakers . . . of gun deaths: Spitzer, *Politics of Gun Control*, p. 82.

6. In 2017, for example . . . suicides that year: Gramlich, "Gun Deaths in U.S."; Centers for Disease Control, Fatal Injury Reports.

6. Some people think . . . that impulse: Spitzer, *Politics of Gun Control*, pp. 82–86; Cook and Goss, *Gun Debate*, pp. 42–43.

7. There are also . . . deaths in 2017: Gramlich, "Gun Deaths in U.S."; Centers for Disease Control, Fatal Injury Reports.

7. These deaths are . . . in the home: Centers for Disease Control and Prevention, "2017 United States Firearm Deaths and Rates per 100,000," WISQARS Fatal Injury Reports 1981–2017, webappa.cdc.gov/sasweb/ncipc /mortrate.html.

7. As you can see . . . most gun deaths: Violence Policy Center, "States with Weak Gun Laws."

8. it spends millions . . . Hillary Clinton: Soo Rin Kim, "Which Lawmakers Got the Most NRA Money?," ABC News, February 20, 2018, abcn.ws/2EKwPhu.

8. There are also . . . than the NRA: Cook and Goss, *Gun Debate*, p. 191; Adam Winkler, *Gunfight: The Battle Over the Right to Bear Arms in America* (New York: W. W. Norton, 2011), p. 82.

8. Shortly after . . . in schools: Mark Berman and David Weigel, "NRA Goes on the Offensive After Parkland Shooting, Assailing Media and Calling for More Armed School Security," *Washington Post*, February 22, 2018, washingtonpost.com/news/post-nation/wp/2018/02/22 /after-silence-on-parkland-nra-pushes-back-against-law -enforcement-the-media-and-gun-control-advocates.

9. As Wayne LaPierre . . . "all registered firearms": Scott Melzer, *Gun Crusaders: The NRA's Culture War* (New York: NYU Press, 2009), p. 98.

10. The Early History of the Gun: In discussing the history of the gun, I drew from these sources: Chuck Wills, *The Illustrated History of Guns: From First Firearms to Semiautomatic Weapons* (New York: Skyhorse, 2017), p. 76; Alfred W. Crosby, *Throwing Fire: A History of Projectile Technology* (New York: Cambridge University Press, 2002), pp. 97–98; Alexander DeConde, *Gun Violence in America: The Struggle for Control* (Boston: Northeastern University Press, 2001), pp. 7–8, 10, repository.library.northeastern .edu/downloads/neu:m039kr671; Jim Supica, "A Brief History of Firearms," NRA Museums, nramuseum.org/gun -info-research/a-brief-history-of-firearms.aspx; Bill Warder, "History of Armour and Weapons Relevant to Jamestown," National Park Service, November 1995, nps.gov/jame/learn /historyculture/history-of-armour-and-weapons-relevant -to-jamestown.htm; Weeks Linton, "The First Gun in America," NPR, April 6, 2013, npr.org/2013/04/06 /176132730.

10. The AR-15 . . . 9mm handgun: Heather Sher, "What I Saw Treating the Victims from Parkland Should Change the Debate on Guns," *Atlantic*, February 22, 2018, theatlantic.com/politics/archive/2018/02/what-i-saw -treating-the-victims-from-parkland-should-change-the -debate-on-guns/553937.

12. the potato chip theory . . . you can't stop: Osha Gray Davidson, *Under Fire: The NRA and the Battle for Gun Control*, 2nd ed. (Iowa City: University of Iowa Press, 1998), p. 45.

12. twelve hundred teens . . . Parkland shooting: Kevin G. Hall, "12 Months, Nearly 1,200 Deaths: The Year in Youth Gun Violence Since Parkland," *Miami Herald*, February 12, 2019, miamiherald.com/news/nation-world /national/article224680840.html; "Since Parkland," sinceparkland.org.

CHAPTER 2

13. Protestants don't trust . . . the country: John Miller, *The Glorious Revolution*, 2nd ed. (London: Routledge, 1997), pp. 1–2; Winkler, *Gunfight*, p. 100; Michael Waldman, *Second Amendment: A Biography* (New York: Simon & Schuster, 2014) p. 59.

13. First, Imagine . . . Houses left standing: Charles Blount, *An Appeal from the Country to the City for the Preservation of His Majesties Person, Liberty, Property, and the Protestant Religion* (London, 1679), p. 2, hdl. handle.net/2027/uc1.31822035067651.

14. James supports . . . for Catholics: Steven C. A. Pincus, *England's Glorious Revolution, 1688–1689: A Brief History with Documents* (New York: Macmillan, 2006), p. 14; Miller, *Glorious Revolution*, p. 4.

15. Even though Monmouth's . . . overthrow him: Winkler, *Gunfight*, p. 100–101; Richard E. Boyer, "English

Declarations of Indulgence of 1687 and 1688," *Catholic Historical Review* 50, no. 3 (October 1964), p. 335, jstor.org /stable/25017471.

15. In 1687 . . . support only him: Pincus, *England's Glorious Revolution*, pp. 14, 28, 132–35; Boyer, "English Declarations of Indulgence," pp. 345–46; Winkler, *Gunfight*, p. 100; Miller, *Glorious Revolution*, pp. 7–8.

16. We have great . . . made public: The letter of the seven noblemen appears in the appendix of Michael Barone, *Our First Revolution: The Remarkable British Upheaval That Inspired America's Founding Fathers* (New York: Crown, 2007), pp. 254–56. [Note spelling has been corrected for clarity.]

18. And so William and Mary . . . group of volunteers: Pincus, *England's Glorious Revolution*, pp. 2–3; Winkler, *Gunfight*, p. 101; Waldman, *Second Amendment*, p. 59.

20. Adam Winkler . . . disarming people: Winkler, *Gunfight*, p. 102; Waldman, *Second Amendment*, p. 59; Pincus, *England's Glorious Revolution*, p. 16.

20. Well, sort of . . . upper class: Winkler, *Gunfight*, p. 115; Waldman, *Second Amendment*, p. 59.

21. The colonists formed . . . man's gun: Winkler, *Gunfight*, p. 113.

21. "Muster days . . . and revelry": Saul Cornell, *A Well-Regulated Militia: The Founding Fathers and the Origins of Gun Control in America* (New York: Oxford University Press, 2006), p. 3.

21. In some colonies . . . people owned: Winkler, *Gunfight*, p. 113.

21. The colonists . . . everyday people: Waldman, *Second Amendment*, pp. 7–8.

21. While the militia would protect . . . "slave patrols": Roxanne Dunbar-Ortiz, *Loaded: A Disarming History of the Second Amendment* (San Francisco: City Lights, 2018), pp. 36, 57.

22. A 1727 Virginia law . . . Black people: An Act for Making More Effectual Provision Against Invasions and Insurrections (1727), *The Statutes at Large, being a Collection of All the Laws of Virginia, from the First Session of the Legislature, in the Year 1619* vol. 4, ed. William Waller Hening (Richmond, 1814), p. 202, books.google .com/books?id=wvRGAQAAMAAJ&pg=PA202.

22. Pennsylvania, for example . . . "special licence": An Act for the Tryal of Negroes (1705), *The Laws of the Province of Pennsilvania Collected into One Volumn* (Philadelphia, 1714), p. 77, hdl.handle.net/2027/mdp .35112203944147.

22. Virginia demanded . . . "or defensive": An Act Directing the Trial of Slaves, Committing Capital Crimes; and for the More Effectual Punishing Conspiracies and Insurrections of Them [. . .] (1723), *Laws of Virginia*, p. 131.

22. And South Carolina . . . "take them away": An Act for the Better Ordering and Governing of Negroes and Slaves (1712), *The Statutes at Large of South Carolina* vol. 7, ed. David J. McCord (Columbia, 1840), p. 353, hdl.handle.net /2027/nyp.33433090745146.

23. Sometimes white people . . . buy a gun: Winkler, *Gunfight*, p. 116.

23. In 1686, for example . . . "other necessary defense": An Act Against Wearing Swords, &c. (1686), *The Grants, Concessions, and Original Constitutions of the Province of New Jersey* (reprinted, Somerville, NJ, 1881), p. 289, hdl .handle.net/2027/mdp.35112103318665; An Act for the Preservation of Deer, and Other Game, and to Prevent Trespassing with Guns (1771), *Laws of the State of New-Jersey* (Trenton, NJ, 1821), p. 28, archive.org/details

/lawsstatenewjer00penngoog; Mark Frassetto, "Firearms and Weapons Legislation up to the Early 20th Century" (January 15, 2013), pp. 19, 34, 88, 103, ssrn.com/abstract =2200991.

23. several colonies had . . . floor of buildings: Winkler, *Gunfight*, pp. 116–17.

25. One thing to keep in mind . . . "voting, or marriage?": Adam Winkler, "Gun Control Is 'Racist'? The NRA Would Know," *New Republic*, February 4, 2013, newrepublic.com /article/112322.

25. Per King George III's . . . to the colonies: Winkler, *Gunfight*, p. 103.

26. On April 18 . . . to stop him: Winkler, *Gunfight*, p. 104; Alan Taylor, *American Revolutions: A Continental History, 1750–1804* (New York: W. W. Norton, 2016), p. 132.

27. The states functioned . . . European Union: Gordon S. Wood, *American Revolution: A History* (New York: Random House, 2002), pp. 71–72.

27. In 1783 . . . went bankrupt: Taylor, *American Revolutions*, p. 361.

27. Before other folks . . . ideal political system: James Madison, "Notes on Ancient and Modern Confederacies," [April–June?] 1786, Founders Online, National Archives, founders.archives.gov/documents/Madison/01-09-02-0001; Waldman, *Second Amendment*, p. 20.

28. Madison has been . . . "weak of voice": Taylor, *American Revolutions*, p. 371; Waldman, *Second Amendment*, p. 19; *Encyclopaedia Britannica*, s.v. "James Madison," by Irving Brant, britannica.com/biography/James-Madison.

28. George Washington . . . "in the nation": Taylor, *American Revolutions*, pp. 374.

29. A lot of people . . . and take away their weapons: Winkler, *Gunfight*, pp. 24, 207; Waldman, *Second Amendment*, pp. 21–24, 31.

30. And as we discussed . . . protect their rights: Waldman, *Second Amendment*, pp. 7–8.

30. Many states recommended . . . "Actual Rebellion": Winkler, *Gunfight*, pp. 108–9; Taylor, *American Revolutions*, p. 387; "Ratification of the Constitution by the State of New Hampshire," June 21, 1788, *Documentary History of the Constitution*, vol. 2 (Washington, DC, 1894), pp. 141–44, hdl.handle.net/2027/mdp.39015053273523; Waldman, *Second Amendment*, pp. 36–37.

35. Some scholars argue . . . New Jersey: Waldman, *Second Amendment*, pp. 123–24.

35. Others suggest . . . a "free country": Eugene Volokh, "Necessary to the Security of a Free State," *Notre Dame Law Review* 83, no. 1 (November 2007), p. 105, scholarship .law.nd.edu/ndlr/vol83/iss1/1.

38. These guns . . . "national defense": Pamela Haag, *The Gunning of America: Business and the Making of American Gun Culture* (New York: Basic Books, 2016), pp. 8–9, 11–12.

38. Remington . . . farm equipment: For the history of Remington firearms, I consulted Albert N. Russell, "Ilion and the Remingtons," September 14, 1897, in *Papers Read Before the Herkimer County Historical Society During the Years 1896, 1897 and 1898*, vol. 1, ed. Arthur T. Smith (Herkimer and Ilion, NY, 1899), pp. 78, 81–82, 87–88, archive.org/details/papersreadbefore04herkpage/76; and Roy Marcot, *History of Remington Firearms: The History of One of the World's Most Famous Gun Makers* (Guilford, CT: Lyons Press, 2005), pp. 8, 12–13.

38. "Anticipating a decline . . . those of peace": Russell, "Ilion and the Remingtons," p. 87; Haag, *Gunning of America*, pp. 60–61.

39. Colt was issued . . . boxes labeled HARDWARE: For the history of Colt firearms, I consulted Wills, *Illustrated History of Guns*, pp. 62, 64; and Haag, *Gunning of America*, pp. 25, 33–34, 66–67.

40. Smith & Wesson . . . Company: For the company histories of Smith & Wesson and Winchester, I used these sources: Jeff Kinard, *Pistols: An Illustrated History of Their Impact* (Santa Barbara, CA: ABC-CLIO, 2003), p. 112; Thomas Henshaw, ed., *The History of Winchester Firearms 1866–1992* (Clinton, NJ: Winchester Press, 1993), pp. 4–8; Haag, *Gunning of America*, p. 55, 56.

40. After the Civil War . . . international markets: Haag, *Gunning of America*, pp. xvi–xvii, 110, 113.

CHAPTER 3

41. In January 1811 . . . along the river: Daniel Rasmussen, *American Uprising: The Untold Story of America's Largest Slave Revolt* (New York, NY: HarperCollins Publishers, 2011), pp. 1, 97, 102, 105, 126–28, 137–40, 142, 147–48; Winkler, *Gunfight*, p. 132.

42. Starting in the 1600s . . . "was not a lie": Nikole Hannah-Jones, "Our Democracy's Founding Ideals Were False When They Were Written. Black Americans Have Fought to Make Them True," *New York Times Magazine*, August 14, 2019, nyti.ms/2H63ygp; Equal Justice Initiative, "Slavery in America: The Montgomery Slave Trade," 2018, eji.org/reports/slavery-in-america; California Newsreel, "Go Deeper: Race Timeline," *Race—The Power of an Illusion*, 2003, PBS, pbs.org/race/000_About/002_03 -godeeper.htm.

43. White settlers were . . . land on their own: Dunbar-Ortiz, *Loaded*, pp. 29–35.

44. But the deed is . . . up to Slavery: *Burlington Free Press*, "The Press on Nebraska," June 2, 1854, p. 1, chroniclingamerica.loc.gov/lccn/sn84023127/1854-06-02/ed -1/seq-1.

44. "most famous preacher in America": Winkler, *Gunfight*, p. 138.

44. Henry Ward Beecher . . . "hundred Bibles": *New-York Daily Tribune*, "Ward Beecher on the Observer," February 8, 1856, p. 6, chroniclingamerica.loc.gov/lccn /sn83030213/1856-02-08/ed-1/seq-6.

44. Beecher's supporters . . . "Beecher's Bibles": Winkler, *Gunfight*, p. 138.

45. Political Parties: In discussing the development of our political parties, I drew from these sources: *Encyclopedia Britannica*, s.v. "Democratic-Republican Party," britannica.com/topic/Democratic-Republican-Party; "The Federalist and the Republican Party," *American Experience*, PBS, pbs.org/wgbh/americanexperience /features/duel-federalist-and-republican-party/; Scott Bomboy, "On This Day, the Whig Party Becomes a National Force," *Constitution Daily*, December 4, 2018, constitutioncenter.org/blog/on-this-day-the-whig-party -becomes-a-national-force; Allen C. Guelzo, review of *The Rise and Fall of the American Whig Party: Jacksonian Politics and the Onset of the Civil War* by Michael Holt, *Journal of the Abraham Lincoln Association* 22, no. 2 (Summer 2001), hdl.handle.net/2027/spo.2629860 .0022.206; Nicole Etcheson, *Bleeding Kansas: Contested Liberty in the Civil War Era* (Lawrence: University Press of Kansas, 2004), p. 23; *Encyclopedia Britannica*, s.v. "Republican Party," britannica.com/topic/Republican -Party.

47. The President of . . . that *posse comitatus*: A. P. Butler, speech in U.S. Senate, March 5, 1856, *Congressional Globe*, 34th Congress, 1st Session, p. 587, memory.loc.gov/cgi-bin/ampage?collId=llcg&fileName=039 /llcg039.db&recNum=589.

48. "Really, sir . . . constitutional liberty": Charles Sumner, speech in U.S. Senate, May 19–20, 1856, pub. as *The Crime Against Kansas* (Boston, 1856), pp. 64–65, www .senate.gov/artandhistory/history/resources/pdf /CrimeAgainstKSSpeech.pdf.

50. "Times now . . . gratify this spirit": Scott v. Emerson, 15 Mo. 576 (1852), cite.case.law/mo/15/576/.

50. "What had . . . political significance": Paul Finkelman, *Dred Scott v. Sandford: A Brief History with Documents*, 2nd ed. (Boston: Bedford/St. Martin's, 2017), p. 25.

50. This was . . . "American history": Waldman, *Second Amendment*, p. 69.

51. Writing for the majority . . . "grant them": Scott v. Sandford, 60 U.S. 393 (1856).

52. Akhil Reed Amar . . . "could never be": Akhil Reed Amar, *The Bill of Rights* (New Haven, CT: Yale University Press, 1998), p. 236.

52. An 1825 Florida . . . "weapons, and ammunition": An Act to Govern Patrols (1825), *Acts of the Legislative Council of the Territory of Florida Passed at Their Fourth Session* (Tallahassee, 1826), p. 55, edocs.dlis.state.fl.us /fldocs/leg/actterritory/1825.pdf.

53. Some were freed . . . 500,000 Black people: *Population of the United States in 1860: Introduction*, Bureau of the Census (Washington, D.C., 1864), p. ix, census.gov/library /publications/decennial/1860/population/1860a-02.pdf.

53. In *Dred Scott* . . . unconstitutional: Finkelman, *Dred Scott*, p. 33; Waldman, *Second Amendment*, p. 69.

53. Taney's goal . . . "abominable": Finkelman, *Dred Scott*, p. 39–41.

54. One of the witnesses . . . John Wilkes Booth: Fergus M. Bordewich, "John Brown's Day of Reckoning," *Smithsonian Magazine* (October 2009), smithsonianmag .com/history/john-browns-day-of-reckoning-139165084/.

54. And Democrats . . . support of Black people: David S. Reynolds, *John Brown, Abolitionist: The Man Who Killed Slavery, Sparked the Civil War, and Seeded Civil Rights* (New York: Knopf, 2005), p. 8.

55. He opposed . . . already legal: Eric Foner, *The Fiery Trial: Abraham Lincoln and American Slavery* (New York: W. W. Norton, 2010), p. xviii.

55. And even though . . . "political equality": Abraham Lincoln, "Fourth Debate with Stephen A. Douglas," September 18, 1858, Charleston, IL, in *Collected Works*, vol. 3, ed. Roy P. Basler (New Brunswick, NJ: Rutgers University Press, 1953), p. 145, archive.org/details /collectedworksof0003linc.

55. While his views . . . "like Charles Sumner": Foner, *Fiery Trial*, p. xviii.

55. You charge that . . . Harper's Ferry?: Abraham Lincoln, "Address at Cooper Institute," February 27, 1860, New York City, in *Collected Works*, vol. 3, pp. 538–40.

57. The Union army . . . protect themselves: Winkler, *Gunfight*, p. 135; Waldman, *Second Amendment*, p. 72.

57. Bans on concealed . . . first adopted them: Winkler, *Gunfight*, p. 166.

57. An 1820 Indiana law . . . "thirty-five dollars": Frassetto, "Firearms and Weapons Legislation," pp. 20–21, 24.

58. In 1845, Connecticut . . . "twenty-five cents": Frassetto, "Firearms and Weapons Legislation," p. 47, 75–76, 81.

59. "These laws weren't . . . among whites": Winkler, "Gun Control Is 'Racist'?"

62. In its first issue . . . "care nothing": *Army and Navy Journal*, "The Army and the Nation," August 29, 1863, p. 8, hdl.handle.net/2027/coo.31924015232758.

62. the Church brothers . . . "the United States": *New York Times*, "United States Army and Navy Journal, Vol. 2," October 16, 1865, nyti.ms/2sYxjvB.

62. Church published editorial . . . *Manual for Rifle Practice*: James B. Trefethen, *Americans and Their Guns* (Harrisburg, PA: Stackpole, 1967), p. 31–32, 34; Winkler, *Gunfight*, pp. 63–64; DeConde, *Gun Violence*, p. 89; Davidson, *Under Fire*, p. 21.

62. "to promote" . . . "push it into life": *Army and Navy Journal*, "Rifle-Shooting Association," August 12, 1871, pp. 836–37, hdl.handle.net/2027/coo.31924069759904.

63. Not long after . . . "of other States": National Rifle Association, "By-Laws and Charter," in *1873 Annual Report*, p. 148, books.google.com/books?id =OMECAAAAYAAJ&pg=RA1-PA148.

63. "Out of ten" . . . "side of a barn": John Houston Craige, *The Practical Book of American Guns* (New York: Bramhall House, 1950), pp. 84–93, in David Cole, *Engines of Liberty: How Citizen Movements Succeed* (New York: Basic Books, 2016), p. 100.

63. Church became . . . group's leaders: Trefethen, *Americans and Their Guns*, p. 37; Davidson, *Under Fire*, p. 22.

64. At its start . . . around $500,000 today: Davidson, *Under Fire*, p. 22; Winkler, *Gunfight*, p. 64; Trefethen, *Americans and Their Guns*, pp. 39–41.

64. New York continued . . . "shooting at Creedmoor": Trefethen, *Americans and Their Guns*, p. 88; Waldman, *Second Amendment*, p. 87; Davidson, *Under Fire*, p. 26.

65. As journalist and historian . . . excellent at rifle shooting: Davidson, *Under Fire*, p. 27.

65. while historian Robert . . . Spanish-American War: Spitzer, *Politics of Gun Control*, p. 131; Trefethen, *Americans and Their Guns*, p. 117.

65. "the association . . . everywhere": DeConde, *Gun Violence*, p. 103.

CHAPTER 4

67. "It is also . . . as soldiers": Abraham Lincoln, "Last Public Address," April 11, 1865, *Collected Works*, vol. 8, p. 403, archive.org/details/collectedworksab08linc.

67. Lincoln's speech infuriated . . . would ever make: Jolyon P. Girard, Darryl Mace, and Courtney Michelle Smith, eds., *American History Through Its Greatest Speeches: A Documentary History of the United States*, vol. 1 (Santa Barbara, CA: ABC-CLIO, 2017), p. 216.

67. President Johnson was horribly . . . opposed Black suffrage: Eric Foner, *Reconstruction: America's Unfinished Revolution, 1863–1877*, updated ed. (New York: HarperPerennial, 2014), p. 179; Winkler, *Gunfight*, p. 140.

67. "man of narrow mind . . . mental disease": E. P. Whipple, "The Johnson Party," *Atlantic*, September 1866, theatlantic.com/magazine/archive/1866/09/the-johnson -party/518748.

68. Under Johnson's plan . . . before the war: Foner, *Reconstruction*, p. 199; Winkler, *Gunfight*, p. 135.

68. Louisiana Republican . . . "slavery as possible": Benjamin F. Flanders to Henry C. Warmoth, November 23, 1865, Warmoth Papers, in Foner, *Reconstruction*, p. 199.

68. In Alabama . . . "deadly weapon": Reconstruction debate in U.S. House of Representatives, April 7, 1866, *Congressional Globe*, 39th Congress, 1st Session, p. 1838 in Nicholas J. Johnson, David B. Kopel, George A.

Mocsary, and Michael P. O'Shea, *Firearms Law and the Second Amendment: Regulation, Rights, and Policy* (New York: Wolters Kluwer, 2012), p. 292.

68. Florida's Black Code . . . seize the weapon: "An Act Prescribing Additional Penalties for the Commission of Offenses Against the State and for Other Purposes," December 18, 1865, Laws of Florida, ch. 1466, no. 3 in Johnson et al., *Firearms Law*, p. 290.

68. And the Black Codes of Mississippi . . . default of bail: "An Act to Punish Certain Offences Therein Named, and for Other Purposes," November 29, 1865,1865 Mississippi Laws 166 in Johnson et al., *Firearms Law*, pp. 290–91.

69. "seen those . . . in its defense": George McKee, speech in U.S. House of Representatives, April 3, 1871, *Congressional Globe*, 42nd Congress, 1st Session, p. 426, memory.loc.gov/cgi-bin/ampage?collId=llcg&fileName=099/llcg099.db&recNum=541.

69. "The only case . . . in self-defense": Ida B. Wells, *Southern Horrors and Other Writings: The Anti-Lynching Campaign of Ida B. Wells, 1892–1900*, ed. Jacqueline Jones Royster (Boston: Bedford Books, 1997), p. 70.

69. It defined . . . "by white citizens": An Act to Protect All Persons in the United States in Their Civil Rights, and Furnish the Means of Their Vindication, April 9, 1866, 14 *U.S. Statutes at Large* 27, loc.gov/law/help/statutes-at-large/39th-congress/session-1/c39s1ch31.pdf.

70. After the Civil Rights Act . . . only Black people: Foner, *Reconstruction*, p. 201.

71. "Between 1775 . . . Carolina freedman": Amar, *The Bill of Rights*, p. 266.

71. Other scholars . . . people of all races: Waldman, *Second Amendment*, p. 75.

72. KKK sought . . . daily violence: Foner, *Reconstruction*, p. 426, 429–33; Winkler, *Gunfight*, p. 135.

73. "operated like a huge slave patrol": Dunbar-Ortiz, *Loaded*, p. 69.

73. And when we came . . . "men and freedmen": C. Caldwell et al., "Report of the Committee of Lawlessness and Violence," June 30, 1868, *Journal of the Reconstruction Convention: Which Met at Austin, Texas, 1868–1869*, pp. 196–99, tarltonapps.law.utexas.edu/constitutions/files/journals1868/1868_07_02_jnl.pdf.

74. Local officials . . . "you cannot convict him": David Montgomery, November 11, 1871, "Testimony Taken by the Joint Select Committee to Inquire into the Condition of Affairs in the Late Insurrectionary States: Florida," 42nd Congress, 2nd Session, House Report 22, pt. 13, p. 125, in Foner, *Reconstruction*, pp. 434–35.

74. As the Texas convention . . . "outrages upon them": C. Caldwell et al., "Lawlessness and Violence," p. 197.

74. At the same time . . . *Harper's Weekly*: *Harper's Weekly*, "The Labor Question at the South," January 13, 1866, p. 19, archive.org/details/harpersweeklyv10bonn/page/18.

75. The Supreme Court made . . . right to bear arms: Winkler, *Gunfight*, pp. 143–44; Waldman, *Second Amendment*, pp. 76–77.

76. The second amendment . . . of the United States: United States v. Cruikshank, 92 U.S. 542 (1875).

76. For gun owners . . . white vigilantism: DeConde, *Gun Violence*, p. 78.

77. In Bennettsville . . . to attack the KKK: Foner, *Reconstruction*, p. 435.

77. Civil rights scholar . . . "federal intervention": Charles E. Cobb Jr., *This Nonviolent Stuff'll Get You Killed: How Guns Made the Civil Rights Movement Possible* (New York: Basic Books, 2014), p. 43.

77. In 1871, Kentucky . . . "ordinary pocket-knife": An Act to Prohibit the Carrying of Concealed Deadly Weapons, 1871 Ky. Acts 89, in Frassetto, "Firearms and Weapons Legislation," p. 27.

77. That same year Texas . . . "on his person": An Act to Regulate the Keeping and Bearing of Deadly Weapons, 1871 Tex. Gen. Laws, ch. 34, p. 25, lrl.texas.gov/scanned/sessionLaws/12-0/CH_XXXIV.pdf.

77. And Wyoming in 1875 . . . "town or village": An Act to Prevent the Carrying of Fire Arms and Other Deadly Weapons, December 2, 1875, Wyo. Comp. Laws (1876), ch. 52, p. 352, hdl.handle.net/2027/nyp.33433007185477.

79. Some scholars have . . . "in mind": Robert J. Cottrol and Raymond T. Diamond, "'Never Intended to Be Applied to the White Population': Firearms Regulation and Racial Disparity—The Redeemed South's Legacy to a National Jurisprudence?," *Chicago-Kent Law Review* 70, no. 3 (April 1995), p. 1310.

79. Other scholars disagree . . . perpetrated by whites: Mark Anthony Frassetto, "The Law and Politics of Firearms Regulation in Reconstruction Texas," *Texas A&M Law Review* 4, no. 1 (2016), p. 122, scholarship.law.tamu.edu/cgi/viewcontent.cgi?article=1106&context=lawreview.

82. In the West, guns . . . pick them up later: Winkler, *Gunfight*, pp. 160, 165–66; Waldman, *Second Amendment*, pp. 77–78.

82. Ordinance No. 9 . . . "permit in writing": Gabrielle Giffords, Mark Kelly, and Harry Jaffe, *Enough: Our Fight to Keep America Safe from Gun Violence* (New York: Scribner, 2014), p. 29.

82. The truth is many . . . people were killed: Richard Shenkman, *Legends, Lies, and Cherished Myths of American History* (New York: William Morrow, 1988), p. 112, in Spitzer, "Gun Law History," p. 66.

82. William Frederick Cody . . . states do today: Winkler, *Gunfight*, pp. 164–65; Shenkman, *Legends, Lies, and Cherished Myths*, p. 112.

CHAPTER 5

83. The population of New York City . . . in 1920: *Total Population NYC and Boroughs, 1900 to 2010*, prepared by NYC City Planning Department with U.S. Census Bureau data, www1.nyc.gov/site/planning/data-maps/nyc-population/historical-population.page.

83. For comparison . . . same timeframe: Decennial Census of Population and Housing by Decade, U.S. Census Bureau, www.census.gov/programs-surveys/decennial-census/decade.html.

83. By the time of the . . . American history: History: Urban and Rural Areas, U.S. Census Bureau, census.gov/history/www/programs/geography/urban_and_rural_areas.html.

83. Nationally, the homicide rate . . . "law enforcers": Jeffrey S. Adler, "Less Crime, More Punishment: Violence, Race, and Criminal Justice in Early Twentieth-Century America," *Journal of American History* 102, no. 1 (June 2015), p. 36, doi.org/10.1093/jahist/jav173.

85. John T. Thompson . . . "engine of death": DeConde, *Gun Violence*, p. 126; Winkler, *Gunfight*, p. 190–91.

85. News and radio . . . "public's distress": Winkler, *Gunfight*, p. 193.

85. For example . . . "gun bullets": NPR, "Prohibition-Era Gang Violence Spurred Congress to Pass First Gun Law," June 30, 2016, npr.org/transcripts/484215890.

85. In 1921 . . . "of the mails": DeConde, *Gun Violence*, p. 121.

85. In September 1922 . . . to the source: William B. Swaney et al., "For a Better Enforcement of the Law," *American Bar Association Journal* 8 (September 1922), p. 591, in DeConde, *Gun Violence*, p. 121.

86. Gun control advocates . . . should be disarmed: DeConde, *Gun Violence*, p. 122.

86. In 1911 . . . weapon such as a handgun: Waldman, *Second Amendment*, p. 79; Winkler, *Gunfight*, p. 205; *New York Times*, "Bar Hidden Weapons on Sullivan's Plea," May 11, 1911, nyti.ms/2Psnhuh; Cottrol and Diamond, "Never Intended," p. 1334.

86. New York City had passed . . . a state law: Lee Kennett and James LaVerne Anderson, *The Gun in America: The Origins of a National Dilemma* (Westport, CT: Greenwood Press, 1975), pp. 171–72; DeConde, *Gun Violence*, p. 107.

86. Similarly, in 1913 . . . to purchase handguns: Kennett and Anderson, *Gun in America*, pp. 167–68.

86. In 1923, Arkansas . . . of Tennessee: DeConde, *Gun Violence*, pp. 122–23, 124, 126.

87. And the criminal laws . . . dismissing cases: Adler, "Less Crime, More Punishment," pp. 36–38.

88. "unless something . . . will be threatened": Lawrence Veiller, "The Way to War on Crime," *World's Work* 51 (April 1926), p. 609, in Adler, "Less Crime, More Punishment," p. 36.

88. "this new breed . . . outgunned police": DeConde, *Gun Violence*, pp. 128–29.

88. The gun control advocates found . . . Federal authority: *Christian Science Monitor*, editorial, October 12, 1925, in DeConde, *Gun Violence*, p. 126.

88. "the gangster life . . . local communities": November 5, 1932, *Public Papers of the Presidents of the United States: Herbert Hoover, 1932–33* (Washington, D.C.: Government Printing Office, 1977), p. 742, in DeConde, *Gun Violence*, p. 134.

89. By the time FDR became . . . build up federal power: Adler, "Less Crime, More Punishment," pp. 39–40.

91. Before he was elected . . . any other crimes: Winkler, *Gunfight*, pp. 201–3.

91. Frederick told Congress that . . . "reasonable" legislation: Karl T. Frederick, testimony, April 18, 1934, in *National Firearms Act: Hearings Before the Committee on Ways and Means, House of Representatives, Seventy-Third Congress, Second Session, on H.R. 9066* (Washington, D.C.: U.S. Government Printing Office, 1934), pp. 58–59, books.google.com/books?id=8AsvAAAAMAAJ&printsec=frontcover.

92. DeConde explains that . . . fount of patriotism: DeConde, *Gun Violence*, p. 142.

93. The NRA asked . . . "for the Attorney General": DeConde, *Gun Violence*, p. 143.

93. Indeed, Frederick . . . "in the Constitution": Karl T. Frederick, "Pistol Regulation: Its Principles and History Part III," *Journal of Criminal Law and Criminology* 23, no. 3 (Fall 1932), p. 541, scholarlycommons.law.northwestern.edu/jclc/vol23/iss3/14.

93. As Franklin L. Orth . . . "in 1871": Alan C. Webber, "Where the NRA Stands on Gun Legislation: 97-Year Record Shows Positive Approach to Workable Gun Laws," *American Rifleman*, March 1968, p. 22, keepandbeararms.com/images/NRA_AR_03-1968_p22.jpg.

95. "The apparent aims of the 1938 legislation . . . class of society": Franklin E. Zimring, "Firearms and Federal Law: The Gun Control Act of 1968," *Journal of Legal Studies* 4, no. 1 (January 1975), p. 140, jstor.org/stable/724104; Alfred M. Ascione, "The Federal

Firearms Act," *St. John's Law Review* 13, no. 2 (April 1939), p. 438, scholarship.law.stjohns.edu/lawreview/vol13/iss2/27/.

95. the purpose was . . . "undesirable hands": "Firearms: Problems of Control," *Harvard Law Review* 80, no. 6 (April 1967), p. 1331.

95. The NRA was okay . . . "by lying": DeConde, *Gun Violence*, p. 146–47.

95. Zimring agrees . . . to purchase guns: Zimring, "Firearms and Federal Law," pp. 140–41.

96. The FBI: For the early history of the FBI, I drew from these sources: Tim Weiner, *Enemies: A History of the FBI* (New York: Random House, 2012), pp. 9–11, 33–35; Waldman, *Second Amendment*, pp. 81–82; Winkler, *Gunfight*, p. 200; DeConde, *Gun Violence*, pp. 138–41; Adler, "Less Crime, More Punishment," pp. 40–41, 46.

97. In a unanimous ruling . . . "well-regulated militia": United States v. Miller, 307 U.S. 174 (1939).

98. "In its early days . . . oppose gun regulation": Cole, *Engines of Liberty*, p. 100.

98. The NRA itself . . . "on their own": NRA, "A Brief History of the NRA," accessed December 10, 2019, home.nra.org/about-the-nra/.

98. They weren't interested . . . much of military life: Davidson, *Under Fire*, p. 28.

98. "leaders to acknowledge . . . hunting": DeConde, *Gun Violence*, p. 157.

CHAPTER 6

99. But it wasn't until . . . she had lied: Richard Pérez-Peña, "Woman Linked to 1955 Emmett Till Murder Tells Historian Her Claims Were False," *New York Times*, January 27, 2017, nyti.ms/2kd16uE.

99. Mamie Till . . . lynched in Mississippi: *American Experience*, "The Murder of Emmett Till: Timeline" PBS, pbs.org/wgbh/americanexperience/features/till-timeline/; "Emmett Till's Death Inspired a Movement," blog, National Museum of African American History & Culture, nmaahc.si.edu/blog-post/emmett-tills-death-inspired-movement; Emmett Till Project, emmetttill-project.com/home2.

100. Years later . . . "keeping her seat": Mamie Till-Mobley and Christopher Benson, *Death of Innocence: The Story of the Hate Crime That Changed America* (New York: Random House, 2003), p. 257.

100. But Parks's actions . . . bus system: Margot Adler, "Before Rosa Parks, There Was Claudette Colvin," NPR, March 15, 2009, npr.org/2009/03/15/101719889.

103. MLK applied for . . . denied it: Cobb, *This Nonviolent Stuff*, p. 7; Winkler, *Gunfight* p. 235.

103. While he didn't . . . "self-defense": Cobb, *This Nonviolent Stuff*, p. 7.

103. "evolved beyond" . . . keeping guns around: David Barden, "NRA Savaged for 'Disgraceful and Exploitative' MLK Tweet," *HuffPost*, January 22, 2019, huffpost.com/entry/5c469950e4b0bfa693c66e21.

104. It might seem surprising . . . "to provide it": Cobb, *This Nonviolent Stuff*, pp. 1, 7–8, 129.

104. Even though white . . . "kill you": Ronnie Moore, interview, February 26, 1993, in Lance Hill, *The Deacons for Defense: Armed Resistance and the Civil Rights Movement* (Chapel Hill: University of North Carolina Press, 2004), p. 27.

106. On January 5 . . . "civil rights movement": Hill, *Deacons*, p. 48.

106. "The concept . . . totally discarded": Adam Fairclough, *Race & Democracy: The Civil Rights Struggle in Louisiana, 1915–1972* (Athens: University of Georgia Press, 1995), p. 341, in Cobb, *This Nonviolent Stuff*, p. 198.

106. "CORE nonviolence . . . a strategy": James Farmer, introduction to Inge Powell Bell, *CORE and the Strategy of Nonviolence* (New York: Random House, 1968), p. v., in Cobb, *This Nonviolent Stuff*, p. 205.

106. While CORE accepted . . . "struggle for freedom": Cobb, *This Nonviolent Stuff*, pp. 214, 223–226, 228.

107. In his book *Seize* . . . "we left Africa": Bobby Seale, *Seize the Time: The Story of the Black Panther Party and Huey P. Newton* (Baltimore: Black Classic Press, 1991), pp. 60–62.

108. At that time, . . . with iron pipes: Winkler, *Gunfight*, pp. 231–32.

108. Newton and Seale . . . "for self-defense": Seale, *Seize the Time*, pp. 67–68.

108. "While they . . . the extreme": Winkler, *Gunfight*, p. 235.

108. It was around this . . . pro-gun groups: Winkler, *Gunfight*, pp. 96–97.

109. "The Second . . . to bear arms": Seale, *Seize the Time*, pp. 67–68.

109. "Huey told" . . . "*Don't go anywhere*": Seale, *Seize the Time*, pp. 86–87, 89.

110. That very day . . . "our programs": Seale, *Seize the Time*, pp. 71, 93.

111. In 1967 . . . conviction was overturned: *People v. Newton*, 8 Cal. App. 3d 359, casetext.com/case/people-v -newton-72; KPIX, "Shooting of Oakland Police Officer John Frey," Bay Area Television Archive, diva.sfsu.edu /collections/sfbatv/bundles/206883.

111. For police agencies . . . powerless to act: Cynthia Deitle Leonardatos, "California's Attempts to Disarm the Black Panthers," *San Diego Law Review* 36, no. 4 (1999), pp. 989–90.

111. Mulford wound up . . . suggests otherwise: Winkler, *Gunfight*, pp. 244–45; Leonardatos, "California's Attempts," pp. 989–90.

112. "The American people" . . . increasing terror: Hugh Pearson, *Shadow of the Panther: Huey Newton and the Price of Black Power in America* (Cambridge, MA: Addison-Wesley, 1995), pp. 131–32.

114. Shortly after . . . disturbing the peace: Winkler, *Gunfight*, p. 243.

114. The next day . . . profile of Newton: Giovanni Russonello, "Fascination and Fear: Covering the Black Panthers," *New York Times*, October 15, 2016, nyti.ms/2e6M3Q6; Wallace Turner, "A Gun Is Power, Black Panther Says," *New York Times*, May 21, 1967, nyti.ms/1VZf5RT.

114. Republicans in California . . . in public places: Winkler, *Gunfight*, p. 245.

114. And indeed, in 1967 . . . least ninety days: Commonwealth v. Ray, 218 Pa. Superior Ct. 72 (1970), law .justia.com/cases/pennsylvania/superior-court/1970/218-pa -super-72-1.html.

116. "What more do we . . . for crime?": 109 Cong. Rec. S22868 (daily ed. November 27, 1963) (statement of Sen. Dodd), govinfo.gov/app/details/GPO-CRECB-1963-pt17 /GPO-CRECB-1963-pt17-8-1/.

116. The NRA had mobilized . . . "past situations": DeConde, *Gun Violence*, pp. 172–73, 179.

116. Many people . . . more gun control: Winkler, *Gunfight*, p. 247.

116. "I hope that this brutal" . . . "were too permissive": Thomas Dodd, April 5, 1968, in Jason Sokol, *The Heavens Might Crack: The Death and Legacy of Martin Luther King Jr.* (New York: Basic Books, 2018), p. 198; David Halberstam, *The Unfinished Odyssey of Robert Kennedy* (New York: Random House, 1968), p. 93; both in Rich Benjamin, "Gun Control, White Paranoia, and the Death of Martin Luther King, Jr.," *New Yorker*, April 3, 2018, newyorker.com/news/news-desk/gun-control-white-paranoia -and-the-death-of-martin-luther-king-jr.

118. On the day he died . . . READY, AIM, LOVE: DeConde, *Gun Violence*, p. 183.

118. President Johnson said . . . old, unwanted guns: June 19 and 24, 1968, *Public Papers of the Presidents: Lyndon B. Johnson, 1968–69*, vol. 1 (Washington, D.C.: U.S. Government Printing Office, 1970), pp. 726, 739, quod.lib.umich.edu/p/ppotpus/4731573.1968.001.

119. The NRA went into . . . "control legislation": DeConde, *Gun Violence*, pp. 185–86.

119. "I asked for the . . . an election year": October 22, 1968, *Public Papers of the Presidents: Lyndon B. Johnson, 1968–69*, vol. 2, pp. 1059–60, quod.lib.umich .edu/p/ppotpus/4731573.1968.002.

CHAPTER 7

121. The leadership of the NRA . . . "can live with": Winkler, *Gunfight*, p. 253; Waldman, *Second Amendment*, pp. 89–90.

121. "it was the concept . . . even hated": Davidson, *Under Fire*, p. 30.

121. "gun violence . . . public controversy": Waldman, *Second Amendment*, p. 88.

121. "even minor measures . . . claimed rights": DeConde, *Gun Violence*, p. 205.

122. "The advent . . . to 1968": Cole, *Engines of Liberty*, p. 102.

122. "Second Amendment . . . under the Constitution": Melzer, *Gun Crusaders*, p. 37.

123. "went back . . . other alone": Davidson, *Under Fire*, p. 29.

123. "aimed largely . . . the Black Panthers": Winkler, *Gunfight*, pp. 230–231.

123. The group's leader . . . gun as well: Richard Harris, "A Reporter at Large: Handguns," *New Yorker*, July 26, 1976; Johnson et al., *Firearms Law*, p. 431–32.

124. The law was passed . . . supported the ban: CBS News, "Has DC's Handgun Ban Prevented Bloodshed?," March 4, 2008, cbsnews.com/news/has-dcs-handgun-ban -prevented-bloodshed/.

124. Long Guns vs. Handguns: Cook and Goss, *Gun Debate*, pp. 10, 12–13; Spitzer, *Politics of Gun Control*, pp. 80–81.

124. The group wanted . . . "Washington, D.C.": Melzer, *Gun Crusaders,* p. 37; Waldman, *Second Amendment*, p. 90; Paul W. Valentine, "After Threatening to Leave, Rifle Group Elects to Stay," *Washington Post*, June 23, 1977, washingtonpost.com/archive/politics/1977/06/23/after -threatening-to-leave-rifle-group-elects-to-stay/810e9a5b -bfd7-4013-b62d-6d3406563af6.

125. More politicians . . . out of politics: Melzer, *Gun Crusaders*, pp. 83–84.

125. "The very idea . . . butchered game": Davidson, *Under Fire*, pp. 31–32.

126. he started scheming with . . . Federation of the NRA: Winkler, *Gunfight*, p. 67.

126. the idea was . . . "right to bear arms": Valentine, "After Threatening to Leave."

126. Over a thousand . . . organization: Waldman, *Second Amendment*, p. 90.

126. And the Old Guard . . . "what was coming": Winkler, *Gunfight*, p. 67.

126. The convention . . . end sooner: Waldman, *Second Amendment*, p. 90; Joel Achenbach, Scott Higham, and Sari Horwitz, "How NRA's True Believers Converted a Marksmanship Group into a Mighty Gun Lobby," *Washington Post*, January 12, 2013, wapo.st/Xu0cF3.

127. In a letter . . . "No gun legislation": Achenbach, Higham, and Horwitz, "NRA's True Believers."

127. "so strong . . . our legitimate goals": Davidson, *Under Fire*, p. 81.

127. This new NRA . . . "Second Amendment": Melzer, *Gun Crusaders*, p. 37.

127. As Adam Winkler . . . *Firearms Control*: Winkler, *Gunfight*, p. 65.

127. After the revolt . . . "collective militia": Cole, *Engines of Liberty*, p. 103.

CHAPTER 8

129. First, the NRA . . . national level: Cole, *Engines of Liberty*, pp. 99, 101–2.

131. "control indiscriminate . . . use firearms": Republican Party Platform of 1968, American Presidency Project, eds. Gerhard Peters and John T. Woolley, presidency.ucsb.edu /node/273407.

131. "the passage . . . gun control legislation": 1968 Democratic Party Platform, American Presidency Project, presidency.ucsb.edu/node/273244.

131. "great respect . . . 'not be infringed'": May 6, 1983, *Public Papers of the Presidents: Ronald Reagan, 1983*, vol. 1 (Washington, DC: U.S. Government Printing Office, 1984), p. 660, quod.lib.umich.edu/p/ppotpus/4732328.1983.001.

132. "clear . . . American citizen": Orrin G. Hatch, preface, *The Right to Keep and Bear Arms*, report of Subcommittee on the Constitution of the Judiciary Committee of the U.S. Senate, 97th Cong., 2d. Sess. (February 1982), p. viii, hdl .handle.net/2027/mdp.39015005397099.

132. This has been . . . deal with at will: Warren Burger, interview with Charlayne Hunter-Gault, *MacNeil / Lehrer NewsHour*, December 16, 1991, transcript, American Archive of Public Broadcasting, americanarchive.org /catalog/cpb-aacip_507-sx6445j916#at_0.0_s.

133. For example, in 1987 . . . (italics added): Constitutional Resolutions of the State of Maine, ch. 2 (1987), lldc.mainelegislature.org/Open/Laws/1987/1987 _CR_c002.pdf.

135. as of 2019 . . . have similar laws: "Concealed Carry," Giffords Center to Prevent Gun Violence, lawcenter.giffords.org/gun-laws/policy-areas/guns-in -public/concealed-carry/.

136. "If George Zimmerman . . . himself or another": State of Florida v. George Zimmerman, 18th Circuit, Seminole County, no. 2012 CF 1083 AXXX, jury instructions, law2 .umkc.edu/faculty/projects/ftrials/zimmerman1 /Zimjuryinstructions.pdf.

136. Reacting to Martin's murder . . . NRA's board today: "'Trayvon Got Justice,' Ted Nugent Says in Interview Aired on Maine Radio Station," *Bangor Daily News*, August 4, 2013, bangordailynews.com/2013/08/04/politics/trayvon-got -justice-ted-nugent-says-in-interview-with-maine-radio -station/.

136. "conspicuous . . . have been armed": Adam Serwer, "The NRA's Catch-22 for Black Men Shot by Police,"

Atlantic, September 13, 2018, theatlantic.com/ideas /archive/2018/09/the-nras-catch-22-for-black-men-shot-by -police/570124/.

137. "companies knew . . . states like New York": Elisa Barnes, counsel for plaintiffs, quoted in Mark Hamblett, "Solo Counsel in Gun Case Gets Win with a Little Help," *New York Law Journal*, February 18, 1999, p. 8, in Matthew Pontillo, "Suing Gun Manufacturers: A Shot in the Dark," *St. John's Law Review* 74, no. 4 (Fall 2000), p. 1185, scholarship.law .stjohns.edu/lawreview/vol74/iss4/6; Hamilton v. Accu-tek, 935 F. Supp. 1307 (E.D.N.Y. 1996).

137. The city of Chicago . . . $1.4 billion: Spitzer, *Politics of Gun Control*, pp. 136, 211–12.

137. In 1999, Charlton . . . "our fight": Sharon Walsh, "Double-Barreled Fight Against Gun Litigation," *Washington Post*, February 2, 1999, washingtonpost.com /archive/politics/1999/02/02/double-barreled-fight-against -gun-litigation/dd8131f8-25c0-4bf5-9749-724c027208e1/.

137. "manufacturers could not . . . defective product": Cole, *Engines of Liberty*, p. 109.

137. Nonetheless, some people . . . of state law: Ryan Lindsay, "Lawsuit by Sandy Hook Victims Against Gun Manufacturer Allowed to Move Forward," NPR, March 14, 2019, npr.org/2019/03/14/703439924/lawsuit-by-sandy -hook-victims-against-gun-manufacturer-allowed-to-move -forward.

138. Why did the NRA . . . at gun manufacturers: Spitzer, *Politics of Gun Control*, pp. 135–36.

138. From 2005 . . . $6 million per year: Cole, *Engines of Liberty*, p. 141; Cook and Goss, *Gun Debate*, pp. 200–1.

138. In 2017, the NRA . . . that same year: Cole, *Engines of Liberty*, p. 140–1; Spitzer, *Politics of Gun Control*, pp. 135–36.

139. "Many firearms . . . National Rifle Association": B. Drummond Ayres Jr., "Gun Maker on Mayhem: That Is Not Our Doing," *New York Times*, March 19, 1994, nyti. ms/2snvLL8.

139. "Would I . . . answer was yes": Jeffrey L. Seglin, "When Good Ethics Aren't Good Business," The Right Thing, *New York Times*, March 18, 2001, nyti.ms/34lLsQF.

141. Today, these anti-government . . . under President Obama: Antigovernment Movement, Southern Poverty Law Center, splcenter.org/fighting-hate/extremist-files /ideology/antigovernment.

141. "It's no coincidence" . . . Black political power: Serwer, "The NRA's Catch-22."

143. "the real source . . . at the ballot box": Cole, *Engines of Liberty*, p. 142.

143. "the more significant . . . in action": Cook and Goss, *Gun Debate*, p. 197.

143. NRA members . . . members of Congress: Cole, *Engines of Liberty*, p. 110; Cook and Goss, *Gun Debate*, pp. 196–98.

143. My conversations with . . . losing their freedoms: Melzer, *Gun Crusaders*, p. 1.

143. The biggest jump . . . were enacted: Cook and Goss, *Gun Debate*, p. 76.

144. "Yeah, I'm like . . . Second Amendment rights": Melzer, *Gun Crusaders*, p. 118.

145. The truth is . . . genuinely afraid: Jann S. Wenner, "Bill Clinton: The Rolling Stone Interview," *Rolling Stone*, December 28, 2000, rollingstone.com/politics/politics-news /bill-clinton-the-rolling-stone-interview-2-40256/.

145. Scholars agree . . . "hassle factor": Spitzer, *Politics of Gun Control*, p. 144.

145. The NRA . . . "interrupting you": Davidson, *Under Fire*, p. 66.

145. As an aide . . . "are risk averse": Cole, *Engines of Liberty*, pp. 142–43.

145. "I went out . . . that's deadly": Scott Higham and Sari Horwitz, "NRA Tactics: Take No Prisoners," *Washington Post*, May 18, 2013, wapo.st/10F9TA9.

146. "Victory springs . . . example to others": George Skelton, "James Brady Out to Disarm Roberti Foes," *Los Angeles Times*, April 7, 1994, latimes.com/archives/la-xpm -1994-04-07-mn-43297-story.html.

147. The law's supporters . . . "acquiring guns": Davidson, *Under Fire*, p. 194.

148. But the new NRA . . . "registered firearms": Melzer, *Gun Crusaders*, p. 98.

149. "You do know . . . further delay": Ronald Reagan, speech, March 28, 1991, George Washington University, C-SPAN, transcript and video, c-span.org/video/?17318-1 /gun-control-legislation.

149. Today, to conduct . . . denies the sale: Rich Barbieri and Aaron Smith, "How Gun Background Checks Work," CNN Money, January 5, 2016, shar.es/a3G6yn.

149. One result . . . "to just 16%": Cook and Goss, *Gun Debate*, p. 84.

150. FOPA said . . . by the government: Public Law No. 99–308, 100 *U.S. Statutes at Large* 450, govinfo.gov /content/pkg/STATUTE-100/pdf/STATUTE-100-Pg449.pdf.

150. "central thrust . . . sales as a business": David T. Hardy, "The Firearms Owners' Protection Act: A Historical and Legal Perspective," *Cumberland Law Review* 17 (1987), p. 632.

150. This was supposed to . . . a background check: Winkler, *Gunfight*, pp. 73–74; Cook and Goss, *Gun Debate*, p. 143; Audrey Carlsen and Sahil Chinoy, "How to Buy a Gun in 16 Countries," *New York Times*, March 2, 2018, nyti.ms/2FNXPu4.

150. Secondary-market . . . go unregulated: Jens Ludwig and Philip J. Cook, "Homicide and Suicide Rates Associated with Implementation of the Brady Handgun Violence Prevention Act," *Journal of the American Medical Association* 284, no. 5 (August 2, 2000), doi.org/10.1001 /jama.284.5.585.

151. The law banned . . . "design characteristics": Cook and Goss, *Gun Debate*, p. 102; Public Safety and Recreational Firearms Use Protection Act, Public Law 103–322, *U.S. Statutes at Large* 1996.

152. The friend later testified . . . faced a background check: Robyn Anderson, testimony before Colorado House of Representatives Judiciary Committee, January 26, 2000, in 146 Cong. Rec. S555 (February 9, 2000) (statement of Sen. Lautenberg), govinfo.gov/ content/pkg/CREC-2000-02-09/html/CREC-2000-02-09 -pt1-PgS555-2.htm.

152. Less than two weeks . . . "Webb finally said": For a fuller account of the protest at the NRA convention in Denver, see Dave Cullen, *Columbine* (New York: Hachette, 2009), pp. 210–11; Knight Ridder, "Still-Grieving Colorado Turns Out to Protest NRA Meeting; Gun Group Remains Defiant as 8,000 Oppose Presence in Light of Columbine Tragedy," *Baltimore Sun*, May 2, 1999, baltimoresun.com/news/bs-xpm-1999-05-02 -9905020166-story.html.

153. Two weeks before . . . one such gun: Cullen, *Columbine*, p. 211.

153. Wayne LaPierre . . . costs on gun buyers: Katharine Q. Seelye, "A Defiant N.R.A. Gathers in Denver," *New York Times*, May 1, 1999, nyti.ms/2qOj4st.

153. "absolutely gun-free . . . security personel": Wayne LaPierre, "Address to Members," May 1, 1999, Denver, web.archive.org/web/20000312035941/http://nrahq.com /transcripts/denver_wlp.shtml.

154. The NRA spent . . . Al Gore: Cole, *Engines of Liberty*, p. 130.

154. "I believe . . . hurt us bad": Joe Conason, "The Salon Interview: Bill Clinton," June 26, 2004, Salon, salon.com /2004/06/25/clinton_101.

154. "In retrospect . . . turned out differently": Cole, *Engines of Liberty*, p. 136.

155. "the NRA worked . . . arms": Cole, *Engines of Liberty*, p. 135.

155. But when Dick Heller . . . in their favor yet: Cole, *Engines of Liberty*, p. 132; Waldman, *Second Amendment*, p. 119; Winkler, *Gunfight*, p. 7; Spitzer, *Politics of Gun Control*, p. 151; Cook and Goss, *Gun Debate*, p. 93.

CHAPTER 9

156. It all started . . . the Supreme Court: Winkler, *Gunfight*, p. 5.

157. In fact . . . only about eighty: "Supreme Court Procedure," *SCOTUSblog*, scotusblog.com/reference /educational-resources/supreme-court-procedure/.

158. "the Firearms Control Act . . . crime": U.S. Conference of Mayors, *The Analysis of the Firearm Control Act of 1975: Handgun Control in the District of Columbia* (Washington, D.C., July 1980), p. 17, in Edward D. Jones III, "The District of Columbia's 'Firearms Control Regulations Act of 1975': The Toughest Handgun Control Law in the United States—Or Is It?," *Annals of the American Academy of Political and Social Science* 455 (May 1981), p. 143, jstor.org/stable/1044076.

158. the NRA suggested . . . down anyway: Jones, "Toughest Handgun Control Law?," p. 144.

158. In 1991 . . . 100,000 people: FBI, Uniform Crime Report statistics, 1991, ucrdatatool.gov/Search/Crime /State/RunCrimeStatebyState.cfm.

158. That same year . . . each year: Colin Loftin et al., "Effects of Restrictive Licensing of Handguns on Homicide and Suicide in the District of Columbia," *New England Journal of Medicine* 325, no. 23 (December 5, 1991), p.1615–20, doi.org/10.1056/NEJM199112053252305.

160. Indeed, they . . . would be moot: Winkler, *Gunfight*, p. 7, 57; Waldman, *Second Amendment*, p. 119.

160. The NRA released . . . "policy debates": NRA-ILA, "NRA Joins in Day of Mourning," April 20, 2007, web .archive.org/web/20070422145113/http://www.nraila.org/.

161. While Alan Gura walked . . . "More death!": Winkler, *Gunfight*, pp. 3–8.

169. "outrageous conduct" . . . First Amendment: Snyder v. Phelps, 580 F. 3d 206 (2011).

172. Originalism became . . . judicial restraint: Emma Long, "Why So Silent? The Supreme Court and the Second Amendment Debate After *DC v. Heller*," *European Journal of American Studies* 12, no. 2 (Summer 2017), journals .openedition.org/ejas/11874.

173. "Good moring, Mr. Chief Justice": The following exchange between Dellinger and the justices is from the oral argument transcript, March 18, 2008, in *District of Columbia v. Heller*, pp. 3–5, 7, supremecourt.gov/oral _arguments/argument_transcripts/2007/07-290.pdf; Winkler, *Gunfight*, pp. 174–175.

174. It seemed as . . . subway system: Winkler, *Gunfight*, p. 274.

175. Applying originalism . . . "case of confrontation": District of Columbia v. Heller, 554 U.S. 570, 577, 592, 599 (2008); Long, "Why So Silent?"

176. "In *Heller* . . . amendment's enactment": J. Harvie Wilkinson III, "Of Guns, Abortions and the Unraveling Rule of Law," *Virginia Law Review* 95, no. 2 (April 2009),

p. 265, virginialawreview.org/sites/virginialawreview.org /files/253.pdf.

176. In a piece . . . "living Constitution": Reva B. Siegel, "Dead or Alive: Originalism as Popular Constitutionalism in *Heller*," *Harvard Law Review* 122, no. 1 (November 1, 2008), p. 192, harvardlawreview.org/2008/11/dead-or-alive -originalism-as-popular-constitutionalism-in-heller/.

177. Instead, Justice Scalia . . . sensitive areas: D.C. v. Heller, 554 U.S. 570, 622 (2008).

177. "The Second Amendment . . . constitutional law": NRA-ILA, "Supreme Court Declares That the Second Amendment Guarantees an Individual Right," June 26, 2008, nraila.org/articles/20080626/supreme-court-declares -that-the-second.

177. "As a longstanding . . . bear firearms": June 26, 2008, *Public Papers of the Presidents of the United States: George W. Bush, 2008–2009*, vol. 1 (Washington, D.C.: U.S. Government Printing Office, 2012), p. 889, govinfo.gov /content/pkg/PPP-2008-book1/pdf/PPP-2008-book1-doc -pg889.pdf.

178. Newspapers . . . control in America: Linda Greenhouse, "Justices, Ruling 5–4, Endorse Personal Right to Own Gun," *New York Times*, June 27, 2008, nyti. ms/2ltLliV.

179. The United States . . . the case: Small Arms Survey, "Global Firearms Holdings," 2017, smallarmssurvey.org /weapons-and-markets/tools/global-firearms-holdings .html.

180. In a 2016 test . . . in Philadelphia: Helen Ubinas, "I Bought an AR-15 Semi-Automatic Rifle in Philly in 7 Minutes," *Philadelphia Daily News*, June 13, 2016, inquirer.com/philly/columnists/helen_ubinas/20160614 _Ubinas__I_bought_an_AR_15_semi-automatic_rifle_in _Philly_in_7_minutes.html.

183. The United Kingdom . . . the United States: Institute for Health Metrics and Evaluation, "Deaths by Physical Violence by Firearm, Both Sexes, All Ages," 2017, University of Washington, ihmeuw.org/4zvu.

184. Similarly, Australia . . . new laws: Australasian Police Ministers' Council, Resolutions of Special Firearms Meeting, May 10, 1996, Australasian Legal Information Institute, austlii.edu.au/au/other/apmc/#RTFToC11.

184. In the years . . . and accidents: S. Chapman et al, "Australia's 1996 Gun Law Reforms: Faster Falls in Firearm Deaths, Firearm Suicides, and a Decade Without Mass Shootings," *Injury Prevention* 12, no. 6 (December 2006), p. 365–372, injuryprevention.bmj.com/content/12/6/365.

184. In 2016 . . . million: New Zealand Police National Headquarters, *Police Statistics on Homicide Victims in New Zealand 2007–2016* (July 2018), police.govt.nz/sites /default/files/publications/homicide-victims-report-2017 .pdf; Stats NZ, "Population," stats.govt.nz/topics /population.

185. In Japan, gun licenses . . . every three years: Max Fisher, "A Land Without Guns: How Japan Has Virtually Eliminated Shooting Deaths," *Atlantic*, July 23, 2012, theatlantic.com/international/archive/2012/07/a-land -without-guns-how-japan-has-virtually-eliminated -shooting-deaths/260189/.

185. there were three . . . in total: Philip Alpers and Marcus Wilson. "Japan—Gun Facts, Figures and the Law," October 15, 2019, Sydney School of Public Health, University of Sydney, GunPolicy.org, gunpolicy.org /firearms/region/japan.

185. Much like the . . . more gun deaths: Violence Policy Center, "States with Weak Gun Laws and Higher Gun Ownership Lead Nation in Gun Deaths, New Data for 2017 Confirms," news release, January 23, 2019, vpc.org

/press/states-with-weak-gun-laws-and-higher-gun -ownership-lead-nation-in-gun-deaths-new-data-for-2017 -confirms.

185. Other studies . . . doesn't include suicide: Paul M. Reeping et al., "State Gun Laws, Gun Ownership, and Mass Shootings in the US: Cross Sectional Time Series," *BMJ* 364 (March 6, 2019), p. l542, doi.org/10.1136/bmj .l542.

187. Indeed, one study . . . robbery stayed the same: Philip J. Cook, "The Effect of Gun Availability on Robbery and Robbery Murder: A Cross Section Study of Fifty Cities," in *Policy Studies Review Annual*, vol. 3, eds. Robert H. Haveman and B. Bruce Zellner (Beverly Hills, CA: Sage, 1979), pp. 752–3, in Spitzer, *Politics of Gun Control*, pp. 100–1.

187. other scholars have . . . committed with guns: Franklin E. Zimring and Gordon Hawkins, *Crime Is Not the Problem: Lethal Violence in America* (New York: Oxford University Press, 1997).

187. The NRA likes . . . "more deaths": Cook and Goss, *Gun Debate*, pp. 1–2, 41, 59.

188. While the numbers vary . . . 1 percent of cases: Jongyeon Tark and Gary Kleck, "Resisting Crime: The Effects of Victim Action on the Outcomes Of Crimes," *Criminology* 42, no. 4 (March 7, 2006), pp. 861–910, in Cook and Goss, *Gun Debate*, p. 17.

188. In a study . . . considered illegal: D. Hemenway, M. Miller, and D. Azrael, "Gun Use in the United States: Results from Two National Surveys," *Injury Prevention* 6, no. 4 (December 2000), p.263–67, doi.org/10.1136/ip.6.4 .263.

189. However, studies show . . . "unreliable": Cook and Goss, *Gun Debate*, pp. 25–26, 130.

190. First, when you introduce . . . by suicide: Spitzer, *Politics of Gun Control*, p. 106.

CHAPTER 10

191. On December 14 . . . "saw Jessica alive": Krista Rekos, "About Jessica," Jessica Rekos Foundation, jessicarekos.org/about-jessica.

191. The majority of those . . . adults who were lost: Barack Obama, news conference, White House, December 15, 2012, CNN, transcripts.cnn.com /TRANSCRIPTS/1212/17/sn.01.html.

192. Two days later . . . were crying: Barack Obama, "Guns in America Town Hall," interview by Anderson Cooper, January 7, 2016, CNN, cnn.com/videos/politics /2016/01/08/obama-guns-in-america-crying-newtown -shooting-town-hall-ac-07.cnn.

193. Wayne LaPierre . . . in the country: Wayne LaPierre, interview by Stuart Varney, *Varney & Co.*, March 4, 2013, Fox Business, video.foxbusiness.com/v /2202824240001.

193. He said . . . who was ineligible: Wayne LaPierre, testimony in *What Should America Do About Gun Violence? Hearing Before the Committee on the Judiciary U.S. Senate 113th Congress, 1st Session*, January 30, 2013 (Washington, D.C.: U.S. Government Publishing Office, 2017), p. 19, govinfo.gov/content/pkg /CHRG-113shrg98436/pdf/CHRG-113shrg98436.pdf.

193. He also mocked . . . "every single school?": Wayne LaPierre, "Remarks from the NRA Press Conference on Sandy Hook School Shooting," *Washington Post*, December 21, 2012, washingtonpost.com/bd1841fe-4b88 -11e2-a6a6-aabac85e8036_story.html.

193. One of those Democrats . . . against the legislation: Higham and Horwitz, "NRA Tactics: Take No Prisoners."

194. "The ability . . . otherwise have": Cole, *Engines of Liberty*, p. 146.

194. "When the Supreme . . . constitutional rights": Waldman, *Second Amendment*, pp. 159, 169.

194. "monumental . . . local officials": Dan Balz and Keith B. Richburg, "Historic Decision Renews Old Debate," *Washington Post*, June 27, 2008, washingtonpost.com/wp-dyn/content/article/2008/06/26/AR2008062604247.html.

194. All he said . . . "old fart": Dick Metcalf, "Target: Me," *Politico*, January 14, 2014, politico.com/magazine/story/2014/01/guns-second-amendment-target-me-102133.

195. In 2014 . . . gun the person has?: Tom Ramstack, "Maryland Gun Store Drops Plans to Sell 'Smart Guns' After Threats," Reuters, May 2, 2014, reuters.com/article/idUSBREA410SD20140502; Andy Raymond, excerpt from Facebook video, *All In with Chris Hayes*, May 5, 2014, transcript, nbcnews.com/id/55116841

195. "the right . . . primary election": Patrick J. Charles, "Second Amendment in the Twenty-First Century: What Hath *Heller* Wrought?," *William and Mary Bill of Rights Journal* 23 no. 4 (2015), pp. 1143, 1149, 1178, scholarship.law.wm.edu/wmborj/vol23/iss4/6.

196. Black and Brown . . . gaining national attention: Yolanda T. Mitchell and Tiffany L. Bromfield, "Gun Violence and the Minority Experience," National Council on Family Relations, January 10, 2019, ncfr.org/ncfr-report/winter-2018/gun-violence-and-minority-experience.

197. "As mothers . . . cup of coffee": Mark Follman, "These Women Are the NRA's Worst Nightmare," *Mother Jones*, September-October 2014, motherjones.com/politics/2014/09/moms-demand-action-guns-madd-shannon-watts-nra/.

197. In the 2018 midterm . . . won the election: Danny Hakim and Rachel Shorey, "Gun Control Groups Eclipse N.R.A. in Election Spending," *New York Times*, November 16, 2018, nyti.ms/2DqkXzF.

198. In the year after . . . gun regulations): Karen Yourish et al., "State Gun Laws Enacted in the Year After Newtown," *New York Times*, December 10, 2013, archive.nytimes.com/www.nytimes.com/interactive/2013/12/10/us/state-gun-laws-enacted-in-the-year-since-newtown.html.

198. Companies trying . . . We call BS: CNN, "Florida Student Emma Gonzalez to Lawmakers and Gun Advocates: 'We call BS,'" February 17, 2018, cnn.com/2018/02/17/us/florida-student-emma-gonzalez-speech/.

199. They started the . . . the shooting: Dankin Andone, "In Just 3 Days, Parkland Students Have Raised $3.7 Million. Here's How They'll Spend It," CNN, February 22, 2018, cnn.com/2018/02/22/us/iyw-march-for-our-lives-gofundme-trnd/.

199. "Parkland . . . is the hurt": Melissa Chan, "'They Are Lifting Us Up.' How Parkland Students Are Using Their Moment to Help Minority Anti-Violence Groups," *Time*, March 24, 2018, time.com/5201562/parkland-students-minority-groups/.

202. Teachers . . . make use of: Emma González, "Parkland Student Emma González Opens Up About Her Fight for Gun Control," *Harper's Bazaar*, February 26, 2018, harpersbazaar.com/culture/politics/a18715714/protesting-nra-gun-control-true-story/.

202. "She put my kid . . . with the families": Jared Moskowitz, speech on SB 7026, Florida House of Representatives, March 7, 2018, Florida Channel recording, 2:25:11 mark, thefloridachannel.org/videos/3-7-18-house-session-part-3/.

203. Within a year . . . for a gun: Allison Anderman, *Gun Law Trend Watch: 2018 Year-End Review* (Giffords Law Center, December 14, 2018), lawcenter.giffords.org/wp-content/uploads/2018/12/Giffords-Law-Center-Year-End-Trendwatch-2018_Digital-Spreads.pdf.

203. Florida voter . . . 2 percent: Tom Bonier, memorandum, July 19, 2018, "Analysis: After Parkland Shooting, Youth Voter Registration Surges," TargetSmart, targetsmart.com/analysis-after-parkland-shooting-youth-voter-registration-surges/.

203. Just institutionalizing . . . gun regulation: Angelo McDade, interview by David Greene, February 14, 2019, "Chicago Group Joins Parkland Survivors to Address Gun Violence," *Morning Edition* transcript, NPR, npr.org/2019/02/14/694635050/.

EPILOGUE

205. "Joaquin brought . . . were here?": Patricia Oliver, interview by Jennifer Medina, in "Two Days, Two Cities, Two Massacres," *The Daily* podcast hosted by Michael Barbaro, August 5, 2019, transcript, *New York Times*, nyti.ms/2yGtOta.

205. He said . . . "of Hispanics": Mitch Smith, Rick Rojas, and Campbell Robertson, "Dayton Gunman Had Been Exploring 'Violent Ideologies,' F.B.I. Says," *New York Times*, August 6, 2019, nyti.ms/2YFJpUw.

205. The NRA . . . from Mexico: Jessica Schulberg, "The NRA Has Long Urged Americans to Arm Themselves Against an Immigrant Invasion," *HuffPost*, August 6, 2019, huffpost.com/entry/5d49b2d8e4b0d291ed07a824.

205. Latinos across . . . "American dream": Simon Romero et al., "'It Feels Like Being Hunted': Latinos Across U.S. in Fear After El Paso Massacre," *New York Times*, August 6, 2019, nyti.ms/2yHmiya.

206. That same weekend . . . in Chicago alone: Elizabeth Thomas, "In Bloody August Weekend, Gun Violence Beyond Mass Shootings," ABC News, August 4, 2019, abcn.ws/2GMkgRR.

206. "What do we . . . Now!": Smith, Rojas, and Robertson, "Dayton Gunman."

207. "Most often . . . public gatherings": Timothy Williams, "What Are 'Red Flag' Gun Laws, and How Do They Work?," *New York Times*, August 6, 2019, nyti.ms/2YMXQq3.

207. So what does . . . "any other available option": John Paul Stevens, "Repeal the Second Amendment," *New York Times*, March 27, 2018, nyti.ms/2pIaPuh.

208. "I think . . . a background check?": Adam Winkler in *Clog x Guns* (September 2017), p. 216.

208. Indeed, after the shootings . . . Republican platform: Sheryl Gay Stolberg, Maggie Haberman, and Jonathan Martin, "Trump Weighs New Stance on Guns as Pressure Mounts After Shootings," *New York Times*, August 8, 2019, nyti.ms/2YUYi9E.

209. "People with mental . . . afoul of the law": Cook and Goss, *Gun Debate*, p. 72; "Gun Violence and Mental Health," AFT, aft.org/childrens-health/mental-health/gun-violence-and-mental-health.

209. "Federal law . . . does for citizens": Pema Levy, "Why Gun Control Backers Love to Talk About Duck Hunting," Talking Points Memo, January 30, 2013, talkingpointsmemo.com/dc/why-gun-control-backers-love-to-talk-about-duck-hunting.

212. "We are going . . . to change the law": CNN, "Emma González: 'We call BS.'"

214. Families of Sandy Hook . . . trial in 2021: Dave Altimari, "After long delay, lawsuit by Sandy Hook families against gun maker Remington Arms will go to trial in 2021," *Hartford Courant*, December 11, 2019.

INFOGRAPHIC SOURCES

2. Chris Nichols, *How Is a "Mass Shooting" Defined?*, PolitiFact (Oct. 4, 2017), politifact.com /california/article/2017/oct/04/mass-shooting-what-does-it-mean/; William J. Krouse & Daniel J. Richardson, *Mass Murder with Firearms: Incidents and Victims, 1999–2013*, Congressional Research Service (July 30, 2015), fas.org/sgp/crs/misc/R44126.pdf; Mark Follman, "How Many Mass Shootings Are There, Really?" *The New York Times* (December 4, 2015), nytimes .com/2015/12/04/opinion/how-many-mass-shootings-are-there-really.html. **4.** Mark Abadi and James Pasley, "18 of the Deadliest Mass Shootings in Modern US History," *Business Insider* (Aug. 5, 2019), businessinsider.com/deadliest-mass-shootings-in-us-history-2017-10. **5a.** Harry Enten, "There's a Gun for Every American. But Less Than a Third Own Guns," CNN Politics (Feb. 15, 2018), cnn.com/2018/02/15/politics/guns-dont-know-how-many-america /index.html. **5b.** Alex Yablon, "Gun Sales Fell in 2018, Despite Parkland-Inspired Activism," The Trace (Feb. 5, 2019), thetrace.org/2019/02/gun-sales-trump-slump-parkland-activism/. **7.** Andy Kiersz and Brett LoGiurato, "Here's Where You're Most Likely to Own a Gun," *Business Insider* (July 3, 2015), businessinsider.com/gun-ownership-by-state-2015-7; Bindu Kalesan, Marcos D. Villarreal, Katherine M. Keyes & Sandro Galea, "Gun Ownership and Social Gun Culture," *Injury Prevention* (June 29, 2015), injuryprevention.bmj.com/content/injuryprev/early/2015/06/09/inju ryprev-2015-041586.full.pdf?keytype=ref&ijkey=doj6vx0laFZMsQ2. **8.** John Gramlich, "What the Data Says About Gun Deaths in the U.S.," Pew Research Center (August 16, 2019), pewre search.org/fact-tank/2019/08/16/what-the-data-says-about-gun-deaths-in-the-u-s/. **24.** Robert J. Spitzer, "Gun Law History in the United States and Second Amendment Rights," *Law and Contemporary Problems* 80, no. 2 (2017), pp. 59–60, 62–69, scholarship.law.duke.edu/lcp/vol80 /iss2/3; Frassetto, "Firearms and Weapons Legislation." **42.** Doug MacCash, "The U.S.'s Largest Slave Revolt to Be Reenacted by a Crowd Marching Toward New Orleans Nov. 8 and 9," Nola.com (Sept. 10, 2019), nola.com/entertainment_life/article_ec7904dc-d40d-11e9-9db4-abb635976c5c .html. **59.** Spitzer, "Gun Law History," pp. 59–60, 62–69; Frassetto, "Firearms and Weapons Legislation." **78.** Spitzer, "Gun Law History," pp. 59–60, 62–69; Frassetto, "Firearms and Weapons Legislation." **130.** David Cole, *Engines of Liberty: How Citizen Movements Succeed*, New York: Basic Books (2016), p. 118. **135.** David Cole, *Engines of Liberty: How Citizen Movements Succeed*, New York: Basic Books (2016), p. 106; Philip J. Cook & Kristen A. Goss, *The Gun Debate: What Everyone Needs to Know*, Oxford University Press (2014), p. 199. **141.** Scott Melzer, *The NRA's Culture War*, New York: NYC Press (2009), p. 39. **142.** OpenSecrets.org, "Gun Rights vs Gun Control"; opensecrets.org/news/issues/guns/ (retrieved September 2019). **144.** Gregor Aisch and Josh Keller, "What Happens After Calls for New Gun Restrictions? Sales Go Up" *The New York Times* (June 13, 2016), nytimes.com/interactive/2015/12/10/us/gun-sales-terrorism-obama- restrictions.html. **180.** Small Arms Survey, as found in German Lopez, "America's Unique Gun Violence Problem, Explained in 16 Maps and Charts," *Vox* (August 31, 2009), vox .com/policy-and-politics/2017/10/2/16399418/us-gun-violence-statistics-maps-charts. **181.** Gunpolicy.org, United Nations Development Programme, as in Lopez, "America's Unique Gun Violence Problem." **182.** Jeffrey Swanson, International Crime Victims Survey, Gallup Europe, as in Lopez, "America's Unique Gun Violence Problem." **183.** Max Fisher and Josh Keller, "What Explains U.S. Mass Shootings? International Comparisons Suggest an Answer," *The New York Times* (November 7, 2017), nytimes.com/2017/11/07/world/americas/mass-shootings-us-interna tional.html. **184.** Gun Policy, Australia, gunpolicy.org/firearms/region/australia. **186–187.** Paul M. Reeping, Magdalena Cerdá, Bindu Kalesan, Douglas J. Wiebe, Sandro Galea & Charles C. Branas, "State Gun Laws, Gun Ownership, and Mass Shootings in the US: Cross Sectional Time Series." *The BMJ* (Clinical research ed.), vol. 364:l542 (March 6, 2019), bmj.com/content/364 /bmj.l542; Joanna Pearlstein, "Guns in America: Our Relationship with Firearms in 5 Charts," *Wired* (November 12, 2018), wired.com/story/guns-in-america-five-charts/. **200–201.** Twitter, as in Amy Held, "One by One, Companies Cut Ties with the NRA," NPR (February 23, 2018), npr .org/sections/thetwo-way/2018/02/23/588233273/one-by-one-companies-cut-ties-with-nra.

INDEX